The Weatherwomen

The Weatherwomen

*Militant Feminists of
the Weather Underground*

MONA ROCHA

McFarland & Company, Inc., Publishers
Jefferson, North Carolina

This book has undergone peer review.

ISBN (print) 978-1-4766-7665-4
ISBN (ebook) 978-1-4766-3880-5

LIBRARY OF CONGRESS AND BRITISH LIBRARY
CATALOGUING DATA ARE AVAILABLE

Library of Congress Control Number 2020002125

Front cover: Mugshots of female members of the Weather
Underground from 1972 (Federal Bureau of Investigation).

Printed in the United States of America

*McFarland & Company, Inc., Publishers
Box 611, Jefferson, North Carolina 28640
www.mcfarlandpub.com*

For James

Contents

Acknowledgments

A great number of people assisted in the research and development of this project. I am grateful for all of the assistance they provided along the way and would like to acknowledge some of them here. A very early version of this project was presented at the Western Association of Women Historians conference and at the Popular Culture Association/American Culture Association national meeting, where I received insightful questions and useful comments. I am also grateful to my students in my Women's History class at LSU and to those in my Radical Women in History class at Fresno State, whose shrewd discussions and cogent remarks spurred me in new and interesting directions.

Some of my greatest assistance came from my graduate school advisors when I was originally writing on the Weatherwomen for my dissertation. I am grateful to Charles Shindo for all his enthusiasm and his invaluable suggestions. Alecia Long's astute comments were always beneficial, as were Kate Bratton's. Significantly, I am immensely grateful to Carolyn Lewis for her many discerning observations and continued support.

I also give thanks to the anonymous reviewers of this manuscript for their valuable suggestions and incisive remarks.

Librarians on both coasts of the country helped me track down documents and archival materials. I am particularly grateful to Michele Wesling of the Southern California Library, as well as to David Olson, Brianne LaCamera, and Kristen La Follette of the Columbia University Center for Oral History. Additionally, I thank Bolerium Books.

I also give thanks to David Gilbert, whose letters provided guidance and insight.

Importantly, I am also grateful to the folks at McFarland. Thank you for your advice and guidance throughout this process, Charlie Perdue and Gary Mitchem.

My wonderful mother, Carmen Constantinescu, is owed a great debt of gratitude. She supported me every step of the way, and without her influence I would not be where I am today. She constantly inspired me to work hard and follow my dreams. My extended family also deserves many thanks: I really appreciate all the love and support I have received from Bridget Brown, Greg Brown, Kimi Rocha, Derrick Rocha, Stephanie Fish, Rex Fish, Savannah Brown, Katherine Rocha, and Kyle Rocha. I especially appreciate Deanna Rocha and Jim Rocha for their invaluable support and belief in me.

Finally, there is one person who weathered every step of this project and read every draft of every chapter. He was there while I paged through FBI files, made charts, wrote and rewrote sections; he spent countless hours discussing the Weatherwomen, their politics, and the turbulent sixties. I am incredibly grateful to James Rocha for all that he has done to make this possible.

Introduction

On March 6, 1970, Diana Oughton's life came to a sudden and violent end as a bomb assembled by members of the Weather Underground Organization (WUO) blew up in a Greenwich townhouse. Newspaper accounts after the explosion characterized Diana's involvement in the WUO as inauthentic and misled, stemming from the greater-than-life personality of her lover, Bill Ayers. Defining Ayers as "charming, manipulative, and a bit cruel," contemporary accounts concluded that he "probably exercised the single most powerful influence over Diana until her death."[1] This treatment reflects the dominant historical narrative of women involved in the WUO and other militant leftist organizations of the late 1960s and 1970s. While there is no doubt that the ideology, goals, and methods advocated by this group were inherently problematic, it is a mistake to dismiss the participation of women such as Oughton as being motivated by simple, misguided infatuation. Dedicated revolutionaries in their own right, the women of the Weather Underground deserve serious consideration.

Arguing that violence can be justified in the pursuit of feminist aims, and that justified violence can be used by women just as easily as by men, the women of the WUO articulated and embodied militant feminist principles. This book excavates their long-buried history and reclaims the voices of the "Weatherwomen," a name they gave themselves.[2] I will employ the term "Weatherwomen" throughout the manuscript in accordance to what the WUO female members called themselves in their pamphlets and publications. Assertive, tough, and idealistic, but far from naive, these Weatherwomen were determined to stamp out sexism and social injustice. As such, the Weatherwomen asserted that militancy was necessary in the pursuit of a socialist revolution that would produce a society rooted in gender, racial, and class equality. As one anonymous Weatherwoman

1

wrote in their self-published book of poetry, *Sing a Battle Song*, "to achieve the full liberation of women means to end the ways we are dehumanized and exploited because of our sex, race or class."[3]

To argue that the Weatherwomen are militant feminists, it is necessary to establish both their militancy and their feminism. Their militancy is easier to establish since the WUO engaged in the bombings of symbolic targets, such as buildings or statues. Let's say that an organization can be militant through direct acts of personal violence, such as by intentionally harming people, who may be combatants or civilians, symbolic acts of violence, such as destroying property (as the WUO did), threats to commit acts of violence, or through associating with symbols of violence, such as by openly carrying guns or using a bomb as a organizational symbol. Thus, an organization can be militant without being actively violent, such as an organization arming itself with weapons in open displays of self-defense (such as the Black Panther Party), but without ever using those weapons or even having any intention to use those weapons. Further, an organization can be militant while being committed to never using violence against persons, such as an organization that sends in bomb threats without actually planting any bombs or even an organization that works very diligently to ensure that their bombs never harm people (as the WUO did). These latter organizations are aggressive and disruptive in ways that conjure up thoughts of violence without actually being physically violent against persons. Hence, there can be militant organizations that attempt to limit their militancy so that they do not harm any persons. The WUO attempted to be militant in this sense: they did not wish to actively harm anybody, but they did use violence symbolically and against buildings and statues.

Feminism, in itself, is an open-ended term that includes anyone who accepts, in some form, three propositions: (a) men and women are equal (in any morally significant sense of "equal"), (b) we live in a society that does not treat men and women as equal, and (c) something should be done to improve our society to obtain gender equality. Someone could not be a feminist and deny the first claim since any claim of gender superiority, such as the belief that men are superior to women, is the essential meaning of being sexist. A feminist argues for the second claim merely by pointing to sexist practices that exist within society. Furthermore, if someone believes the first two, they are likely to accept the third as a practical consequence: if men and women are equal and society fails to recognize this equality, then something should be done to rectify the situation.

This general baseline for feminism thus captures a wide range of possible feminist positions. Feminists are not a monolithic category: feminists can largely agree on these foundational claims while having a plethora of disagreements on what gender equality means, where sexism exists within our society, what should be done to bring about gender equality, etc. One standard way employed to distinguish feminists so as to note these potential disagreements has been to use the historical wave metaphor. While the wave metaphor has provided some useful distinctions in the history of feminism, this book will argue that it is ultimately misleading and we should be wary of relying on it as a historical category. In particular, we will find that the women of the Weather Underground were active during the historical period of the second wave, but they exhibited clear positions that are more representative of the later, third wave. Before arguing for that point, we should begin by briefly looking at how the wave metaphor is typically laid out.

Women's and feminist historians roughly identify the first wave as the period focused on obtaining the right to vote for women in the United States, and thus this wave has been located from the 19th century to the passing of the Nineteenth Amendment in 1920. The first wave therefore encompassed the fight to get fundamental political rights for women. The second wave aimed to obtain a broader specter of rights for women, from rights in the workplace and the home, to educational access, as well as social and economic rights. It drew on the language of civil rights to call for female liberation and gender equality. Feminist historians typically describe the second wave as starting in the 1960s and continuing into the 1980s. The second wave pushed for women's equality in all areas of life and fought against gender discrimination, but was dominated by a white, middle-class perspective.[4]

The third wave of feminism, roughly placed as starting somewhere in the 1980s, was an attempt to meld feminist practice with the values of diversity and inclusion. Furthermore, the third wave focused on broadening that point of view to address the needs of all women, regardless of race, class, sexuality, or other identity markers. As such, this wave practiced inclusion in terms of all identity types. This concept is usually referred to as intersectionality, which is a term that Kimberlé Crenshaw coined. Intersectionality denotes an awareness that different folks might experience different combinations of oppressions based on their class, the color of their skin, their gender identity, their sexual orientation, etc. Third wavers are aware that, based on someone's particular identity type and their interaction with the world around them, various oppressions can compound and intersect.[5] The third wave also embraced sex positivity as an aim. For third wavers, sex positivity meant including not only all sexual identities, which means embracing women of all sexual orientations and treating trans and cis women equally, but also embracing women's sexual lives, whatever women wished to do with their sexuality. Where the second wave critiqued certain kinds of sexuality, such as that found in pornography or prostitution, the third wave was much more welcoming of all kinds of sexuality. Some feminist scholars argue that we are currently in the fourth wave of feminism. This wave can be characterized through cyber feminism, with technology offering feminist activists a platform to effectively spread their messages and promote action through platforms such as Twitter.[6] In this work, we will concentrate only on the first three waves and take no stance on whether there is yet a fourth wave.

As this book reveals, the WUO's feminism derived in large part from the second wave feminist movement that was developing contemporaneously with them. Even though the WUO severely critiqued some aspects of second wave feminism, they also articulated and replicated many, though certainly not all, of the second wave views of the women's liberation groups of their time period. Specifically, the WUO criticized the role of women in the home, was concerned with the subordination of women to men, attacked the gender pay gap, and supported female bodily integrity—which were all issues at the forefront of female liberation groups from the time period.[7]

Yet, the WUO saw the second wave's women's groups' foundational concern with gender as overly indulgent and not responsive to the needs and concerns of *all* women. Hence, this book also explores how the women of the WUO—previewing later third wave feminists—critiqued feminist groups of their historical period for their self-involvement, while articulating a feminist ideology that would incorporate multiple identity perspectives.[8] Since their concern with intersecting identities occurred well before what is normally taken to be the beginning of third wave feminism (which can be dated either to 1981 when *This Bridge Called My Back* was published, or 1991 when Rebecca Walker coined "third wave feminism" in her famous piece "Becoming the Third Wave"), this book calls into question the accuracy of the wave motif as a historical construction.

Other works have rethought the wave metaphor; here I add to that discussion through the use of the WUO.[9] In particular, I will argue that the literature up to now has conflated two distinct ways of looking at the waves of feminism: a historical approach and a conceptual approach. The historical approach distinguishes the three waves by their historical periods (the first wave being up to 1920, the second wave being from 1960 to the 1980s, and the third wave being from the 1990s arguably to the present). The conceptual approach distinguishes the waves by their conceptual commitments (among other things, the first wave concerns securing political rights, the second wave concerns securing other rights such as economic rights or rights in the home, and the third wave concerns including women of all backgrounds). It is easy to conflate these approaches because they appear to largely overlap: the time periods in question appear to be dominated by the issues in question (it was up to 1920 when women were seeking the vote, it was after 1960 when women sought a broader array of rights, and it was in the 1990s when mainstream feminism became more inclusive). The problem with conflating these approaches is that the conceptual issues, while largely linked to the relevant time periods, also spread beyond and cannot be contained within the time periods in question. As I will discuss briefly within the first chapter, there are in fact multiple feminist groups that existed within the second and even the first waves that held third wave positions. For instance, anarcha-feminists from the historical period of the first wave held onto numerous views that would later be considered to be defining of the third wave.[10] Significantly, there are also women of color who actively pursued third wave feminist aims during the period that is designated to be second wave. For instance, Patricia Robinson argued for the sexual autonomy of black women in the 1968 position paper "Poor Black Women," and she also argued in favor of birth control.[11] The Third World Women's Alliance, with Black, Puerto Rican, and Asian American women members, was organizing across racial and ethnic groups to fight capitalism, displaying what historian Benita Roth calls "feminist organizing as intersectional."[12] Members of the Black Panther Party (an organization to which we will return shortly) were organizing, among other things, for the rights of Black women and advocating for gay rights.[13] As Bobby Seale, one of the co-founders of the Black Panther Party (BPP), put it, the BPP was an "'All Power to All the People!' organization…. Women of Black Panthers were an integral, critical influence in the feminist/women's rights movement. These black women were at the activist forefront of establishing more freedom and rights for women of every color."[14] Thus, the BPP included many women and some men who were fighting for the rights of black women in particular and for third wave feminist views in general, and their actions predate the typical start of the third wave by roughly two decades.

Thus, by conflating the two approaches, we risk alienating or even silencing women who held onto conceptual positions in different historical periods, such as women who held third wave views in the second wave period or even women who continue to hold second wave views during the third wave period. Once we tease apart these two approaches, we quickly see that the historical approach on its own loses its usefulness. If the "second wave" was used to pick out any feminism that happened in the 1960s through 1980s, then there would be no point to make the distinction other than to simply say when a particular feminist was alive. That is, we could say Patricia Robinson is a "second wave feminist" in this sense, but all we would mean by that is that Robinson was active during the 1960s and 1970s. The motif becomes much less useful to us if it is merely pointing to dates. Thus, in criticizing the wave metaphor, the point is to say that it is not useful in a purely historical approach and it is misleading in a mixed historical and conceptual approach since the two approaches do not perfectly overlap (as, for example, Patricia Robinson supported third wave concepts in the second wave time period). We then could instead concentrate on the conceptual points we want to make with the wave metaphor while also noting that largely these points followed, but were not limited to, certain historical periods.

Given a more conceptual approach to the wave metaphor, this book will argue that the women of the WUO were in some ways second wave feminists but were at the same time third wave feminists in other ways. This position is possible because the waves are being thought of here in the conceptual sense. From here on, I will specify when I mean to use the waves in a historical sense, and otherwise I will use the waves in conceptual senses as explained here, often without further specification as to the conceptual usage.

The WUO's feminism, while situated in the time period of the historical second wave, promoted conceptual views associated with the third wave. International and multiethnic in its worldview, the feminist philosophy of the Weatherwomen in particular, and the WUO in general, moved beyond the white, American, middle-class perspective to include the experiences of working class and Third World women. The Weatherwomen stated, "we are joining our lives with the needs and aspirations of poor and working class women."[15] Their actions attempted to make good on this third wave promise.

It is important to note that the WUO's work on this issue neither predated nor was more significant than similar work from working class women and women of color. While it is true that the Weatherwomen were largely white and middle to upper class, their work was heavily influenced by and derived from the work of the oppressed women whom they were attempting to support. The claim of significance here is that the WUO represented the first organization that both is largely made up of white and fairly privileged individuals (both men and women), and presented third wave conceptual positions, including the recognition that all feminists should fight for the rights of all women. Specifically, the WUO aimed to become allies to the oppressed, along the lines that BPP leader and co-founder Huey P. Newton was recommending. Newton had asked for white allies to make a choice: "they have a choice to make between whether they will be a friend of Lyndon Baines Johnson or a friend of Fidel Castro. A friend of Robert Kennedy or a friend of Ho Chi Minh."[16] By turning away from establishment politics and aligning themselves with the beleaguered, the WUO saw itself as answering that call from Huey P. Newton and the BPP.

The Weatherwomen's particular brand of feminism—a brand that incorporated second wave positions, a cogent critique of the second wave's insularity, early adoptions of third wave positions, and embraced militant tactics to bring about a socialist society with true gender equality—may be difficult to label precisely. As mentioned previously, feminism is quite diverse. U.S. women's history records a plethora of feminist movements forming in the second half of the 20th century: radical feminism, Marxist feminism, cultural feminism, sex-positive feminism, postmodern feminism, among many others. With this slew of distinct standpoints, one position—the one that will provide the background in this work for analyzing the WUO's own version of feminism—stands out in its absence: militant feminism. Perhaps this position has been overlooked because of the seeming contradiction of its terms: militant action appears to embrace masculine traits and endorse patriarchal values, accepting tactical violence over collaboration and peaceful resistance.[17]

Actual militant feminist groups—ones that embraced militancy in the pursuit of just and feminist aims—provided their own answers to this seeming paradox. While it may appear to the philosopher that feminism and militancy are contradictory, or at least inconsistent, the historical record offers several examples of groups in the second half of the 20th century in the United States that attempted to combine a principled feminist stance with a methodology that they felt required militancy. A couple of other groups that could arguably qualify for this label would be the Black Panther Party (BPP) and Cell 16.

Despite the lack of significant scholarly recognition for their feminist leanings, the Black Panthers represent one of the earliest proponents and developers of militant feminism in modern U.S. history.[18] Though much is made of the sexism that abounded within the ranks and even the leadership of the BPP, the BPP supported the advancement of women to leadership positions especially at local levels, demanded an environment inclusive of and respectful to women, modeled egalitarian and gender breaking behavior, and supported community programs that fit within feminist aims. These programs, run by both men and women, ensured the well-being of the black community and were responsive to the various needs of community members, with the BPP acting as "an ombudsman for many of the community's residents."[19] Among others, the BPP operated the breakfast program and the summer free lunch program, which fed hungry children and preteens, the clothing giveaway program that supported those seeking employment, medical clinics that provided accessible health care, legal clinics to familiarize individuals with their rights, and busing programs to prisons that attempted to keep family structures intact while family members were incarcerated.[20] Weekly political education classes offered analysis of everything from black history to socialism.[21] However, these grassroots and feminist organizing efforts were often times diminished in historical accounts in favor of sensationalized reports of the BPP as violent, which led them to be "relegated to the status of an outlaw fringe group."[22]

While the BPP certainly counts as an early militant feminist group, there were also clear limitations to their feminism, such as a lack of gender parity among national leadership. It wasn't until 1971 (five years after BPP was founded) that a woman took on an important leadership role at the national level as Elaine Brown became Minister of Information. Brown later became the Chairperson of the Party in 1974, but other female leaders in the BPP on the national stage were rare. Other notable women who played important roles in the BPP, such as Angela Davis or Assata Shakur, did not rise to national leadership.[23]

Roxanne Dunbar-Ortiz founded Cell 16 in 1968 as a Marxist radical feminist organization. She envisioned the group as part of the women's liberation movement, but also as independent, acting on its own in militant fashion if necessary. Dunbar-Ortiz stated that "masters do not relinquish power; it is wrestled from them," and that doing so might necessitate "warfare (guerrilla style)."[24] Cell 16's mission was to advance female liberation and "destroy the three pillars of class (caste) society—the family, private property, and the state—and their attendant evils—corporate capitalism, imperialism, war, racism, misogyny."[25] Consequently, Cell 16 can be characterized as a militant organization, while at the same time was also quite dedicated to feminist ideals.

This book considers how the WUO, which was heavily influenced by the BPP and, in turn, influenced Cell 16, was a militant feminist organization that worked to achieve gender parity in leadership, put forth a feminist agenda, and made strides in advancing feminist thinking. In fact, the WUO saw itself as a white ally of the Black Panther Party, fighting in solidarity with the group and in support of national liberation struggles. They were using their white privilege and putting their white bodies on the line in defense of what Newton called the black colony; they were building a white revolutionary movement aimed to take on structural racism.[26]

The Weatherwomen firmly committed themselves to militancy, as a 1969 statement made clear: "Our liberation as individuals and as women is possible when it is understood as a political process—part of the formation of an armed white fighting force. Political power grows out of the barrel of a gun, and the struggle to gain and use political power against the state is the armed struggle for our liberation."[27] The WUO believed that liberation and an achievement of true equality were only going to happen when women actively seized their freedom in a militant fashion. The WUO's combination of militancy with feminism certainly brought together conflicting viewpoints: it borrowed heavily from Marxist analysis, insisted on the importance of the intersections of race, class, and gender when assessing oppression, forged aims aligned to second wave feminism, and adopted conceptual third wave feminist positions.[28] As such, WUO's militant feminism was nuanced, layered, rich, and, thereby, worthy of further study.

The WUO therefore blended radical aims with feminist goals to respond to the problems that they perceived in the political and social milieu of their time period. This general openness to feminist aims, coexisting alongside a militant agenda and thriving in spite of macho posturing, is precisely why the concept of militant feminism fits the WUO so well. Militant feminism, as defined in this book, tempers outright militancy with a respect for and adherence to ethical and feminist values. While this book concentrates on the militant feminism of one group, the WUO, it is a significant movement among numerous groups, such as the BPP, Cell 16 and others, from this time period. Thus, militant feminism, especially as exemplified in the WUO, emerges as an important historical movement of the 1960s and 1970s that is often overlooked in histories of leftist social movements, of feminism, and of militant groups.

Though numerous commentators, including some of the Weatherwomen themselves, object to labeling the WUO as feminist, this work asserts that there is definitive evidence of the organization's substantive feminist aims.[29] As the following chapters reveal, this feminism flourished despite the undeniable sexism within the WUO, especially from many of the male leaders. These male leaders encouraged macho attitudes within WUO collectives and took sexual advantage of female members, all while paying lip service to sexual liberation. The main chroniclers of the WUO focus on these instances of sexism and male chauvinism and conclude that Weather's inherent sexism held back the Weatherwomen.[30]

The secondary literature's emphasis on this sexism overshadows the struggles and contributions of Weatherwomen to their own project of militant feminism. Neither did the sexist male leaders of WUO make up the whole of the organization, nor was the WUO organized in such a linear, hierarchical fashion that we could pinpoint the organization's positions simply by examining its male leadership. The WUO was a fluid organization whose leadership had a variety of messages, some of which were conflicting and varied over time. Focusing only on the sexism present in the WUO ignores the Weatherwomen's very real efforts to smash sexism both in society in general and in the WUO itself in particular. Such a one-sided focus also erases the many sites of empowerment that the Weatherwomen experienced—both of a personal nature and as exemplified through leadership positions and activities. Insofar as many of the women of the WUO, and some of the men, were both feminist and influential, it would be a mistake to dismiss out of hand the idea that the organization was feminist in a significant way.

Just as the overt sexism within the WUO has skewed its historical representation, so, too, has the organization's decentering of gender. Feminists of the era did not recognize the WUO as feminist because the group did not place gender at the forefront of their movement as second wave groups tended to do.[31] For some early radical feminists, such as Shulamith Firestone, women's oppression *qua women* was the core of identity politics and was not to be diluted with other identity or political issues.[32] The primary job of feminists was to fight for gender equality, just as it was the primary job of other oppressed groups to fight for their own empowerment. This second wave position of course relies on the lack of an intersectional analysis: it assumes that one can separate sites of oppression and feminists could concentrate only on gender and have no concern with race, class, sexuality, etc. Thus, to be a feminist, these second wavers felt that one had to put the fight for gender equality first and foremost.

The WUO did not accept this primacy of gender, which led many activists of the era or historical accounts of second wave feminism to not include the WUO as feminist. Yet, as this work makes clear, the group's political analysis most certainly included gender as a special category of women's oppression. The WUO furthered that feminist analysis with an articulation of how that oppression functioned as it intersected with class, race, and political status within the imperialist structure.[33] Drawing upon the work of bell hooks, who is more clearly a conceptual third wave feminist, and other third wave feminists who argue for a definition of feminism as a political consciousness that is both inclusive of differences and critical of privilege, this book considers how WUO members struggled to incorporate multiple subjectivities and experiences in the brand of feminism that they were forging.[34] The militant feminism that members of the WUO were fashioning recognized differences in class, race, and (to a lesser extent) sexuality, and it attempted to acknowledge the subjectivities of all women. Thus, the WUO's feminism is more reminiscent of third wave feminism's inclusiveness of multiple subjectivities than the more primarily gender-focused second wave feminist groups of their time period. By looking through a broader lens, we can reestablish the Weatherwomen as feminist according to today's more inclusive perspective.

This work locates the WUO's militant feminism in the pages of the organization's numerous pamphlets, communiqués, position papers, and newspaper articles. Memoirs of former WUO members add insight into the personalities, conflicts, and gender dynamics present within the WUO. Even FBI files and FBI informants support the idea that the WUO was concerned with female liberation. These various sources offer a great deal of information about the contributions—both theoretical and material— that the Weatherwomen made both to their organization and to the cause of feminism.

By shifting the focus from the male leadership and machismo of the group, which the literature on the WUO has emphasized up to now, to the Weatherwomen's roles and actions, the following chapters enlarge the current historical discourse and contribute a new and unique perspective on the WUO. In doing so, this book also offers a broader understanding of militant feminism and its place in the women's liberation movement, the leftist social movements of the 1960s, and social activism in 20th century U.S. history. In this context, militant feminism holds that the use of violence is justified if it is done in the pursuit of just ends, including ends that are required for the building of a feminist society. Militant feminism holds that women can use violence just as capably as men and that their use of it is justified as long as it is in the pursuit of morally required ends.

To understand how the WUO developed and put into practice its own version of militant feminism, this work begins by tracing the historical and theoretical roots of the organization, along with the personal inspirations of the individual members who took up this particular cause. While this book is providing a historical perspective on an actual, existing militant feminist organization, it is also developing a theoretical argument that recreates the Weatherwomen's own militant feminist position, in spite of the numerous detractors that argue that they have no such viewpoint. Due to this complexity, the book will not follow a traditional, chronological timeline that merely lays out what happened and when it happened. Instead, the chapters will lay out a case for militant feminism by first briefly laying out the chronological history (Chapter 1), examining the sexism of the WUO and the Weatherwomen's critical and constructive responses to it (Chapter 2), analyzing key examples of female leadership in the WUO (Chapter 3), and then showing the WUO's second wave (Chapter 4) and third wave elements (Chapter 5). Therefore, the book presents an overall argument with precise steps represented in each chapter: the Weatherwomen were actively fighting the WUO's sexism, they were developing their own version of militant feminism, they worked their way up to leadership in the organization, and their feminism is both second and third wave, disrupting the usual feminist wave metaphor that spells out the waves as distinct historical periods. Based on this argument, if it were to be persuasive, we would have to conclude first that we need to reexamine historical accounts of the WUO that deny their feminism. Second, we would also have to note that the WUO's feminism is historically significant in that it both represents its own, unique version of feminism (militant feminism) and it challenges the widespread, historical wave motif. Let's examine the major moves of this argument in a bit more detail before starting.

Chapter 1 provides a brief history of how the WUO developed out of another organization, the Students for a Democratic Society, including a discussion of how the WUO's leadership derived their theoretical views from the works of Karl Marx, Herbert Marcuse, Ernesto "Che" Guevara, and Regis Debray. The first chapter also looks at how WUO members saw the implementation of United States policies, both at home and abroad, as leading them to develop personal commitments to do something to foment meaningful change, which they believed would involve some level of militancy that would be both necessary and justified.

Having established the historical, theoretical, and some of the personal underpinnings for the WUO's belief that a revolution was needed to achieve feminist goals, Chapter 2 continues this discussion by highlighting the key contributions of Weatherwomen, both to the fight against the sexism of the WUO and to the production of the WUO's feminist mission. The second chapter navigates the complex waters that include the sexism present within the WUO (and its predecessor, Students for a Democratic Society), as well as how female members of the organization resisted this sexism by fighting it at an organizational level both through questioning male leadership and through creating feminist position papers and communications. Weatherwomen also fought against sexism on individual levels, speaking against the macho and overly-sexual attitudes of particular male WUO members.

By listening more carefully to the Weatherwomen's voices, we learn that many women found the WUO to be a locus of agency, autonomy, and empowerment. Chapter 3 explains how various women within the organization felt that the WUO allowed them to excel as persons in ways that were not otherwise possible given the pervasive and intense sexism that abounded throughout mainstream society in the late 60s and early 70s. To this end, the third chapter discusses various instances of female leadership within local WUO collectives and at the national level. Personal histories establish how individual Weatherwomen were able to express their political perspectives, to prove their full capabilities, and to establish their vision for a better society, which they were taking steps to enact. These women embraced militancy in a way that shattered gender constraints that painted them as passive, weak, and incapable of working to change the patriarchal society they found themselves trapped inside of. Though their methods may be morally suspect, the historical record ought to reflect that the Weatherwomen autonomously chose these methods in their attempt to break free from sexist constraints that would restrain them to the small set of gender roles that were recognized by and accepted within mainstream society. In short, despite claims that they were coerced or blinded by passion, the Weatherwomen were autonomously militant and active agents in their own right.

Chapter 4 begins the exploration of the particular brand of feminism that the Weatherwomen articulated. Though the WUO was highly critical of the women's liberation groups of their own time period, the WUO's feminism had clear connections to second wave objectives and positions. These connections include the WUO's positions and analyses on housework, childrearing, welfare, rape, sterilization, and, generally speaking, the right to be free of patriarchy. Since the current literature usually dismisses the feminism of the WUO, this chapter brings to light the many clear feminist concerns that the WUO articulated via women's quality of life.

Chapter 5 further elaborates on the WUO's brand of feminism as it contrasted with the second wave positions of their time period. This chapter argues that the WUO's feminism was adopting concepts from the third wave in substantial ways. The WUO maintained that the hegemonic second wave feminism of its time period did not address the needs or experiences of women of color, Third World women, or poor women. The WUO envisioned a version of feminism that would establish an alliance with all of these women while showing a concern with responding to *all* sorts of oppressions as they intermixed and intersected in most ordinary persons' real lives. Traditionally, this stance on the part of the WUO has been interpreted as the WUO dismissing female liberation, or really feminism itself, as a bourgeois concern. This chapter shows that such a characterization is misleading and uncharitable. A more accurate interpretation that fits the Weatherwomen's own writings focuses on the various ways in which the WUO was inclusive and anti-racist in its feminist vision. In other words, Chapter 5 argues that the WUO was concerned with female liberation, but was aiming to include all women, with their various, unique subjectivities. This chapter also explores instances of the WUO's position in regard to women's sexual experimentation, which will further establish that the WUO is more akin to a sex positive, third wave group when it comes to sexual issues.

The book's conclusion notes that the WUO offered a complex feminist agenda that was concerned with smashing sexism, breaking gender norms, and solving concrete social problems for women. Though they believed in using militancy to achieve social change, Weatherwomen also put limits on the use of violence, so that aggression would only be employed for the pursuit of just and feminist aims.

Overall, then, this work aims to correct certain misunderstandings of the WUO by concentrating on the actions and writings of its female members. This book puts the Weatherwomen at the forefront—asking how they managed to toil and thrive in the turbulent and patriarchal sixties. While other women fought to get out of the kitchen or the secretarial pool, these women were stepping onto the battlefield and into positions of organizational leadership. By highlighting their contributions and experiences, this work allows the Weatherwomen to speak for themselves as the strong, autonomous, revolutionary agents of change that they were.

CHAPTER 1

Militant Feminism in the Weather Underground Organization

On March 6, 1974, a blast rocked the federal offices of the Department of Health, Education, and Welfare (HEW) in San Francisco. The bomb had been set by the Women's Brigade of the Weather Underground Organization (WUO) to draw attention to the plight of poor women, especially welfare recipients. The communiqué accompanying the bombing pronounced that this action is for all women who:

> —wait in lines for too few food stamps and brave food distribution lines because our families have to eat;
> —worry through degrading forms and humiliating rule and regulations;
> —are kept out of paying jobs because there are no child care programs;
> —struggle to raise our children while we're called "pigs at the trough" and "lazy parasites" by reactionary male politicians....[1]

The communiqué was delivered in commemoration of International Women's Day, March 8, "in solidarity with the rising resistance of women."[2] It outlined a plethora of issues that marginalized women faced, from sterilization abuses to denying them welfare benefits.[3] The communiqué listed a number of complaints, including criticisms of Ronald Reagan (then Governor of California) and Caspar Weinberger (Secretary of Health, Education, and Welfare from 1973 to 1975), who both blamed women for their poverty while simultaneously trying to cut back welfare benefits in the name of fiscal responsibility.[4] The Weatherwomen felt so strongly about the unfair treatment that these women experienced that they believed that radical acts—such as bombing a federal office building—were appropriate courses of action.

How had the members of the Women's Brigade gotten to the point where militancy had become just another tool to affect political and social change? In asking this question, we must note that "militancy" is used as a term inclusive of violence, in that it denotes an aggressive, non-peaceful method of protest or resistance. Furthermore, militancy refers to a combative way of achieving political change. Thus, a political organization can be militant by being violent (against persons or non-persons, including buildings or statutes), by threatening violence, or by merely taking up the tools of violence in a militant posture (as the Black Panther Party did when they openly carried guns).[5] The WUO employed militant methods to achieve social and political change or to raise awareness of issues it deemed problematic in some way— and it arrived at these methods gradually, over the course of its existence.

The WUO was born amidst the turmoil of the sixties and was very much shaped and influenced by the political unrest of that time period. Against the background of the Vietnam War with its rising death toll, various social movements were taking shape at home, fomenting change in myriad ways. From the fight for civil rights, to national liberation struggles, to anti-imperialist organizing, to the anti-war movement, and to the women's movement, the sixties were filled with political rebellion and a search for justice and equality.

Through their militant stances and actions, the WUO was attempting to find a path to their vision of a just society, which would be a society devoid of sexism, racism, and capitalist exploitation. From the very beginning of its emergence from the Students for a Democratic Society (SDS), the WUO was not only committed to militancy, but also explored feminist aims. The organization exemplified militant feminism: it believed that a just society would be a feminist society, while also holding that militant methods were justified in the attempt to bring that society about. The following sections briefly trace the development of this organization in an effort to both understand militant feminism as a position and to locate the WUO's position in history as a militant feminist group. Overall, this chapter analyzes the organization's genesis, ideology, and proper place in the history of the sixties, radical leftist organizations, and feminist organizations.

White Mother Country Radicals: Increasing Militancy, Creating a White Fighting Force and Embracing Manliness[6]

Often described as a turbulent decade, the 1960s in the United States could reasonably be characterized via a series of leftist reactions to perceived instances of injustice, which many of those leftists believed were largely perpetrated by the United States government and U.S. corporations through imperialist policies (where imperialism is defined as one country's systematic method of gaining controlling influence over at least one other country through coercion, force, and manipulation).[7] These injustices revolved around the mistreatment of African Americans, women, LGBTQ individuals, impoverished individuals, and other oppressed groups at home, along with wars of aggression and alleged coup d'états abroad, such as wars in Korea (1950–1953) and Vietnam (1955–1975), and coups in Iran (1953), Guatemala (1954), Indonesia (1958), Cuba (1959), the Congo (1960), Dominican Republic (1961), Ghana (1966), and others.[8] While President Lyndon B. Johnson presented the Vietnam War as necessary to stop "godless communism," anti-war demonstrators characterized it as unbridled imperialism and a denial of democracy abroad.[9]

Initially, leftist organizations reacted to these perceived injustices through almost entirely non-violent means, such as forming non-violent organizations, arranging protests, and engaging in civil disobedience. The National Association for the Advancement of Colored People (NAACP), Congress of Racial Equity (CORE), Southern Christian Leadership Conference (SCLC), Student Nonviolent Coordinating Committee (SNCC), churches, and other grassroots organizations took direct action through voting registration projects, sit-ins, boycotts, mass protests, and Freedom Rides. These actions relied on mass mobilization and non-violence—in fact, the quiet determination and dignity of African Americans protesting at lunch counters or on buses emphasized the inhumanity of white bigots.[10]

Unfortunately, attacks on activists continued. For just a few examples, let us consider how Fannie Lou Hamer was grossly beaten, on the back of her head and her "hands till they turned blue,"[11] for her efforts at voter registration in the south in Winona, Mississippi, in June 1963, or how James Chaney, Michael Schwerner, and Andrew Goodman, three civil rights activists, were murdered during Freedom Summer in 1964.[12] Activists felt that something needed to be done, as traditional forms of support—such as protection from the Federal Bureau of Investigation (FBI) or the Justice Department under Robert Kennedy—were not ameliorating the violence on the ground. As Hamer explained it:

> I really believed that—believed with all my heart—that they would protect you. Until a certain length of time. So much went on that nothing was done about, and I had a kind of little leery feeling: Would they really protect us or not? ... we would just talk about it among ourselves, and some of them would finally just give up on it and say

there wasn't nothing going to be done. That's when I've seen a lot of people, black young people and white young people, become disgusted and disillusioned with the whole setup, you know. They said, "There ain't nobody going to do nothing," and all of that.[13]

Hence, the non-violent movement felt, to many of the young people of the time, to require positive responses from people outside of the movement. One key goal of relying on non-violence was to establish a clear distinction between those who used violence (who at the time were the bigots and the oppressors) and those who used non-violence (who were the civil rights activists). Yet, the more time went on, the less it seemed that the outside world was tracking this distinction: the violence of the oppressors seemed to be rewarded either by being ignored or by receiving implicit support from people who were not troubled by the oppression of others who were so different than them, so many young people became disenchanted with the non-violent approach.

Activists grew weary of the non-violent principles that they felt were bringing change too slowly and leaving them with no defense against harm. In fact, the FBI, through its Counterintelligence Program (COINTELPRO), was keeping track of activists involved in the Civil Rights Movement, and of organizations such as SCLC, CORE or SNCC, but not to offer help.[14] As a memo dated August 25, 1967, detailed, the purpose of COINTELPRO was to "expose, disrupt, misdirect, or otherwise neutralize the activities of black nationalist, hate-type organizations and groupings, their leadership, spokesmen, membership, and supporters."[15] As such, activists turned increasingly toward self-defense. Organizers Kwame Ture (who was then known as Stokely Carmichael) and Charles V. Hamilton, for example, said, "Black people in America have no time to play nice, polite parlor games—especially when the lives of their black children are at stake."[16]

As such, militant organizations began to emerge during this period of discontent in the mid to late 60s. One of the first large militant leftist groups was the Black Panther Party for Self Defense (BPP), founded in 1966. Developing from a platform of protecting community neighborhoods from the brutality of police to a broader appeal for social justice, equality, and political self-determination for African Americans, the BPP quickly gained national prominence and acquired a reputation for militancy, mainly due to its protest against gun control in May 1967 at the statehouse in Sacramento.[17] The BPP held that "liberties are not given they are taken," and that doing so is a constitutional right of Black people.[18] The FBI, under its Counterintelligence Program (COINTELPRO), kept track of the BPP's activity throughout the country, warning that "the organization is growing in influence and is very attractive to militant youths" and cautioning of "connections with foreign revolutionaries."[19] Indeed, by 1968, the Black Panther Party was working toward an agenda of international socialist revolution.[20]

During this time period, Puerto Rican activists likewise formed their own organization, the Young Lords, on September 23, 1968.[21] A militant leftist group modeled along the lines of the BPP, the Young Lords united around the aims of Puerto Rican self-determination and neighborhood control, developing programs aimed at improving conditions in local communities. The organization also created a Thirteen Point Program, akin to the BPP's Ten Point Program. Both of these programs outlined their organizations' platforms and visions, from fighting for "the liberation of all oppressed people" (from the Young Lords' Thirteen Point Program) to demanding "Power to Determine the Destiny of Our Black Community" (from the BPP's Ten Point Program).[22]

Asian American activists were also organizing. As activist Warren Furutani put it, "our 'Movement' was the result of the racial, social, and economic oppression of Asian Pacific American and people of color in America."[23] Activist Amy Uyematsu added that "the blacks and yellows have suffered similar consequences as Third World people at the hands of American capitalist power."[24] Alongside African American activists, Asian American activists "were protesting their maltreatment in this country, struggling with the prospect of fighting against an enemy whom they in some cases resembled [in Vietnam], while both decried the hypocrisy of America's neocolonialist aggression abroad."[25] Asian-American anti-racist struggles were modeled on a BPP style, and Asian American activists began to see themselves as an internal colony that was being oppressed within the United States, necessitating active resistance.

In the same time period, as other organizations moved from dedicated non-violent stances to more militant and international outlooks, the organization Students for a Democratic Society (SDS) followed suit. Formed in 1962, SDS became a nation-wide student organization for young activists, with numerous chapters across college campuses. SDS originally upheld a non-violent platform that was designed to achieve change through community organizing, student activism, alliances with labor or civil rights leaders, and electoral politics.[26] Following the BPP's prescription that white activists should not spearhead the protests for civil rights, SDS maintained a policy that it was improper for white activists to lead efforts for black self-determination. First, they acted through the Economic Research and Action Project (ERAP), which aimed to address economic and political inequality in predominantly black neighborhoods. Here, they tried to form community-based grass-roots organizations to ameliorate conditions in each locality, offering anything from information, to childcare, to access to legal help. Later, they worked with the Columbia University student protest of 1968, supporting black student organizers who were resisting the building of a gymnasium in Harlem's Morningside Park. Overall, SDS tried to work in a supportive role, embracing an agenda of racial integration and multi-racial alliance.[27]

SDS also identified U.S. policy in national and international matters as problematic and unjust: they saw the United States' domestic and foreign policies as supporting a racist system designed to maintain U.S. political and economic hegemony through a repression of national liberation struggles.[28] As the Vietnam War escalated, SDS also adopted an international outlook supporting revolutionary activity, thus moving SDS closer to a militant stance.[29]

Bernardine Dohrn, an SDS member who rose to national leadership—and later also became a WUO leader—explained that for 1968–1969, SDS's national strategy was multi pronged:

1. promote power-structure research into war-related institutional activity in colleges and universities (including ROTC) to focus and inform local campaigns against the Vietnam War;

2. encourage SDS chapters to engage with and act in solidarity with emerging black student unions on campuses, to support calls for black studies, community worker solidarity, and to demand open enrollment;

3. escalate educational tactics of direct action, civil disobedience, and militancy.[30]

This militancy became more pronounced during 1968, as SDS became focused on stopping U.S. imperialism through political *and* combative means.[31] As Dohrn recalled, "action merged with anger and anxiety about the draft and rebellious alienation from the established order. We were not afraid to offend. Increasingly, the talk was of revolution."[32]

The year 1968 was generally a time of increasing disruption and disturbance, which inspired activists to become more radical. For example, in terms of the Vietnam War, at the end of January, the National Liberation Front launched a coordinated attack against Southern Vietnamese and U.S. forces, illustrating the weakness of U.S. policy in Vietnam. The assault was large-scale: over 120 cities and the U.S. Embassy in Saigon were attacked.[33] In the wake of the Tet Offensive, as the attack was called—and its accompanying television coverage that brought the carnage into living rooms—not only was it increasingly apparent that the war was immoral and problematic, but also that the cost of a U.S. victory would be extremely high. On April 4 of that same year, Martin Luther King, Jr., was assassinated, sowing further upheaval and distrust throughout the nation. As historian Max Elbaum puts it, King's assassination "convinced thousands that the nonviolent road he advocated was a dead end."[34] Another assassination soon followed on June 5, as Robert Kennedy—the Democratic anti-war candidate for President of the United States—was assassinated in Los Angeles after winning the California presidential primary. Folks were stunned and angered, as death seemed to follow respected leaders who offered peace and hope for a better future.

Unrest followed with the August Democratic Convention in Chicago, where police attacked demonstrators indiscriminately. With this event also being televised—and as demonstrators were chanting, "The Whole World is watching!"—it became more apparent than ever to the young generation of the time that working within the system was fruitless.[35] As Elbaum explains, "the combination of unrestrained police violence with Humphrey's election—which meant that both major parties fielded pro-war presidential candidates—drove the final nail in the coffin of the work-within-the-system formulas."[36] A revolutionary, militant spirit, fed up with the ineffectiveness of the system, was permeating the nation.

Following up on all of these events, in the spring of 1969, SDS members authored position papers, such as "Hot Town: Summer in the City or I Ain't Gonna Work on Maggie's Farm No More," which openly alluded to an increased revolutionary militancy ("Maggie's Farm" stood for the Pentagon in SDS/WUO speak).[37] "Hot Town: Summer in the City" explicitly stated that public fights with the repressive state apparatus—and not just a sense of solidarity with those who are oppressed—would serve a strategic function in raising political consciousness and would build solidarity. Jim Mellen and Bill Ayers, the authors of the paper, wrote that "there should be involvement by SDS people in the neighborhood issues as they come up: a fight in the park, a protest against the pigs" as part of coalition building and "political outreach into the community."[38] This fighting, revolutionary spirit was no mere intellectual opposition, but rather was developing into a militant stance.

Not all SDS members accepted this growing embrace of militancy; as a result, tensions rose within the group. In the spring of 1969, building on this fissure, two separate factions of SDS each published conflicting revolutionary platform papers, prefacing SDS's eventual split. The Worker Student Alliance (WSA), which was organized and putatively controlled by the non-student organization, the Progressive Labor Party (PL), released "Revolutionaries Must Fight Nationalism."[39] PL was a Maoist organization that believed that the Communist Party USA (CPUSA) had become too subservient to the Soviet Union, and supported non-revolutionary actions, such as participating in elections.[40] The PL/WSA's paper took a strong stance against nationalism, which involves active, political support for a specific national identity. A nation is a collection of people who see themselves as inherently connected through their membership in the regional group, such as the French nation, the nation of Venezuela, the Mongolian nation, etc. Importantly, while a nation can be seen as identical to an internationally recognized country, a nation often is something different: we think of many groups as having national identities even when they do not have legal control over a specific country. For instance, we can talk about the Kurdish national identity (even though there is currently no Kurdistan) or the French-Canadian national identity (even though the country Canada is not exclusively made up of French Canadians). Given this understanding of nation, we can roughly think of nationalism as the promotion of a distinct, collective ideology associated with a given nation and the pursuit of a given set of national interests for the group of people associated with that given nation. Therefore, one usual sense of nationalism connects it to a national identity that is connected to being patriotic within a certain country, such as American patriotism, Romanian patriotism, Vietnamese patriotism, Botswanian patriotism, etc. Yet, we also see, especially during the 1960s, nationalism spread among oppressed groups, such as a sense of collective African American belonging (black nationalism) or Latinx identity (Latinx nationalism). This second type of nationalism can be seen as a response to colonialism (such as Algerians insisting on their nationalism during French occupation) or racial oppression (such as African Americans insisting that they feel a sense of black nationalism in contrast to their feeling that their country did not represent them). In this manner, nationalism is seen as a way to unify identity to help in resisting oppression.

The PL/WSA's "Revolutionaries Must Fight Nationalism" paper argued that all forms of nationalism—whether in the hands of oppressive colonial powers or oppressed groups that sought freedom for their peoples—were reactionary and contrary to the mission of communism. As David Gilbert explained it, this position "denied the very independence and self determination that oppressed people had been fighting for."[41] Nevertheless, the PL/WSA felt that nationalism of any kind was divisive and ultimately needed to be torn down.

Since this PL/WSA paper appeared to attack many groups that other SDS members allied themselves with, such as the BPP who took a stance in favor of black nationalism or the Young Lords who supported Puerto Rican nationality, and it represented a substantial departure from SDS's previous position that national liberation groups were justified in developing a political and socio-cultural agenda in response to attacks on their culture, society, or lives from U.S. imperialism, it was intensely controversial. Further, nationalism was also important over issues related to Vietnam. It is common in wars of aggression that imperial (or neo-imperial) powers critique liberation armies as merely engaged in nationalism insofar as liberation armies are putting their national interest above the interests of the imperial power. Thus, in a war like the Vietnam War, it made sense for the SDS to support the National Liberation Front in its struggle for self-determination: that is, the Vietnamese had more right to determine the future of Vietnam than imperial powers like the French or the United States did (the PL did support Vietnam, but only because it was being attacked by the United States). Thus, this paper was instantaneously and extremely divisive. Contrary to the message of the PL/WSA position paper, just a couple of months prior, an SDS resolution had clearly articulated SDS's "support for the Black Panther Party and their essentially correct program for the liberation of the black colony" as well as its "commitment to defend the Black Panther Party and the black colony against the vicious attacks of the racist pig power structure."[42] In other words, up to this point, SDS had envisioned itself as a backer of the BPP, and abandoning it, as the WSA suggested, seemed inimical to what many felt SDS purportedly stood for. As Dohrn put it, the BPP was leading the way to their own national liberation and, as white allies, SDS members needed to form a white revolutionary movement that would support the BPP and would work on anti-racism in an allied fashion.[43]

The immediate dispute with the WSA position led to a response paper from the other main faction of SDS, the Revolutionary Youth Movement (RYM), entitled "You Don't Need a Weatherman to Know Which Way the Wind Blows."[44] This piece staked out a position that, among others, (a) identified black people within the United States as an oppressed colony that needed support in achieving self-determination; (b) pointed to the youth as an ally of oppressed factions within the United States and abroad; and (c) pointed out that nationalism, in certain forms, is a significant tool to fight colonialism, and therefore, imperialism. These positions went against those of the PL and the WSA. To draw a clear distinction between the nationalism of oppressed groups and that of imperialist states, RYM identified black nationalism in particular as a necessary step in the worldwide struggle that stood in opposition to U.S. imperialism. This statement, referred to for short as the "Weatherman" paper, also pointed toward the goals that RYM would try to achieve through SDS: the creation of a broad coalition to throw out imperialism, which would include groups that embraced their own nationalism (contrary to the PL's demands that these groups overcome their nationalism), followed by the installation of worldwide socialism. To achieve these goals, they would build a revolutionary youth movement (from which their name derived) that would fight the agents of the imperialist state at every opportunity.

At the June 1969 SDS National Convention in Chicago, the two sides found no way to resolve their stark differences in this factionalist divide. Their impasse led to a fracturing of the organization. Members of RYM, encouraged by the BPP, voted to expel PL members, and seized the SDS national office, which contained the national member list.[45] Essentially, what was left of the SDS organization, after this move, was a national office that was staffed by RYM members; the WSA and their PL backers effectively were removed from power in SDS. RYM later split into multiple organizations, with the largest one being the Weathermen—an organization named after the "Weatherman" paper, which represented the SDS's final rupture as an organization. As WUO chronicler Harold Jacobs puts it, "from the destruction of SDS something new was created—a small, tightly organized revolutionary fighting force of white youth."[46] Initially known simply as Weatherman or the Weathermen Organization, this group later changed its name to the Weather Underground Organization in December 1970 so as to indicate inclusivity and less gender bias.[47] As a remnant of SDS, it had a presence across the nation, with "collectives in Boston, Cleveland, New York, Denver, Pittsburgh, Chicago, Detroit, Cincinnati, Columbus, and Grand Rapids."[48]

The organization had a multi-faceted ideology, based not only in theory, but also in practice. The "You Don't Need a Weatherman" paper not only gave the budding Weatherman organization their name, but also stated their initial ideology, viewpoints, and methodology. Building on the militancy previously expressed in "Hot Town: Summer in the City," the "Weatherman" paper stated that a fighting force was needed to take on the massive imperialist system. The Weatherman strategy was to reach out to those disenfranchised by the current political system, especially the youth, and to tap into their discontent:

> They are the ones who most often get drafted, who get the worst jobs if they get any, who are the most abused by the various institutions of social control…. And their day

to day existence indicates a potential for militancy and toughness. They are the people whom we can reach who at this stage are most ready to engage in militant revolutionary struggle.[49]

Mobilizing and assembling the oppressed masses into a fighting force was part and parcel of creating change for the Weathermen. As the militant stance of the Weathermen became more pronounced, they openly espoused revolutionary struggle as a way to address political problems. WUO historian Ron Jacobs explains that "weather, on the other hand, had fewer qualms [about violence] and was convinced that planned offensive actions were necessary because what was at stake was no longer proving that it was on the right side, but seizing military power."[50] They felt that the time for negotiation or peaceful protest was over, largely because they now saw these methods as ineffective—the imperialist system could eventually accommodate these less invasive methods and continue on uninterrupted. In the 1969 pamphlet "Bringing the War Home," Weathermen Kathy Boudin, Bernardine Dohrn, and Terry Robbins articulated this belief, stating that "all those who are orderly, polite, and well behaved are welcomed to imperialism and will be absorbed."[51] Thus, their strong, militant views derived from their frustrations with the ways in which they saw the well known, more pacifist methods previously employed throughout the 1960s as ultimately ineffective in stopping the mechanisms of imperialism, racism, and sexism. These were also a direct outcome with the disenchantment and frustration brought about by all the traumatic events of 1968 in particular and the sixties in general.

Their openly militant stance also appeared in the Weathermen newspaper, *The Fire Next Time,* or *FIRE!* for short. For example, the November 7, 1969, issue of *FIRE!* stated that "it is neither numbers nor loud voices alone that will bring imperialism down, but real material attacks on the state."[52] Following up on that pugnacious stance, the December 6, 1969, issue of *FIRE!* displayed a cover that openly advocated a confrontational stance: "During the 1960's, the Amerikan [sic] government was on trial for crimes against the people of the world. We now find the government guilty and sentence it to death in the streets."[53] The Weathermen made no attempt to sugarcoat their militancy.[54]

To develop into a fighting force, Weathermen maintained the position that revolutionaries needed to be competent, aggressive, and tough fighters. They needed to attract the kinds of individuals who would be unafraid to engage with the police, if necessary. Cathy Wilkerson, a Weatherwoman, explained that they were actively cultivating a strong and militant stance out of a sense of "trying to reach white youth on the basis of their most reactionary macho instinct, intellectuals playing at working class toughs."[55] In a similar vein, Weathermen Mark Rudd and Terry Robbins also wrote in *The New Left Notes* that the Weathermen needed to be "a movement that fights, not just talks about fighting. The aggressiveness, seriousness, and toughness ... will attract vast members of working class youth."[56]

This tough image of active fighters is gendered male in that it associated revolutionary fitness with hyper-masculine qualities. However, this image did not exclude the organization's female members from full participation. Indeed, some of the Weatherwomen viewed this embrace of traditionally masculine attributes as not only necessary in the pursuit of regime change, but also as personally liberating. As Wilkerson put it, "part of me, however, enjoyed the macho posturing.... The toughness was an ultimate rejection of the image of feminine helplessness that had saturated the literature and manners of my childhood."[57] Susan Stern, another Weatherwoman, explained that acquiring revolutionary toughness and organizing for the revolution made her feel like she "would never again know how to be or want to be Susan Stern—student, housewife, potential mother."[58] Weatherwoman Laura Whitehorn echoed this attitude, stating that as a revolutionary, she thought of herself as something more than a wife or a piece of property; through revolutionary activity she felt empowered.[59] Phoebe Hirsch, another Weatherwoman, explained that after embracing aggressiveness—in particular, after she "socked [a] cop to prove to myself that I wasn't intimidated"—she felt that "if I can do that I can do anything, because that uniform is so scary."[60] This attitude—that the embrace of toughness or violence could be liberating for women—alludes to the tempering of chauvinist tendencies that otherwise could have overtaken the Weathermen.

Though an unreflective embrace of masculine attributes often marks patriarchal thinking in a way that furthers the oppression of women, Weatherwomen were autonomously choosing to accept and adopt these masculine attributes as their own. The acceptance of the masculinity inherent to their organization by the Weatherwomen does not entail that the men were initially right to develop and encourage this movement towards reinforcing gender norms. It does though suggest that a simple denunciation of the practice as a whole ignores how the women themselves responded positively to it. Numerous Weatherwomen embraced these aggressive and militant gender norms, which would elsewhere be oppressive, as they judged them to be subversive and personally liberating, thus prefacing the WUO's militant feminist position.

Living Your Conscience Within the Heartland of a World-Wide Monster: The Theoretical Underpinnings of the WUO's Militancy[61]

The WUO was not afraid to take an openly militant stance; in fact, they saw their militancy as part of a second American Revolution.[62] But the WUO's militancy was not simply coming out of pre-theoretical dissatisfaction with the current political system, but out of a well-developed theoretical analysis, which was heavily indebted to Karl Marx as well as similar theorists such as Herbert Marcuse, Regis Debray, and Ernesto "Che" Guevara.[63] Having examined the historical path that led to the WUO's militant feminism, it is next incumbent on us to seek out the theoretical path that similarly led to militant feminism.

One of the main tenets of Marxism is that capitalism necessarily exploits labor, thus alienating the worker from the daily activity of his or her labor, the products of that labor, the value that derives from that labor, and eventually from the worker's very humanity. When Marx, or other Marxists, argue that capitalism necessarily exploits labor, they simply mean that the worker is always paid less than the value of their labor. This lower pay is necessitated by the capitalist's need to create profit—profit just is what is left over from the full value of the worker's labor after the worker has been paid (and materials have been bought). This initial exploitation then is undeniable. What's more contentious is how the capitalist turns the exploitation of the worker into an alienation of the worker that truly harms the worker in multiple ways. Capitalism alienates the worker from his or her humanity since the capitalist treats the worker as a product-making machine. The worker, as a machine, is reducible to how much monetary value the capitalist can profit from his or her labor. The capitalist has no interest in the worker's humanity since paying the worker enough to show concern for their humanity (i.e., to make sure that the worker has enough money to live a good life) involves taking less profit. Instead, the capitalist only wants to see the worker as a machine (without concern whether the worker's salary would allow for a comfortable life) that creates products that can be transformed into maximum profits for the capitalist.[64] Therefore, the exploitation of the worker's monetary value, which involves ensuring that the worker produces more than they are paid, leads to an alienation of the worker's humanity, which involves reducing the worker into a machine whose exact worth must be calculated and limited so as to maximize profit.

The exploitation and alienation inherent in the capitalist system is also seen in the practice of colonialism, which Marxists have likewise condemned.[65] Just as the capitalist seeks to maximize their own profits, the imperial power seeks to maximize their gains from their colony. It then follows that colonized people are being alienated from their land (it is treated like it is not theirs to value, theirs to protect, or theirs to hold domain over), alienated from the natural resources that derive from their land, alienated from the value they have created in their country, and alienated from their humanity as the colonizers make decisions for them as if they were children. Thus, at both home and abroad, Marxists would necessarily critique an American system that oppressed through capitalist economics and imperialist foreign policy.

As Marxists, members of the WUO critiqued what they saw as the United State's capitalist and imperialist policies. The WUO further believed the entire system was also anchored in white privilege, as the WUO held that white, middle class folks (and those even more affluent than them) "had been bought off by the spoils of Empire, and [were] thoroughly racist and sexist."[66] And as white allies, the WUO saw itself as using its white skin privilege to actually create change: fomenting resistance was thus necessary, through education of the masses, as well as through militancy. The WUO linked labor to the need for socialist revolution, proposing that once the workers realized the extent of their alienation and oppression, the process of dismantling the capitalist system would begin. Historian Harold Jacobs explains that they "argued in this debate that most all Americans are workers in the Marxist sense and that socialist revolution was in almost everybody's objective interest. Instead of seeking to curb student violence, Weatherman [sic] saw the onset of a sustained armed struggle against the state as the best means of creating revolutionary consciousness among American people."[67] In this way, the WUO connected Marxist analysis and militancy, for the aim of destroying imperialism and colonialism.

Moreover, the WUO saw a concrete causal connection between capitalist wealth in the U.S. and imperialist aggression abroad, stating, "We are within the heartland of a world-wide monster.... The U.S. empire channels wealth, based upon the labor and resources of the rest of the world, into the United States."[68] Therefore, the WUO advocated an alliance with all Third World nations, and saw itself as part of an international militant socialist struggle. Summing it up nicely, the WUO's FBI file encapsulated this stance as "an unshakeable faith that imperialism will only be defeated through a world-wide linking up of the revolutionary process."[69]

In addition to Marx, the philosopher Herbert Marcuse offered another theoretical foundation for the WUO. Marcuse, in his 1965 essay "Repressive Tolerance," articulated the foundation for the right to resist oppressive state behavior.[70] This right to active intolerance of the state apparatus served as the WUO's basis for its insurgency as Marcuse allowed for extra-legal measures to achieve social change.[71] Furthermore, Marcuse's *One Dimensional Man* linked the exploitation of labor with social repression and domination, advocating through the concept of the "Great Refusal," which would lead to the abandonment of the entire system.[72] Likewise, in *An Essay on Liberation*, Marcuse also noted that change needed to start in "the advanced capitalist countries" as "the internal weakening of the superpower can finally stop the financing and equipping of suppression" in the rest of the world (especially the Third World).[73] As such, the WUO saw itself as following a Marcusian mandate inside the United States to actively resist the system through their militant actions, disrupt capitalist, imperialist colonialism, and aid in world-wide liberation.[74]

The WUO's militant actions were further styled according to the teachings of Ernesto "Che" Guevara and Regis Debray. Argentine Marxist revolutionary and guerrilla fighter Che had declared that "to wish the victims [of imperialism] success is not enough; the thing is to share their fate, to join them in death or victory" and had also called for the creation of "two, three, many Vietnams" as a way to achieve national liberation and defeat imperialism.[75] The WUO associated itself with Che, and with the tactics he upheld.[76] Che proposed a strategy of mass-guerrilla warfare to lead a revolutionary war, and also supported a *foco* strategy, which was discussed in Regis Debray's *Revolution in the Revolution?*[77] A French journalist who had written his book to communicate the lessons of the Cuban Revolution, Debray explained that a small group of fighters could create a mass revolution. The idea was that a few guerrillas could act together to swiftly attack the enemy, vanishing easily. In the process, they would come to inspire the oppressed masses, raising their consciousness and encouraging them all to engage in revolution.[78] As Ron Jacobs puts it, "The importance to Weatherman of Debray's book is impossible to overstate. In addition to underground newspapers and other Left periodicals, well-thumbed copies of *Revolution in the Revolution?* were to be found in every Weather collective's house."[79] FBI infiltrator Larry Grathwohl corroborated that pronouncement, testifying that well-worn copies of the book were present in each of the collectives he had visited throughout his assignment.[80] The FBI concluded that the heavy influence of Debray's theory showed the WUO's commitment to guerrilla action.[81] *Foco* groups appealed to the WUO: they did not need to be deterred by their small numbers in the struggle against the state. They could attack the state from small autonomous collectives while also inspiring and educating the masses.[82]

Thus, the intellectual background of the WUO pulled together multiple sources, including the works of Karl Marx, Herbert Marcuse, Che Guevara, and Regis Debray. From the works of these writers, the WUO gathered philosophy, theory, and practical ideas. Yet, as we will see next, they also had a wide variety of personal foundations for their beliefs and motivations.

Personal Underpinnings of the WUO's Militancy

In addition to this theoretical commitment to militancy, the members of the WUO felt a deep personal commitment to social change. For many individual members, a sense of duty was born out of a respect for human life and out of a horror at the varied human suffering seen in Vietnam, the Third World, and at home. Whether it was derived from poverty, political repression, or racism, this sentiment moved many members of the WUO to feel they had to do something to try to cease the suffering. For example, Weatherwoman Bernardine Dohrn stated, "In my view white supremacy and anti-imperialism were at the core of what we understood and were right about."[83] For Dohrn, militancy was not about blind rage or a willful destruction of property, but was, at its core, about a dedication to fighting racism and promoting national liberation.

Weatherman David Gilbert expressed much of the same sentiment, articulating that revolutionary struggle was the way to achieve a fairer, more just, less racist society. "I did not want to pass on to my children a society wracked by racism and unjust wars," Gilbert explained, "where the almighty dollar was valued far above human beings. Joining with the Black struggle for human rights was a key to achieving a more humane society for white people also."[84] Sharing in the same convictions, Weatherwoman Kathy Boudin said, "I felt very keenly the decimation and murder created by the United States all over the world. I felt if we didn't commit ourselves to resisting it full time, nothing would change."[85] For Boudin, taking action gave concrete expression to her beliefs—to do any less would have been unconscionable.

Weatherman Shin'ya Ono felt that action in the streets would serve as an example that would encourage others to act against injustice and have an almost transformative effect on their consciousness as they come to realize that they, themselves, were previously racist or bigoted. As he put it,

> To see a group of other whites willing to fight to the very end on the side of the blacks will be a shocking experience for most whites. The existence of such whites, and actually seeing them fight, will hit hard at the core of their racist being in ways no words or analyses alone can do. The resulting fluidity of their consciousness will provide us with a radical space through which we can begin to communicate a class analysis of their own oppression. Without the reality of white groups actually fighting on the side of the blacks, the racism of whites could never be broken through, let alone overcome systematically.
>
> While you confront their racism in this manner, you also must show a concrete alternative by identifying and actually attacking the real enemy, that is, the various imperialist institutions implicated in their class oppression....[86]

As Ono envisioned it, militancy in the streets acted as a model of activist behavior for others to follow. It would especially, as Ono argued, provide alternative visions of what white people could do to reject their white privilege and take up the fight in favor of black people (as well as other minorities) who were being oppressed. In effect, it was a tool to raise the consciousness of others (especially privileged others), and served an important purpose in those folks' revolutionary education. Overall, it would lead to a transformative change of society for the better, as capitalism and imperialism were to be dismantled.

Perhaps it is Weatherwoman Naomi Jaffe who best clarifies the militant commitment of the WUO:

> Violence can mean a lot of different things. We felt that doing nothing in a period of repressive violence is itself a form of violence. That is the part that I think is hardest for people to understand. That if you sit in your house and live your white life and go to your white job, and allow the country that you live in to murder people and to commit genocide, and you sit there and you don't do anything about it, then that's violence.[87]

Here, Jaffe argues that even ordinary people are complicit in the violence committed in their names by their governments. Thus, if you pay taxes that are used for war or you simply do nothing when your government engages in illicit violence, then you are part of the problem in her view. While doing nothing was clearly unacceptable, performing actions that did not create real change was not much better. In the WUO's estimation, tangible actions—neither discussions nor polite demonstrations—were needed to stop the very real oppression that existed in the world. Discussions, polite demonstrations, or the winning of any reform from the government were all equated with ineffective action, and with "selling out" for an insignificant concession. To do any less than taking significant actions to create real changes, was, as the Weathermen saw it, to become part of the problem.[88]

For this reason, the WUO mobilized for the Days of Rage in Chicago in October 1969. Over the summer, individual collectives across the country organized on their own over local issues and also prepared collectively for this national action in Chicago. The national action was planned to last four days, from October 8 to October 11. During those four days, the WUO marched in the streets of Chicago, engaged with police, and caused damage to businesses and private property.[89] As WUO leaders Kathy Boudin, Bernardine Dohrn, and Terry Robbins put it in their position paper planning this national action, titled "Bringing the War Back Home," the point of the Days of Rage was also to model revolutionary action and to create a fighting force—one that could then be used against the Vietnam War or against racism: "Because we know that revolutionaries are created in struggle and not through protest or persuasion, we say clearly that this is an action not to register a complaint … but to make a difference, to create a solution."[90] Hence, they were living according to their beliefs that radical actions, and neither mere words nor demure demonstrations that could be easily ignored, were acceptable in these turbulent times.

As the name suggests, each day of the Days of Rage was envisioned as a chance to engage in radical actions. The first day was meant to build solidarity with the youth of Chicago by "joining with kids from high schools, community colleges, trade schools" through a "Jailbreak," where various WUO members would go onto campuses, interrupt classes, and speak to students about racism, the Vietnam War, and women's liberation.[91] The second or third day (the planning was flexible) would be dedicated to showcasing women's strengths, through a "women's action, planned by women from functioning political collectives all over the country … this action will be an attack on the institutions of racism and imperialism."[92] Here, women would display their physical prowess and dedication to the struggle. We will discuss the women's actions at further length as we proceed. Additionally, a night "youth-rock music festival" was planned for the evening of October 9 to "build culture in struggle," as activism was melded with relaxation—or used to further build solidarity with other groups.[93]

The third day was envisioned as a protest against the trial of the Chicago 8. The defendants were Abbie Hoffman, Jerry Rubin, David Dellinger, Tom Hayden, Rennie Davis, John Froines, Lee Weiner, and Bobby Seale. The Chicago 8 were defendants charged by the federal government with conspiracy, inciting to riot, as well as other charges related to the

Anti-Vietnam protest at the 1968 Democratic National Convention.[94] Bobby Seale, one of the defendants and a BPP member, was denied his Sixth Amendment, Constitutional right to counsel—he had requested a postponement so that his attorney Charles Garry could be allowed to undergo gallbladder surgery. When this motion was denied, Seale asked to represent himself, a request that was likewise denied. In response, Seale argued for his rights, accusing the court of behaving in an illegal and racist manner. The judge, Julius Hoffman, responded by ordering Seale bound, gagged, and chained to his chair in the courtroom, "an extreme measure rarely used in American courtrooms."[95] Nevertheless, Seale had "a white muslin cloth tied around his mouth. He was placed in a steel folding chair to which his ankles were attached with leg irons and arms with handcuffs."[96] Bobby Seale would have his trial severed during the proceedings, and was eventually sentenced to four years in prison for contempt of court for demanding his right to counsel.[97]

The WUO had not yet found out about this outright violation of Seale's constitutional rights when they were planning the Chicago Days of Rage (they were planning in late summer, the action was scheduled for October 8–11, and Seale was gagged on October 29), but they were planning to protest this trial, which had been scheduled for September 24 of that year. WUO members viewed the trial as an example of repressive state power being used against political prisoners, in other words, state power was being used to silence political opposition. Hence, their aim was to "indicate our commitment to fight back when the Man comes down with repression" through their march against the Federal Building in the downtown loop area where the trial was being held.[98]

The final day of the Days of Rage, October 11, was meant for a citywide march (for which the organizers were seeking a permit). The WUO envisioned this action as an important moment in developing resistance to imperialism, capitalism, racism, and the Vietnam War; with a large public demonstration, they believed that they could inspire and create such positive social change. In their planning, the WUO also noted that they expected to be attacked by Chicago police intent on protecting the status quo. While they expected "no guarantee of safety," the WUO organizers denied "organizing white youth to bring guns to Chicago to provoke an armed confrontation."[99] In fact, the WUO cautioned against believing "such bullshit" and pointed out such beliefs would actually hurt the overall action, as "what this obviously does is give the pig an excuse to bring out his shotguns and shoot people down in the streets."[100] And, actually, that is what happened, as "2,633 National Guardsmen were being called to

Chicago to back up police officers," and protesters ended up injured from confrontations with the police, with over 250 of them being arrested.[101] Ron Jacobs reports that it was 284 arrests specifically.[102] Optimistically envisioned as a plan to bring about meaningful political change, the Days of Rage did not actually achieve the results it had set for itself.

All the same, the WUO persisted in their efforts to bring about social change. Their attempts did not endear them to other mainstream activists, as often times WUO tactics were critical of others and thus divisionary. For example, at the end of October, "when Bobby Seale was gagged and shackled in Judge Julius Hoffman's courtroom and other conspiracy defendants sat by and watched, the Weatherpeople denounced them."[103] They next followed up with a critique of the Moratorium Against the Vietnam War on Washington, held later that fall, on November 15, 1969. This march, which brought over 500,000 anti-war protesters to D.C., involved singing and chanting against war at the White House. The WUO denounced it as too peaceful and reasonable, and thus pronounced the Moratorium as ineffective in achieving real change.[104] During this event, the Parade of Death had also taken place down Pennsylvania Avenue. Held as a silent march where "45,000 kids walked five miles single file ... [and] each dropped the name of a dead GI [as well as the name of a destroyed Vietnamese village] on a coffin," the Parade of Death was meant to highlight the death toll of the war. The WUO judged this Parade of Death as a futile effort in achieving social change, whether in stopping the war or the imperialist machine.[105] As they put it, "It's crazy to think that because we walked in front of their houses with a peace sign, the rich fuckers in power would somehow see how they rip people off, and that the people whose power is staked on imperialist wars and forces like teachers and pigs would destroy their own positions to give it all back."[106] The WUO was coming to the conclusion that protests did not make the leaders of imperialism and oppression uncomfortable enough to give up the massive profits they gained through war and violence.

Rather, the WUO encouraged more radical action, which involved using aggression as a tool to force social change:

> Violence by itself is neither good, bad, right nor wrong. The thing is to get a handle on what's necessary to build a revolution in the world. We've got to start looking at things in terms of winning, seeing our actions as part of a strategy for the struggle. We've got to see the connection between the sabotage of the imperialists' office building in New York, the SDS riot in Chicago [the Days of Rage], and the violent motion that came out of Washington. We know that the only way that the fat cats who run this country are going to give up anything—the Vietnam War or their power to suck off everyone else—is when people take it back from them.[107]

As they begin this quotation, they are arguing for their belief that violence in itself is not wrongful. Instead, whether violence is justified or wrongful depends on the motivations for undertaking it. The WUO believed in militancy in the pursuit of what they believed to be justified means, which included taking back power from the people who were "suck[ing] off everyone else" (this phrase likely refers to the Marxist idea of capitalists alienating the workers of the world from their humanity and the value they produce, just like vampires sucking life away). Taking back the power meant using aggressive means. For the WUO, peaceful demonstrations were just "a whole utopian trip" and active fighting was the only way to go.[108]

They were further convinced of the righteousness of this path when the Chicago police murdered Fred Hampton, the Chairman of the Illinois chapter of the BPP, in December of 1969, in his own bed. In a gunfight that lasted seven minutes, as the Chicago police was conducting a raid, Hampton and another BPP member, Mark Clark, were killed while asleep.[109] As a result of the killing, the WUO "condemned ordinary white citizens, white radicals, and themselves too, and decided that no mass, revolutionary movement could or would be formed here, that an underground guerrilla organization had to be started immediately."[110] As Weatherwoman Laura Whitehorn remembered, "When the Chicago cops and FBI assassinated Fred Hampton on December 4, 1969, it made it clear to me what I had already accepted: that the fight of Black people would have to involve armed struggle. Like the people of Puerto Rico, the Native American nations, and the Mexicano Nation within the U.S.—like the struggle of the Vietnamese—the movements fighting against the U.S. government would have to utilize armed power."[111] Whitehorn and the WUO were ready to support what they believed was right, through radical means. As Weatherwoman Cathy Wilkerson put it, "This really is war. I would do anything, I vowed, anything to not let his murder be in vain."[112]

To plan for this change—and still trying to reach out to the rest of the mainstream Leftist movement that it characterized as not radical enough—the WUO planned a so-called War Council for the end of December 1969. This meeting was meant as an organizational tool to develop strategies to reach out to other activists and to pave a way to go underground, away from police and FBI surveillance, from where the WUO and its allies could continue to fight.

The War Council was a steppingstone of sorts for the WUO, which presaged their advent into a frenetic state of mind that was to lead them to a problematic path later on, specifically to the use of bombs. At the time of the War Council, in December of 1969, members and leaders of the WUO were facing felony indictments for their involvement in earlier actions (such as at the Days of Rage) and they felt the pressure of being ostracized from the mainstream Leftist movement due to their criticisms of it as ineffective; they also experienced the pressures of rooting out police or FBI infiltrators in their midst. As such, they came to see themselves not only as under threat, but also as the only viable choice in actually creating real change—and so they became even more committed to militancy.[113]

Following the WUO's developing combative commitments, demonstrations were followed by a series of bombings, from spring 1970 to spring 1975.[114] The bombings were intended to sabotage and protest imperialism and were picked for their symbolic significance in terms of representing people or organizations that were responsible for maintaining or causing oppression.[115] Thus, police stations were targeted in protest of racism or in solidarity with political prisoners, the U.S. Capitol was targeted as a symbolic act for U.S. involvement in Vietnam, and the Federal Offices of Health, Education and Welfare were bombed for the repression and harassment that the WUO members felt these institutions visited on poor women.[116] The special oppression of women—especially poor women and women of Third World nations—was a particular concern of the WUO, and this concern reflected the organization's feminist underpinnings. Weatherman David Gilbert explains that the association of the sites with oppression was a way to raise the consciousness of the people and a way to inspire them to stand up to the oppression that was being targeted.[117] Weatherman Bill Ayers explains a similar position by also noting that these actions were considered "propaganda of the deed."[118] That expression is an old anarchist concept that is used to describe the spreading of propaganda not through words, but through actions, especially militant ones.[119]

Unsurprisingly, as a result of all of this militancy, the WUO was placed under FBI surveillance. One FBI agent, Cril Payne, explained that "the Director of the FBI did not take too kindly to these revolutionary exhortations.... Mr. Hoover was outraged.... From all indications, the Weathermen had officially replaced the Black Panther Party as the most serious threat to internal security. The group was now the potential successor to the 'Communist menace.'"[120] Hence, as the WUO moved more towards militancy, the FBI increased their concerns over the organization.

In spite of this high concern from the FBI, the WUO was not the only group that was using bombs as a form of protest.[121] In April 1970 alone (just a single month), for example, there were 121 bombings, and none were associated with the WUO.[122] By comparison, over a five-year period, the

WUO took credit for 17 bombings.[123] While the WUO was certainly a militant organization, they were neither alone in their militancy nor the most violent organization of the period. As Ayers remembered,

> From early 1969 until the spring of 1970 there were over 40,000 threats or attempts and 5,000 actual bombings against government and corporate targets in the U.S., an average of six bombings a day.... Five thousand bombings, about six a day, and the Weather Underground had claimed six, total.[124]

Whereas the WUO is remembered as *the* most violent group of the sixties and seventies, in actuality, other groups of the decade were even more militant and violent. As chronicler Dan Berger writes:

> In the fall of 1968, there were 41 bombings on college campuses, almost double what the Weather Underground did in total throughout its seven-year existence. In the spring of 1969, before the "Weatherman" statement even appeared, there were 84 bombings on school campuses and then off-campus bombings by movement radicals. In the 1969-1970 school year, extremely conservative estimates say that there were at least 174—and as many as 5000.... From September 1969 to May 1970, there was at least one bombing or attempted bombing somewhere in the United States every day by the progressive and radical movements.[125]

A map printed in the January 1971 issue of the radical journal *Scanlan's Monthly* illustrated that between 1965 and 1970, more than 1,300 incidents of "sabotage and terrorism" had been recorded throughout the United States, including physical attacks on security guards and buildings, as well as fire bombings, arson attacks, and timed bombings.[126] During the month of March 1970 alone, 62 guerrilla attacks had occurred across 17 states.[127] Discussing the period from 1970 to 1974, Larry Grathwohl, who infiltrated the WUO for the Federal Bureau of Investigation (FBI), noted that there was a rising tide of revolutionary violence all around the nation: "Each year since 1970 there have been 2000 bombings in the United States, the great majority of which are attributed to revolutionary groups, according to FBI statistics."[128] Further, of the year in which he was writing (1974), Grathwohl wrote:

> But Weathermen weren't alone in taking credit for bombings this year. The Americans for Justice, the Armed Revolutionary Front of Puerto Rico, the World Liberation Front, and the People's Forces had already boasted of terrorist acts in 1974. The Americans for Justice placed two pipe bombs at the Shell Oil chemical plant in San Ramon, while the New World Liberation Front attacked a subsidiary of ITT.... And these are just five of the 25 revolutionary groups active on a national scale.[129]

The WUO's bombing record is low compared to that of these other groups. Additionally, the WUO's bombings were conducted after extensive reconnoitering and during off work hours, so as to prevent loss of life.[130] As Ayers recalled, "Our signature was a warning call to some sleepy guard inside the building or to the police nearby or to a journalist with calm and detailed instructions to clear a specific area...."[131] In fact, the WUO did not kill anyone throughout their anti-imperialist bombing campaign except for three of their own members in one unintended explosion. This event was the Townhouse explosion in March 1970, where Weather members assembling a bomb blew themselves up. Thus, what emerges from the historical record is that the period was thoroughly tempestuous, so much so that a journalist characterized it as one where "bombing and arson attacks on army installations, federal buildings, corporate and banking headquarters and department stores have escalated into the common place."[132]

Numerous groups saw the suffering caused by their own government and felt that they were justified in using militant means, including violence, to combat the injustices created by a system that perpetrated sexist, racist, and imperialist oppression. As just another quick example, consider the Cattonsville Nine. Catholic activists, the Cattonsville Nine conducted an action in May 1968 where they used hand made napalm to destroy draft records at the Selective Service Office in Cattonsville, Maryland. The protesters were tried in Federal Court, then went underground and were sought by the FBI.[133]

Consequently, from what they witnessed around them, different individuals formed or joined the WUO with the intent to do whatever they could to bring about a more just, socialist, racism free, and feminist society. And they were drawn to militant measures because they witnessed actions around them that they felt were practical failures that did not bring about real change. Frustrated with pacifist and liberal measures, the members of the WUO turned to militancy and violence, which was a prevalent turn in the time period from other disaffected and frustrated young persons on the far left.

A Multifaceted Feminist Stance

The WUO, despite their open militancy and embrace of macho qualities, was nevertheless feminist. In fact, militant feminism was the WUO's answer to the era's "woman question" (the "woman question" referred to issues that revolved around women's rights).[134] Women were well represented in the group's local and national leadership and took an active role in developing WUO papers and positions. In these tracts, the Weatherwomen were able to articulate feminist stances and advocate feminist aims while representing the WUO's position on political issues. Though the WUO was not singularly a feminist organization—it was neither a single-issue organization nor did it escape the sexist trappings of its time period—these key elements (female representation in leadership and the taking of feminist positions) show that feminism was an important part of the organization, especially through the voices of the Weatherwomen.

The heavy inclusion of women in both general membership and leadership positions attests to a commitment to gender equity.[135] For example, Cathy Wilkerson played an important organizational role from the group's beginning, serving as a national secretary for SDS, and then joining the newly formed WUO. Furthermore, Naomi Jaffe, Kathy Boudin, and Diana Oughton helped focus and refine the vision and mission of the WUO. Bernardine Dohrn was influential in leading the WUO from its inception to its demise and acted as the voice of the WUO in publicly announcing its military targets and the reasons behind its bombings.[136]

As the organization matured, it also developed decidedly feminist stances on several issues, some of which fit snugly within second wave feminist aims of their time period, such as a rigid theoretical stance against sexism, a belief in a woman's right to be free of patriarchy, and an opposition to the gender pay gap.[137] At other times, the WUO previewed a third wave feminist vision, one that openly warned against a preoccupation with middle class, straight, white, and American female oppression, and advocated the inclusion of the experiences of poor women, women of color at home, and of Third World women abroad in the fight for female liberation.[138] Overall, the WUO put forth its own feminist program, one that was in certain ways ahead of its time period, weaving together class, race, and gender with a Marxist analysis concerning the need for social and political change. Weatherman David Gilbert explained that, in a conscious effort to signal support for female liberation, and to be "more gender neutral and inclusive," in December 1970, the organization even changed its name from "Weatherman" to "Weather Underground."[139] FBI infiltrator Grathwohl remembered that the change came after the women in the WUO demanded it:

> When I got back to the house [of a collective in Detroit], a meeting was going on. The women were talking about their role in the general structure of Weathermen. They now were objecting to the name Weathermen being applied to the group as a whole. The group, they protested, should be called Weather People, Weather Movement, or Weather Machine. Then, within the group, there would be Weathermen and Weatherwomen.[140]

Weatherwomen demanded a name change that was more appropriate of a group that included both men and women, modeling gender sensitivity, and they were able to enact this name change for the group; as Grathwohl remembered, women had been demanding and gaining more authority "on all levels" within the organization.[141]

The placement of gender equity and militant feminism in the WUO agenda was gradual and by no means without struggle. Clear instances of sexism or machismo within the WUO must be noted. Yet, simply to concentrate on these problems, as most of the existing literature on the WUO has thus far done, ignores the group's feminist leanings and further silences the voices of the Weatherwomen who developed and promoted feminism within the organization. While WUO members were primarily politically oriented, many of them, including people in key leadership positions, saw feminism as central to that orientation. Their position was that the fight against imperialism would lead to an egalitarian, feminist, socialist society. For the WUO, socialist revolution would necessarily lead to gender equality: the revolution would not be complete if it did not include the empowerment of women. Even though feminism was neither the sole nor even the primary focus of their revolutionary struggle, the WUO recognized that it had to be addressed as part of that struggle or else their movement would not be truly revolutionary. As the Weatherwomen wrote, "Women's liberation is a matter of survival. We need food, decent medical care, good schools, and community-run day care. For this, we need revolution."[142]

The struggle to wage a feminist revolution was not without challenges. The following chapter explores the sexism present in the SDS and then the WUO. As such, Chapter 2 considers the sexist challenge against the WUO being feminist, while also expressing the position that while sexism was a significant and unfortunate part of the WUO, it did not represent the organization as a whole.

Chapter 2

Resistance Amidst Sexism

In 1967, Cathy Wilkerson, then editor of the *New Left Notes* (*NLN*), reached out to Jane Adams, a fellow Students for a Democratic Society (SDS) activist, to share a recipe for soup. Wilkerson printed the recipe in the *New Left Notes* for other SDS activists to have on hand. Wilkerson thought that students, who, while living as cheaply as possible, were dependent on donations and fundraising for sustenance, would greatly appreciate having a recipe for a "tasty and nutritious soup, costing almost nothing."[1] Wilkerson saw having this information "as critical a part of building a movement as theory was."[2] After all, large numbers of SDS conference attendees and student workers needed to be fed, and cheaply— idealism and theory alone did not fill a hungry belly. As Wilkerson put it, "In an organization that often had no funds, this was a good way to make the organizing dollar stretch more."[3] What was meant as an act to support the development of the student movement, however, was later misinterpreted. Wilkerson recalls, "Interestingly, in the years to come, the recipe was sometimes cited by feminists as an example of SDS's sexism, a charge I thought revealed some inattention to the challenges of supporting a low budget movement in action."[4]

As illustrated by this vignette, sexism can be misattributed. Additionally, where the historical record accurately notes the presence of sexism or chauvinism, it is necessary to avoid attributing a victimhood mentality to the women involved. To ameliorate such potential flaws in the historical record, it is important to maintain a focus on the possibility that the female protagonists served as active agents on their own behalf— thus necessitating an investigation of what the Weatherwomen did in response to the sexist attitudes of the Weathermen.

One of the main reasons that historians of the Weather Underground

Organization (WUO) do not usually recognize the organization as being feminist is that there was a good deal of sexism in the organizational structure, in the male leadership, and in the sexual attitudes of many of the WUO's members, especially the men.[5] Although there is good evidence for this widespread sexism, a unitary focus on the sexism both oversimplifies the gender relations and gendered positions within the organization and implicitly assumes a privileged male perspective—as if the men of the WUO provided the main, or even the only, representation of what the WUO truly was.

The reality of the WUO is, in fact, much more complicated than a blanket pronouncement of the organization as "fully sexist and not at all feminist" could possibly encapsulate. While it is true that the WUO (much like its predecessor, SDS) had problems with sexism, it also had powerful women in the organization who stood up to that sexism and prescribed solutions for smashing it. As the founding manifesto itself proclaimed, "Revolutionaries must be made to understand the full scope of women's oppression, and the necessity to smash male supremacy."[6] Weatherwomen acted on this revolutionary line, challenging chauvinist and sexist assumptions wherever they found them, all the while carving out positions of leadership for themselves. Since these women were leaders of the WUO and vocal representatives of the WUO's positions, a full analysis of the WUO as an organization requires not only locating the sexism of the group, but also the internal fight against that sexism and the anti-sexism work of the women and some of the men within the WUO.

This chapter seeks to correct the literature's myopic focus on the WUO's sexism by placing the narrative relative to this sexism in its proper historical context. Moreover, this chapter also introduces the manners in which the organization's female members both experienced and responded to the sexism they faced. In doing so, this chapter demonstrates how the naming and eradication of sexism within the organization and larger society actually became an important ideological and material commitment of the Weather Underground Organization.

Tea Time for the Ladies: Gender Contradictions of the 1960s

When future Weatherwomen Diana Oughton and Kathy Boudin were accepted to Bryn Mawr College in the early 1960s, they were counseled to bring a tea service with them, to best partake of the afternoon teas that the ladies—students and professors alike—were expected to enjoy at college every day from four to five in the afternoon.[7] Conservative notions of a woman's place reigned at Bryn Mawr, and elsewhere—the dictum mostly being that women got educated, married, and then died.[8] While the 1960s were bringing a sense of change, at the beginning of the decade, progress was still slow.

The social and cultural milieu of the early 1960s was still imbued with 1950s conservatism, which included the belief that women were of secondary status to men, whether in private or public life.[9] Weatherwoman Cathy Wilkerson remembers that skirts and stockings were mandated in school for women, and that "the role projected for women was very subservient as far as I was concerned."[10] Women were still expected to marry and shape their lives around that of their husbands. Women were still supposed to prioritize being wives and mothers above any other interests or aspirations. Meek, quiet, and in the background, they were meant to occupy a supportive and secondary role to their spouses. As radical feminist Shulamith Firestone said in 1966, it was a time when the primacy of the male gender was recognized, as "boys would say in morning prayers, 'Thank you, lord, for not making me a woman!'"[11] Overall, the remnants of the 1950s "culture of exclusion" when it came to women were hard to dismiss.[12]

Women coming of age during this time period faced a particular challenge borne out of the distinct social expectations—those of 1950s conservatism versus 1960s liberalism—that already were butting heads during the early sixties.[13] Historian Ruth Rosen explains that even though men and women were rebelling against the constraints of the fifties and reaching toward a less rigid way of life, women experienced a crisis that emerged out of these conflicting social tensions: young men rejected their parents' politics, but still insisted on fatherhood and a traditional marriage modeled on the fifties mold.[14] Men also experienced anxiety in regards to women's increasing assertiveness.[15] Thus, women faced an untenable situation: as they reached for liberation from restrictive gender norms, resistance and backlash were a consistent part of their everyday experiences.

These cultural tensions played out on a political level, too. For example, John F. Kennedy appointed a presidential commission to explore women's secondary status in the United States, yet he appointed no women to his cabinet. Importantly, as historian Ruth Rosen explains, Kennedy saw the creation of the commission as a way to avoid "the far more contentious alternative, that of supporting the Equal Rights Amendment" adding that "to Kennedy, a commission seemed a cheap political payoff, a way to reassure the American people that all was well, that women required no drastic or dramatic changes."[16] The commission's report in fact propagated traditional stances, such as raising worries over the erosion of family life and raising concerns over working women destroying families' structures.[17]

Furthermore, the proposed Title VII of the Civil Rights Act, which addressed, among other things, sex and race discrimination, was met with laughs in the House of Representatives when it was introduced "as a poison pill" by a southern conservative opposed to the Civil Rights Movement.[18] Though it eventually passed, it was ridiculed as "the Bunny Law" when newspaper editorials wondered if, in the wake of the law, Playboy clubs would now have to employ male bunnies.[19] A *New York Times* editorial concluded, "This is a revolution, chaos. You can't even safely advertise for a wife anymore."[20] Radical feminist Dana Densmore later recalled, "A thorough-going, smirking disrespect for women permeated every aspect of society."[21]

In the context of this prevalent male chauvinism, it is not surprising to find that student groups and New Left organizations also were infused with sexism. In 1965, activists Casey Hayden and Mary King authored "Sex and Caste: A Kind of Memo" based on their experiences and work within the Student Nonviolent Coordinating Committee (SNCC). Here, they noted that male chauvinism was deeply entrenched, and that an adherence to traditional gender norms permeated even progressive groups.[22] "Sex and Caste" pointed out the inequality in the treatment of men and women in the Movement: women were usually given secretarial work, while men led.

Race also played a role in how women experienced this sexism. White women felt marginalized by secretarial roles. Black women were at times leaders in local, field positions. Still, black women were not recognized as leaders on the national stage, where men were usually identified as either decision makers or Movement leaders.[23] Historian Benita Roth introduces another complication, as she explains that "during the 1960s, masculinism was very much present in other parts of the Left and in other parts of the Black community" and functioned to encourage women to act in supportive and subordinate roles to male activists.[24] Roth goes on to explain that this endorsement of a patriarchal structure could have its root in a response to the racist 1965 Moynihan report (a report on black poverty written by sociologist and Assistant Secretary of Labor for Policy, Planning and Research Daniel Moynihan for the Johnson administration), with its conclusion "that the Black family was 'matriarchal' and 'deviant,' because women held an inappropriately large amount of power."[25] As such, encouraging traditional gender norm adherence as part of black women's activist practices could be read as an attempt by black male activists to refute the report while at the same time compounding the oppression black women were experiencing. In any case, this overall sort of labor division showed that gender role normativity was alive and well within the Movement.

Furthermore, feminist activist Dana Densmore recalls that working for "The Resistance," a group of anti–Vietnam War activists, was an exercise "in self-lacerations for women. It went without saying that we cooked and cleaned up while the men bonded, strategized, and postured."[26] Densmore explains that a gender hierarchy reigned in the group, even though in all reality the female members were just as committed to the cause and acted in concrete ways to support it, even going to jail for their convictions.[27]

Feminist historian Barbara Winslow also recollects a similar experience during her activism in Seattle during the late sixties: "One night at a party, friends told me that they were going to call me Mrs. Vietnam Committee because they didn't know my name."[28] Even though she and her husband shared the same political vision, it was his name that stood out to the group; he was the recognized leader. Her role was to be in a supportive position—encouraging, empathetic, helpful, but not outspoken. In fact, Winslow confesses that she was passive at lectures or meetings and hardly ever spoke up, having internalized proper womanly gender performance. It seemed out of place, even to her, to break out of that pattern.[29]

When women challenged gender normativity, their actions were seen as threatening by their male colleagues. Unsurprisingly, the actions of women's liberation protests were met with derision and violence. Winslow recalls that a protest against a Playboy bunny appearance at the University of Washington was met with aggression on the part of the males in the auditorium. When protesting women took the stage, "a group of fraternity and student government men grabbed the women, started punching them, and dragged them off the stage."[30] Resistance to women's empowerment was strong.

Nevertheless, within this general context of fierce misogyny, the women's movement was born. Despite—or perhaps because of—the resistance they faced, women's liberation took off as, in historian Rosalyn Baxandall's words, "women were catching fire and coming together to change the world."[31] Not surprisingly, women within leftist student organizations were at the forefront of this movement. This phenomenon—of women coming together in the face of sexist opposition—occurred first within SDS, and then again within its offspring organization, the WUO.

The Sexist Ramparts of SDS[32]

Like other leftist groups of the sixties, SDS did not initially have many women in leadership positions, even though women were about one third of the organization's membership.[33] An activist in SDS, and later a Weatherman, David Gilbert recalls that even though, "women were central and critical to the early anti-war movement … as consistent workers but also as initiators and strategists … in those days almost all visible leaders and speakers were male."[34] Cathy Wilkerson, active in SDS and later a Weatherwoman, recalls much of the same, adding that "no women really were listened to when they spoke or when they spoke at meetings."[35]

Many women did not generally feel comfortable speaking up in SDS meetings. But they were deeply interested in the debates, the positions presented, and the pathways etched out; significantly, they found inventive ways of inserting their opinions into the mix. For example, Gilbert recalls that at the June 1967 SDS National Convention in Ann Arbor, Michigan, students were planning workshops for the convention, when "Betty, very bright and extremely shy, was sitting next to me and whispered, 'We should have one on women's liberation.' So I raised my hand and made the proposal, and it was added to the list without any discussion."[36] This anecdote is representative of the slow progress that was being made within SDS: Betty was not comfortable being up front, but easily negotiated an important change—introducing a women's platform workshop into the SDS national conference—through the help of a friendly male colleague, who was immediately taken seriously as a matter of course.

The rest of Gilbert's story illustrates the depth of resistance SDS women faced when they questioned their status within the group or society. SDS member Marilyn Buck was supposed to present the report on the women's liberation workshop to the plenary at the convention. As soon as she expressed that this item was a report on women's liberation, "all hell broke loose. Men hooted and whistled from the floor, threw paper planes at Marilyn, and shouted such gems as 'I'll liberate you with my cock.' The circus response revealed the depth of sexism within SDS."[37] This sexist and even misogynist response exhibits that many men within the SDS membership were quite far from being prepared to accept feminist ideals.

This vicious outburst is a clear testimony to the prevalence of male supremacy within sixties' culture—even in an otherwise broad-minded organization like SDS—but importantly it also serves as an example of persistent female resistance to sexism. In the face of the hostile and misogynist response from the crowd, Marilyn Buck firmly stood her ground and pushed the report through. The report was eventually accepted by the plenary, with other women's (and some men's) voices supporting it. In doing so, Gilbert observed, "women's liberation had breached the sexist ramparts of the New Left."[38] It was a battle hard won, but it paved the way for SDS (and later for the WUO) to become committed to women's liberation.

In fact, in the July 10, 1967, issue of the *New Left Notes*, future Weatherwoman Bernardine Dohrn published a report about the SDS women's findings from this conference. Here, she outlined the demands of the women who attended the Women's Liberation Workshop: an end to traditional gender roles, a call for communal child care centers, access to birth control, and the "availability of a competent medical abortion for all women who so desire."[39] Furthermore, the report explained that "women are in a colonial relationship to men" and therefore have to fight for their own independence, as "only an independent woman can be truly effective in the larger revolutionary struggle."[40] Importantly, the report recognized that women in other parts of the world would likewise have problems with male supremacy, and stressed the idea that those women's experiences would be different. In articulating this position—and in proclaiming solidarity with the women of the Third World—the SDS women were recognizing that other non–U.S. women might have different subjectivities (meaning different perspectives based on their own unique interconnected oppressions in their own life contexts) and were showing themselves as true, respectful allies, not prescribing their own solutions to other women's problems.

Furthermore, the report added that SDS women demanded "full participation in all aspects of movement work, from licking stamps to assuming leadership positions."[41] It continued by demanding that men undergo a shift in how they viewed women, since men had been taught all along, by virtue of living in the United States, to adopt toxic male gender norms and thus to disrespect women.[42] Linking "radical social change" with "the necessity for the liberation of women," the piece communicated the SDS's women new call for "our brothers [to] recognize that they must deal with their own problems of male chauvinism in their personal, social, and political relationships."[43] To support that attitude change, SDS women called for widespread education on the topics of feminist theory and the exploitation of women through SDS's "internal education arm."[44] The Women's Liberation Workshop had delineated a robust program; in spite those initial boos from the audience, women's liberation was here to stay and its message was getting propagated to the group.

Nevertheless, the initial shameful response to the issue of women's liberation in 1967 became one of the least known causes of the split that occurred within SDS two years later. While the usual reason for the split of the SDS is given as the disagreement between the Progressive Labor (PL) and the Revolutionary Youth Movement (RYM) (including the future WUO) faction over the question of national liberation, which was significant and which we already discussed, this concern with female liberation was another important factor. Gilbert explains that

> PL, like many old-line Marxist groups, saw class as the fundamental contradiction, with problems like racism and sexism as secondary. They agreed that the Left should oppose "male chauvinism" which defined the problem mainly in the realm of ideas and culture, and not as a fundamental structural problem that included oppression within the working class and the Left. Women who insisted on independent forms of organization as a power base were accused of being "divisive."[45]

Part of the PL side of the dispute, which ended up splitting SDS's membership, was that Marxism required a primacy of class issues over all other issues, such as gender or race. For the PL, according to Gilbert, if there was a social problem that revolved around race or gender, then either it should be reduced to a class-based problem or, if it could not be reduced in that fashion, then the problem itself should be minimized in importance.

For example, consider the problem of inequality in the home. If women were treated poorly in the home because they were alienated from paid labor and forced to be economically subordinate to their husbands, then this women's issue could be analyzed as a class issue. If, on the other hand, women wanted to have as much power over household decisions as their husbands, but they did not seek economic parity, then this was a lesser problem for people who took the PL position. Gender problems, for the PL, were only important if they were in actuality class problems that just happened to be plaguing women in the current situation. The RYM faction felt this reductionism of gender and racial problems was offensive.[46]

Writing later in 1976, an anonymous Weather group, Sisters of the WUO, also agreed that this disagreement was central to the SDS split and added that the PL's reductionist position was actually incorrect as Marxist analysis.[47] They argued, "This is not a Marxist-Leninist analysis. The material basis of women's oppression, and its concrete expression in the institutions of society—the family, schools, courts, laws, religion and the state—are left out."[48] In other words, any analysis that immediately reduces all social issues to class issues ignores the various human relations that provide the basis for women's oppression. Men and women relate in certain ways to survive and reproduce (roughly speaking, "the base" in Marxism). Those relations are recognized and replicated in cultural, political, and economic institutions (roughly, "the superstructure" in Marxism).[49] An understanding of women's oppression requires a comprehension of these base relations, which are, in a theoretical sense under Marxism, more fundamental than the economic class system that exists under capitalism, which makes up part of the superstructure. Thus, according to the Sisters of the WUO, RYM's complaint was justified: the PL were wrong in their Marxist analysis that reduced gender and racial issues to class issues.[50] In fact, in a more accurate Marxist analysis, power and oppression are connected in a multifaceted way, and women's oppression cannot only be understood through an economic lens. By moving away from PL, the Weather contingent of SDS was separating itself from a significant cause of leftwing sexism (though, by no means, would this separation mean they would be rid of all forms of sexism in the WUO).

Weatherman Jeff Jones also takes up this same point. He explains that due to feminist activity in SDS—particularly that of Naomi Jaffe, Bernardine Dohrn, and Susan Sutheim, who were organizing SDS women— PL saw this concern with sexism and women's liberation as divisive.[51] Conversely, the RYM/WUO faction of SDS saw sexism as a deeper problem that needed to be studied and solved. RYM identified it as a special oppression of women, with the unreceptive, chauvinist men actually being truly divisive.[52]

This viewpoint was expressed in the foundational paper "You Don't Need a Weatherman," which outlined RYM's ideology. This stance would also provide the underpinning for the future WUO's ideology, and also played a part in the split of SDS. The "Weatherman" paper recommended the stomping out of sexism, and labeled the special oppression of women "male supremacy."[53] This position paper also heavily criticized SDS's slow reform in regards to women, stating that "SDS has not dealt in any adequate way with the women question; the resolution passed at Ann Arbor did not lead to much practice, nor has the need to fight male supremacy been given any programmatic direction within the RYM."[54] Additionally, the document recognized the revolutionary potential of women. Drawing a parallel between the alienation of youth/workers within the capitalist system, the tract stated that "the cultural revolt of women against their 'role' in imperialism (which is just beginning to happen in a mass way) should have the same revolutionary potential that the RYM claimed for 'youth culture.'"[55] Furthermore, the essay advocated the breaking of traditional gender norms for women, calling for the creation of a new society not burdened by gender normativity. In fact, "You Don't Need a Weatherman" included an encouragement for women to break out of traditional "female" and "mother" roles as everyone would shape new ways of life not stuck in "the plastic 50s."[56] It also encouraged organizing around issues such as the pay gap, around building self-consciousness, and around analyzing the male supremacy consistently present in women's lives in various instantiations. These issues were seen as tying directly into the economic and social oppression for women—and were clearly tapping into the special oppression of women *qua* women.[57]

Thus, the "Weatherman" paper laid out RYM's feminist stance—thereby previewing the future feminist stance of the WUO—and called for female liberation through revolution. The feminist women of SDS responded to this call, having resisted being cast as second-class citizens through much of the existence of SDS. Prior to the split, SDS women had become increasingly adamant about taking an active role in the organizational life of the group. As SDS Interorganizational Secretary (and future Weatherwoman) Bernardine Dohrn characterizes that period, "Women were speaking up and acting up in droves, pressing against male supremacy and sexist assumptions of our appropriate role."[58] Women's caucuses appeared as part of SDS convention programs. Women insisted on chairing meetings and started becoming public speakers.

Women were also included when SDS traveled to Cambodia to discuss anti–Vietnam War efforts and, once there, they looked to Vietnamese women as worthy revolutionary examples who were achieving equality in terms of access to political and military power in their early attempt to build an independent nation.[59] Cathy Wilkerson states that she believes that the Vietnamese asked for women to be part of the delegation.[60] There are two important things to notice here: (1) the Vietnamese were providing an example of including women in political action and strategy, an example that the WUO takes to heart and follows throughout its career and (2) even if the Vietnamese initiated the idea that women should be involved, SDS went along with the request and the women who went on the delegation became empowered as part of their experiences on the trips—whether it was through their subsequent organizing work, through their speech making, speaking tours, etc. Moreover, Bernardine Dohrn, in her 1968 piece "The Liberation of Vietnamese Women," explains that Vietnamese women, through fighting, were building a new society based in equality. The piece also mentioned that the Democratic Republic of Vietnam's policy included the position that women were equal to men and that the fight for women's rights was an important issue to address as the nation moved forward.[61]

Cathy Wilkerson went on lengthy speaking tours throughout the country in the wake of that trip, raising consciousness as to the Vietnamese people's plight. As she traveled, she learned public speaking, becoming increasingly effective in raising the consciousness of her audiences. In the Seattle chapter of SDS, the Research and Propaganda groups were given female revolutionary names, such as Harriet Tubman, Mother Jones, or Sojourner Truth.[62] Future Weatherwoman Naomi Jaffe reports that women's study groups were also organized within SDS, including a women's group devoted to developing feminist theory.[63] Women's only meetings also gave voice to women's concerns and discussed how to best analyze female oppression.[64]

There are also key examples of SDS men supporting women in these efforts to combat SDS sexism. For example, activist Barbara Winslow remembers that it was an SDS man, Ed Mormon, who encouraged her to speak up in meetings and have her voice heard in the decision-making process.[65] David Gilbert also reports having his own realization that women's voices were not often heard, and that women's ideas were usually recast in male voices.[66] Gilbert reports another incident at which he felt deep outrage for how women were treated by sexist males: right before the split from SDS, in the spring of 1969, he and a fellow organizer (and later a Weatherwoman) by the name of Dionne Donghi, went to Chicago to present a platform demanding open college admissions to the SDS Chicago leadership. Donghi was the one who had developed the platform, with Gilbert's help. After she presented her ideas, only Gilbert was attacked. In his shock he remembers that "they totally disregarded Dionne, treating her as simply a front-woman for me."[67] The sexism was so pervasive that they couldn't even imagine the platform being a woman's idea.

When it came to theorizing, the male leadership of SDS did not usually respect women's contributions.[68] Gilbert recalls that SDS women nevertheless persisted in creating theoretical bases for explaining social or political oppression. Gilbert explains that future Weatherwoman Naomi Jaffe, while still in SDS, was very active in this regard, as she

developed a new working class theory in relationship to the role of women in advanced capitalist society, and we had a lot of discussion, although I ended up receiving more recognition and credit, on analyzing the prodigious drive to boost consumption within the domestic economy—both the economic role and cultural impact. Naomi went on to relate this to the changing sexist stereotypes and the pressures placed on women.[69]

Although Gilbert says he ended up receiving the credit and recognition for these ideas, Naomi Jaffe's sophisticated analysis linked gender oppression to economic oppression, which previewed the Marxist analysis that would later appear in the WUO's own brand of feminism.

Furthermore, in collaboration with future Weatherwoman Bernardine Dohrn, Naomi Jaffe also wrote "The Look Is You." This 1968 piece of feminist theory was penned in response to a *Ramparts* magazine cover that consisted of a headless woman's bust. As such, "The Look Is You" called out the sexism of *Ramparts* (a New Left journal) for allowing such a cover and analyzed the special oppression of women within the Movement and U.S. society. Reducing women to "two tits and no head" was proof positive, per Jaffe and Dohrn, that women were "unfree [*sic*] within the Movement and in personal relationships, and in the society at large."[70] They were the victims of a systematized oppression that taught them specific gender roles and ways of being, and then took advantage of them economically. In other words, "The Look Is You" criticized the objectification and sexualization of women's bodies, linking capitalism and consumerism to proper gender performance for women.

In a Marxist vein, Jaffe and Dohrn explained that economic markets defined persons as consumers and stifled their authentic, autonomous development. They added that women were, paradoxically, both the beneficiaries and victims of the economic system since "the same new things that allow us to express our new sense of freedom and naturalness and movement ... are also used to force us to be the consumers of the endless flow of products necessary for the perpetuation of a repressive society."[71] Jaffe and Dohrn urged women to realize that true independence did not come from buying, but rather from authentic self-growth—"'choosing oneself' in commodity form is a choice pre-defined by a repressive system," they warned.[72] These strands of theoretical thought constitute a complex feminist critique and also a preview of the Marxist tone of the WUO's later feminism—however, this piece is not usually analyzed in the literature, nor is it recognized as significant despite the fact that the authors become influential members of the WUO.[73]

Sexism and Female Leadership

After the split, and despite the militant feminist ideology of many of its members, the WUO did not immediately emerge as a feminist utopia. Indeed, as with SDS, there was a good deal of sexism within the WUO.

However, just as women's liberation broke through SDS's misogynist barricades, so did it slowly pierce through the WUO's chauvinism. While the sexism within the organization was real, it was not the whole story: Weatherwomen stood up to it and pushed through gender equity in leadership, refined theoretical arguments for the oppression of women, and generally fought to "smash sexism," as they would say. Interestingly, one FBI informant, Bill Dyson, noted that in spite of the sexism,

> women seemed, in some cases, to be more dominating than the men were. They had Bernardine Dohrn, Cathy Wilkerson; they had Kathy Boudin, and many others—they had women in prominent positions. And yet there seemed to be this thought within people in the Weather Underground that the women were being regarded as secondary. I don't think it was true. I'm looking from the outside and saying, "Wait a minute, it's the exact opposite!"[74]

As this passage makes clear, even the members of WUO were missing how central women were to their own organization. Instead, it took an outsider to see that women were playing key roles in the development of the WUO. While it is true that Weatherwomen were negatively affected by the sexism of the WUO, they were not just passive victims of it—they fought against it, challenged males' misperceptions, and proved their agency along the way.

One form the WUO's sexism took was in the organizational structure, in that the WUO's political program saw women as potentially capable fighters, but little more. As Gilbert puts it,

> Our political program about women's issues was reduced to extolling women guerillas in the Third World and urging women here to become fighters. Doing so was an important role and contribution of women, but limiting our focus to armed struggle was not only a negation of the many other crucial battles against patriarchy but also tended to promote a macho concept of struggle.[75]

In other words, this charge regarding the WUO's sexism is that the organization limited their positive appraisals of women's abilities to their fighting skills. A closer analysis, though, reveals that through this stance, the WUO was making a small, but significant strike against patriarchy by seeing women just as capable of fighting as the men. The fact that the WUO saw women as potentially proficient fighters—at a time when the U.S. government would not accept women as soldiers, which therefore implied that women were deemed to be second class citizens due to their purported inability to partake in combat or to receive the requisite praise and honor that society bestows on those individuals who take up military service—was a reversal of larger social attitudes.[76] It was also a lesson learned from the women of Vietnam, who were active fighters for their own liberation.[77] This militant position, which involved seeing women as potential fighters, actually enlarged women's gender roles by going beyond the accepted gender roles of the time period, which limited women completely to the home and the hearth.

The Weatherwomen largely embraced this view of themselves as fighters. They found the fighter role emboldening. For example, Weatherwoman Susan Stern found strength and liberation through being a fighter: "the nights of rioting and fighting together had made bonds among the women that years of talking had not done.... We were tasting the macho strength that characterizes men, but we felt it keenly as women. Eyes glowing, we looked at each other warmly. Like a sweet perfume in the air we breathed in our first scent of sister-love."[78] For Stern, the WUO's program of fighting women was akin to liberation. Weatherwoman Laura Whitehorn also interpreted the idea of women fighters as empowering, seeing female fighters as models of women's resistance, with Vietnamese women fighters being clear models for the Weatherwomen in this respect.[79]

Yet, in another sense, even with this gender breaking role, the Weathermen's view of women was overly narrow since they encouraged their female members to see themselves as fighters more easily than they encouraged female roles as leaders or intellectual contributors. As Gilbert put it, the WUO, "lacked any kind of women's program beyond promoting women as fighters."[80] Nonetheless, women would ascend to leadership positions and would carve out positions of influence and power for themselves—a task perhaps made even harder by the fact the WUO did not have a nation-wide, programmatic commitment to women's causes, but the Weatherwomen, nevertheless, would achieve gender equity in leadership in spite of the sexist hurdles that they faced.

Much like they had done within SDS, the women who joined the WUO after the split in the summer of 1969 almost immediately created groups to build female solidarity and to organize against political and social oppression from their male colleagues. Many of the WUO collectives included women's caucuses that challenged male misperceptions of women and worked to advance female leadership. Within the organization at large, these Weatherwomen shared their feminist growth with the rest of the group.

In a piece written by Columbus collective Weatherwoman Lorraine Rosal titled "Who Do They Think Could Bury You?" women's voices came together and discussed the problem of sexism and what women were doing about it. The piece reported that the six Weatherwomen in the collective "dealt with male chauvinism simply by attacking chauvinist and paternalistic remarks by men."[81] The criticisms, it is implied, were numerous, cutting, and of a personal nature, and, as Rosal said, they were "handled liberally and personalistically [*sic*]."[82] These Weatherwomen used their solidarity and power to speak freely as a base from which they could attack the Weathermen's sexism, so that "we began defending each other because we were women, not because we were politically correct."[83] The Columbus Weatherwomen even engaged in "a few fistfights when the men's chauvinist baiting reached an unbearable level."[84] Upon further reflection—and not wanting to engage in a male/female contest of wills and a rumble that would take away from constructive dialogue—the women eventually concluded that they were behaving just as badly as the men, from a position that essentialized gender. Thus, the Weatherwomen decided that they themselves were "using chauvinism as a bludgeon" and that they needed to move toward more fruitful ways of pointing out sexist behavior.[85] Importantly, the women decided that they would still stand up to sexism when men exhibited it, but do so in a constructive manner that allowed men to reflect on their wrong doings in less confrontational environments, so that the men could undergo a transformation in their thinking (and not just stop a conversation for fear of reprimand, without making real progress).

Nevertheless, Rosal reports that the Columbus women did not achieve political respect from men until they began engaging in feminist action against the larger community. In one such activist event, Rosal recounts that the Weatherwomen attended a Stanly party, an affair which a hostess threw so as to get her friends to buy Stanly products, which the Weatherwomen defined as "the more you screw your friends by getting them to buy products they can't use, the more points you get and the more worthless products you acquire; i.e., the more the Stanly Company screws you."[86] The Stanly Company offered an array of products, ranging from household care products, such as cleaners and mops, to personal care items; these items were sold at parties at people's houses. At this particular party, the Weatherwomen interrupted the selling of products and attacked consumerism and gender roles; they discussed family structure and women's wages. As such, the Weatherwomen saw themselves as educating the young partygoers as to their limited roles in society—as subordinate to their husbands and bound by domesticity and lower wages. This kind of organizing was feminist in nature, and also earned the Weatherwomen respect from the male members of their collective.

The sexism of the Columbus Weathermen was real and problematic—so much so that the Weatherwomen had to argue their way to respect (including to the point of having to exchange punches over it), and then prove themselves in action, but eventually the Weatherwomen succeeded in garnering the respect they sought from their male peers. Their reward was access to leadership positions within the Columbus collective.[87] By sharing the experience of the Columbus Weatherwomen in an article entitled "Who Do They Think Could Bury You?," which was published in the nationally distributed newsletter of SDS, the *New Left Notes*, these women could encourage other women to take more direct action in combatting sexism—and perhaps instruct male readers in how not to treat women. "Who Do They Think Could Bury You?" came out during the first few months of WUO's existence (August 1969), after the spring (June 1969) SDS split. Thus, it would have had tremendous instructional value to women of the newly formed WUO collectives and to the former SDS members who had transitioned to the WUO and had brought with them not only their zeal, but also their New Left sexism.

In other collectives, such as in Seattle, women successfully combatted sexism and similarly moved into positions of leadership. According to Susan Stern, another Weatherwoman, Beverly, often made decisions within the group, controlled the group's finances, and everybody looked at Beverly "for direction" (Stern only provides a first name for Beverly—this practice comes up repeatedly in other texts or from other authors, as a means to disguise the identity of group members; other times, the names provided are aliases or pseudonyms).[88] Members of the Seattle collective were also dedicated to smashing sexism, so much so that, at first, they even objected to Stern joining the collective on the grounds that she was living with two men who were notorious chauvinists. Further, they disapproved of Stern working as a go-go dancer, which the Weather members considered to be a job that was not fitting given their commitment to the women's liberation movement.[89] Once she joined, Stern discovered that work within the collective was not divided along gender lines—there was no cleaning set aside for women, no important work set aside for the men (unlike SDS). The point was to get things done in a collaborative manner. Men and women had to learn to be self-sufficient in all aspects of life so that everyone would do traditionally gendered work, regardless of their own genders.[90] Contrary to the implication that women only broke gender roles in terms of fighting, in at least the Seattle collective, women also learned to be automobile mechanics. And everyone, women and men, shared housework. Stern recalls, "We all took turns cooking and cleaning the house.... Suddenly we would get a free half hour and a mop and broom would appear and we would clean frenetically. For a day and a half there would be no dust, and no oily layer of dirt anywhere. Then it would accumulate all over again, and two days later the house looked like a trashcan."[91] In the Seattle collective, the revolution included breaking away from traditional gender roles for both women and men.

As undercover FBI agent Larry Grathwohl infiltrated the Cincinnati collective of the WUO, he noted that various women were contributing significantly to the group and were ascending to positions of leadership within their unit. For example, while at a recruitment meeting for the Cincinnati collective, Grathwohl remembers seeing Weatherwoman Karen Ashley taking "the teacher's position in front of the classroom" and instructing the audience in what it meant to be a revolutionary. Ashley also explained the WUO's political agenda of solidarity with "the struggle of the Vietnamese, the Uruguayans, the Rhodesians, the Blacks—All Third World people who are fighting against U.S. imperialism"—she was entrusted to enlist new members and raise awareness of the WUO's mission in the community.[92] Grathwohl further noted that Weatherwoman Annie Gordon was especially effective in discussing politics with high school students. Part of the high school collective, she not only informed young people about the WUO's political agenda and the problematic nature of the Vietnam War, but also discussed gender inequality with young women, asking, "When you graduate, why shouldn't you have as many opportunities as the boys?"[93] When ran off by the police, this Weatherwoman also thought of recruiting students in the pizza shop next to the high school, the place to which she had noted the hungry teenagers often gravitated.[94] When discussing the Cincinnati collective, Grathwohl also mentions that Weatherwomen Nancy Chiara and Karen Bittner were part of the leadership of the group, with Naomi Jaffe joining them for part of the time (later on, Bittner was solely responsible for the secondary, Vine Street collective, of the WUO in Cincinnati).[95] As Grathwohl reported, the Cincinnati collective was in large part run by women.

Across the organization, as women fought the seemingly never-ending battle against sexism, many of the men responded positively. David Gilbert remembers that women took the time to point out instances of sexism and tried to get men to work on and alter their internalized male supremacy. He saw this effort not only as patient and loving (on the part of the women) and redemptive (for the men), but also as incredibly beneficial to the WUO's overall dynamics. Gilbert says, "There's actually an act of love to try to critique someone in a constructive way ... in that being attuned to relationships, being committed to people to try to develop a more collective approach, I think that all of those things—that the women in general and the women's movement made a real contribution to that."[96] Additionally, WUO chronicler Ron Jacobs agrees that Weatherwomen confronted men within WUO frequently for their sexism.[97]

Weatherwomen also saw their efforts as making important advances within the WUO. Weatherwoman Laura Whitehorn believes that "sexism within the organization would have been much worse if women hadn't been doing some of the best most serious anti-imperialism across the country."[98] Weatherwomen attacked men's sexism in criticism self-criticism sessions (sessions where members would be criticized for any of their actions so that they could improve in their behavior), and men began to self-identify their own problems.[99] For example, Weatherwoman Susan Stern mentions how another member, Weatherman Robby, who self-identified as "the world's worst male chauvinist," developed to the point where "all he wanted to see in the world was for women to get stronger, learn to love each other, and leave rotten men like himself to ponder their atrocities against women."[100] Robby changed so much due to criticism, according to Stern, that he became "fanatical to the point of absurdity."[101] Further, David Gilbert was also made to see that he had a "cavalier" attitude toward women, and that he undercut women; he was confronted and, as he acknowledges himself, he was corrected at a criticism self-criticism session.[102] Hence, while instances of male chauvinism—including the objectification and over-sexualization of women—existed within the WUO, they were fought against, which led to at least some men developing an awareness of their own sexism and eventually even becoming more feminist themselves. In this sense, the WUO's feminist, anti-imperialist revolution literally began at home.

Sometimes Weatherwomen had to take direct action against sexist members. From various direct accounts of WUO gender relations, Weatherman (and WUO leader) Mark Rudd emerges as a living embodiment of the male exploitation and oppression of women.[103] Rudd later confessed to this charge of chauvinism, saying, "Women were definitely to me a type of object, to be used to build up my already inflated ego."[104] But even in the face of this sexist and influential leader, Weatherwomen worked to curtail his negative effects, eventually forcing him out of the WUO. As Weatherwoman Bernardine Dohrn told activist Jane Alpert in a July 1971 meeting, "A lot of our women feel the same way about him that you do [that he is sexist]. It's the main reason he was asked to take some time off."[105] Thus, in at least some cases where men could not reform their sexist ways, the Weatherwomen were able to expel them from the WUO. This point is important since it shows how misled we are in describing the WUO's overall views by relying on men in leadership, such as Rudd, whom the women were powerful enough to expel.

Perhaps one of the WUO's strongest women leaders was Bernardine Dohrn. Integral to the organization from its inception (during its split from SDS) all the way to the time it went underground to escape surveillance, Dohrn was at the forefront of the WUO. But even her leadership was contested. Evidence from 1976, published within a pamphlet of the Prairie Fire Organizing Committee (PFOC, a group formed in 1976 by the above ground portion or supporters of the WUO), charged that women such as Dohrn were promoted to WUO leadership for the wrong reasons or that women were "tokens" within the organizational structure, were not imbued with any real power, and were usually associated with a powerful male.[106] Even Bernardine Dohrn released a tape where she referred to herself as a token, greatly enhancing the evidence for this complaint.[107]

Despite Dohrn's statement, her actions within the group hardly seem to be that of a token. It was Dohrn who led the split of SDS at the Chicago 1969 convention. In July of 1969, Dohrn went to Cuba to formulate strategy for one the WUO's big planned actions, the previously discussed Days of Rage; in October of the same year, it was Dohrn who led women into battle at this event. She also was the one who took the reins of the organization and initiated the strategy of moving away from bombing civilians and to just bombing symbolically. Moreover, Dohrn was the voice of the WUO.[108] She wrote many position papers, developing the WUO's feminism and discussing women's rights. To name just a few of the key papers that are written in whole or in part by her, there's "You Don't Need a Weatherman," "The Look Is You," "Toward a Revolutionary Women's Movement," and "An Open Letter to the U.S. Workers."[109] In fact, the WUO, commenting on Dohrn's contributions as of July 1970, stated that "Bernardine Dohrn is no token; she's one of the strongest revolutionary leaders we have."[110] The FBI's infiltrator, Larry Grathwohl, concurred, identifying Dohrn as one of the "most notorious Weatherman leaders"; FBI files viewed Dohrn as a "leading functionary of the WUO."[111]

The discussion surrounding the WUO points out another issue with female leadership: women who made it into leadership were almost always partners in heterosexual couples, where the male was often a strong leader in his own right. Both David Gilbert and Cathy Wilkerson bring up this point. Gilbert states, "Women's participation and percentage of leadership were very strong, but in practice, a woman had to be part of a heterosexual couple to be a top leader."[112] Wilkerson implies that, for women, power flowed through men to the women.[113] As was the case in SDS and civil rights organizations, such as SNCC, it often seemed as the only route to leadership for women was through their personal relationships with powerful men.[114]

These facts cannot be disputed, but they are not as damning as they initially appear. Not only are there counterexamples to this arrangement—for example, Susan Stern was a leader within her collective and slept with men *outside* of the WUO—but this bias tended to cut both ways.[115] After all, many men in national leadership were also part of heterosexual, power couples (John Jacobs, Bill Ayers, and Jeff Jones stand out as key leaders who were part of power couples). Weatherman David Gilbert, one of the people who made this claim about women, agreed that men in leadership tended to need to be in relationships with powerful women as well.[116] Power in the WUO tended to reside neither in single women nor single men, but in heterosexual couples working together. Therefore, while there is some clear bias here, it is too shortsighted to claim it is merely a sexist bias against women. This criticism may instead point to biases against single people and non-heterosexual relationships, which may be significant for a group that attempted to smash monogamy (which will be discussed more fully later on) but still gravitated towards heterosexual power couples in leadership.

As an example, let us consider Jeff Jones, who dated and eventually married Eleanor Raskin, who was herself active in SDS and then the WUO. Raskin established her revolutionary credentials when she led protesters and picketers in the Columbia protest in 1968 while married to her first husband, Jonah Raskin. In 1969, after her divorce and while acting as a Weatherwoman, she joined the delegation to Cuba led by Dohrn—thus Raskin emerged as politically active in her own right while with her first husband and then as a single woman, *before* her involvement with Jeff Jones. Furthermore, she authored *The Bust Book: What to Do Till the Lawyer Comes* with Kathy Boudin (the bust book was a book dedicated to educating activists as to what to do when they were arrested, before their lawyer arrived). Raskin also was involved in the Weatherwomen's action in Pittsburgh in 1969. After the townhouse explosion (where she acted as a guide to lead Wilkerson—a surviving WUO member—underground), she lived in the Catskills Mountains, where she fell in love with national leader Jeff Jones. Thus, it cannot be argued that Jeff Jones brought Eleanor Raskin into the organization or was responsible for her revolutionary activity—Eleanor Raskin was responsible for her own radicalization and political activity.[117]

Dohrn was part of another power couple. Early on in SDS, and for the first few months of the WUO's existence, Dohrn dated activist John Jacobs (known simply as J.J. in WUO circles), the principal author of the "Weatherman" paper, and a proponent of revolutionary violence. By this time, though, Dohrn had already established her own revolutionary credentials through her work in SDS—she had been elected Interorganizational Secretary of SDS on her own merits and had been active on behalf of the National Lawyer's Guild. She was also another one of the authors of the "Weatherman" document. Significantly, Dohrn acted on her own when it came to organizational matters: for example, she went alone on delegations to Cuba, leaving Jacobs at home.[118] Furthermore, Dohrn threw Jacobs out of the organization when he insisted on using violence against persons, again denoting her higher status and influence within the group.[119] Accordingly, it could be argued that as two dedicated revolutionaries in their own right, each individual saw commonalities in the other that resonated with their own commitments and interests, and therefore entered in a relationship without any machinations as to power or influence.

Later on, Dohrn was also involved with SDS member and then WUO national leader Bill Ayers, but she brought him into national prominence, as Ayers saw himself as unfit for leadership in the years prior to his relationship with Dohrn. Ayers says of his leadership capabilities during that time period: "I had no firm idea, really, of what a collective was, even though I was part of the national leadership collective and a leader in the Detroit collective."[120] In his own estimation as a leader, he emerges as somewhat bewildered and as fueled by theory and idealism. He also adds, when commenting on the Days of Rage, that he would have followed Dohrn anywhere, as she inspired him.[121] In the Dohrn and Ayers leadership couple, it is not that power derives from the man (Ayers) to the woman (Dohrn), but quite the opposite.

Thusly, the critique that that power flowed from men to women makes sense based on certain typical gendered assumptions, but a closer look reveals that in some key instances at least, power also flowed from women to men. We then cannot simply assume from the importance of power couples that men always held more power than women in the WUO. Instead, a more nuanced analysis shows the situation is more complex: power in the WUO was not merely controlled by men but was held by women and men together in a variety of ways that is not easily reducible to the idea that WUO is simply and thoroughly sexist.

Honky Tonk Women in the Heart
of the Mother Country[122]

Weatherwomen fought against sexism in theory as well as in practice. By producing feminist position papers and theoretical frameworks supporting the equality of women, the Weatherwomen and the WUO were engaging in what they identified as feminist work. Because the WUO did not prioritize gender over other sites of oppression, however, self-proclaimed feminist groups of the era, such as the Bread and Roses collective, and feminist thinkers, such as Robin Morgan, dismissed the organization as being not feminist enough or not feminist at all. Rather than replicating this myopia, it might be more useful for us to consider what this suggests about the fluidity of feminist theory and practice in the late 1960s and early 1970s.[123] The feminism practiced within the WUO might have been different from that championed by mainstream feminist organizations, but it cannot thereby be dismissed.

When thinking of feminism, it is sometimes helpful to divide it into periods, or waves. Ultimately, we will see that this historical framework is problematic and may even lead to misunderstanding certain feminist organizations and individuals. Yet, while the historical approach to the wave metaphor is worrisome, we can make use of a conceptual version of this model as an organizational tool. We will organize the major ideas and views of feminism into their standard waves, but in doing so, we will not have to restrict ourselves to the typical historical periods. By delineating the waves into conceptual categories, we can say that a group in the 60s (which historians typically associate with second wave feminism) can count as a third wave group because it holds onto third wave views, such as sex positivism and intersectionality. With such a conceptual organization, we will be able to see how the WUO defies the typical historical organization by being a third wave feminist group, conceptually speaking, during the second wave, historically speaking. This seeming inconsistency, now made perfectly consistent through a conceptual reimagining of the waves, thus indicates the potential dysfunction of over-relying on the historical wave motif, which would have led to severe difficulty in understanding the WUO's own third wave feminism.

As explained in the preface, the historical first wave of feminism is typically defined as the period when activists were dealing with gaining political rights for women (such as the right to vote, gained in 1920). In this sense, the first wave may be the least problematic when one is contrasting the two different approaches: conceptually, the first wave entails the search for political rights with emphasis on the right to vote, which historically finishes in 1920. The second wave, which the consensus historically locates during the time period that we have been discussing (the late 1960s and early 1970s), conceptually deals with enlarging the rights of women by focusing on gender oppression and how that gender oppression functions in various areas of life, such as in education, the workplace, or the home. The second wave is thusly operating, conceptually speaking, from the starting point that oppression *qua* woman is primary, and assumes the category woman is reflective of its own membership (thus replicating white, straight, middle class concerns since other sites of oppression, such as race, sexuality, and class, are being stripped away to concentrate on gender alone). Consequently, historical second wave feminism and conceptual second wave feminism could come apart if, for instance, a person or group were seeking more than political representation any time prior to the 1960s and especially prior to 1920, which would imply such a person or group, such as the anarcha-feminists, could be conceptually second wave prior to the historical start of the second wave in the early 1960s.[124]

Third wave feminism, historically denoted as starting in 1981 or 1991, conceptually picks up on the work of the second wave, but insists that the category woman comes in multiple identity types, such as those based in class, race, health, ability, etc.—third wave feminists point out that these identity markers cause women's experiences and oppressions to differ and interplay with one another. This concept, which is essential to understanding the conceptual version of the third wave, is called "intersectionality," which refers to the idea that identity is never singular, but instead involves an intersection of various traits, and, further, that this intersection brings up unique issues that are not captured by handling each identity trait separately. Thus, an African American lesbian has many identity traits, including being African American, a woman, a lesbian, and many others. Yet, she also has unique experiences that are due to her experiencing life at the intersection of all of her various identity traits. The third wave therefore conceptually operates from an inclusive standpoint, and aims to be responsive to the needs of all women and their various subjectivities that derive from their own intersectional identities.[125] It follows that an organization or person can be third wave conceptually speaking while existing prior to the historical third wave simply by being committed to intersectionality prior to the 1980s and 1990s.

Using this framework, the WUO displayed a feminism that was a conceptual combination of the second and third waves: they were situated in the second wave historically speaking (and held onto some distinctly second wave positions, conceptually speaking, as they were interested in the various kinds of oppressions women experienced as women and sought for women to have rights beyond merely formal political rights), but they were also pushing for greater inclusivity and more recognition of inter-sectional identities (even though the "intersectional" term had yet to be coined), akin to the third wavers. Therefore, the WUO disrupts the his-torical wave schema and pushes for a more conceptual understanding of the waves.[126]

For a different perspective, historians Angie Maxwell and Todd Shields see the (historical) second wave as whitewashed due to an over-reliance, in the media, on its white, affluent female leaders, as well as the subsequent attention that some historians gave to these same white, affluent leaders.[127] Calling to attention the contributions of activists who also happened to be women of color and who operated within the time period of the second wave, Maxwell and Shields conclude that the usual wave metaphor is prob-lematic and that the characterization of the second wave should be more nuanced, and not solely rely on its "failure to understand intersectional-ity."[128] Such an approach attempts to solve the conflation of the historical and conceptual approaches of the wave motif by embracing the historical approach. In this response, intersectionality can be located in the second wave just as easily as the third wave since the waves merely pick out his-torical periods and not key concepts.

The problem with this merely historical approach to the waves is that the conceptual meaning is exactly what feminist scholars rely on and make use of when they apply the wave metaphor to draw distinctions about dif-ferent types of feminism. This attempt to reimagine the second wave as sometimes intersectional blurs the conceptual distinction between the second and third wave and renders the metaphor much less practically useful. That is because what it means to say someone or some organization is "second wave" would no longer provide any information other than what historical period they operated in. There would be no sense of saying things such as "there is a difference between second wave and third wave feminism on the issue of sexuality," or "second and third wave feminism differ in how they look at race." The only difference would be that they are different time periods. In that sense, we could simply stop using the wave metaphor altogether and simply refer to "early 20th century femi-nists," "mid–20th century feminists," and "late 20th century feminists," which would be much more precise if we only were referring to time peri-ods and not conceptual differences.

Regardless of this move, it is important for us—as Maxwell and Shields also point out—to note that contemporary activists and critics of the second wave, such as Audre Lorde, recognized that the second wave tended to ignore the voices and experiences of "poor women, Black and Third-World women, and lesbians."[129] As such, to some contemporaries at least, the second wave seemed overly focused on a white, middle class perspective. And since these contemporary feminists were alive during that time period, they clearly can best be understood, in making this point, as making a conceptual point: the mainstream second wave, conceptually speaking, excluded the voices of women of color. Audre Lorde is clearly not saying that there were no poor women, black women, Third World women, lesbians, etc., during the historical period of the second wave. Hence, to make sense of Lorde's claim, we need to think of the waves in a conceptual manner. The WUO agreed with this concern that the second wave excluded the voices of these women, and saw its own inclusive, anti-racist work as a cornerstone to its brand of feminism. As Weatherwoman Laura Whitehorn put it, "we tried to analyze the affects of white skin privilege on us and on our organizations."[130]

Even though we can understand the waves from a conceptual perspective, that does not entail that each wave is internally uniform. For instance, the second wave had many internal struggles. Conceptually, the second wave is picked out through those feminists' agreement on the primacy of gender, which is encapsulated in their burgeoning theoretical analysis. We also conceptually identify the second wave as lacking in an intersectional analysis, but that leaves quite a lot of room for difference across various second wave feminists. As early feminist writer Jo Freeman puts it in "The Women's Liberation Movement: It's Origins, Structures, and Ideas," second wavers agreed on only two things: (1) a belief that in spite of men and women being the same, they are treated differently by social institutions and (2) a conviction that women experience oppression. Freeman put it thusly: "The feminist perspective starts from the premise that women and men are constitutionally equal and share the same human capabilities. Observed differences therefore demand a critical analysis of the social institutions which cause them."[131] As such, the work of second wavers focused on "the legal and economic difficulties women face."[132] When it came to oppression, second wavers defined it in terms of sexism, which they further broke down:

> For women, sexism describes the specificity of female oppression. Starting from the traditional belief of the difference between the sexes, sexism embodies two core concepts. The first is that men are more important than women.... The second core concept is that women are here for the pleasure and assistance of men. This is what is

meant when women are told that their role is complementary to that of men; that they should fulfill their natural "feminine" functions; that they are "different" from men and should not compete with them. From this concept comes the attitude that women are and should be dependent on men....[133]

Second wave feminists experienced conflicts in how best to address the problems they identified above. There were conflicts as to methodology (for example, the question of whether consciousness raising should be used as a tool to dismantle gender norms or sexist behavior, where consciousness raising means becoming aware of how a systemic problem is experienced and manifested in a particular woman's life); there were differing viewpoints on whether men should be included in consciousness raising sessions or seen as allies in general; there were disagreements over whether self-proclaimed feminists should devote themselves to only feminist aims or work alongside other political platforms.[134] In other words, outside of their commitment to a theoretical foundation that prioritized gender oppression, second wavers engaged in debate over what exactly constituted their own brand of feminism.

Likewise, throughout its existence, the WUO debated which model of feminism to adopt. For example, in the late 1970s, "Letter from Sisters" was a document from some Weatherwomen to the PFOC organization that critiqued seven years of WUO activity as sexist.[135] The Sisters charged the WUO with downplaying women's special oppression in the article "The Women's Question Is a Class Question," which appeared in the winter 1975-76 of *Osawatomie*, the WUO's magazine. The Sisters complained that "the material basis of women's oppression, and its concrete expression in the institutions of society—the family, schools, courts, laws, religion and the state—are left out" and that "male supremacy is liquidated [erased] and sexism seen as unimportant."[136] In essence, the Sisters were saying that "The Women's Question" article did not address the special oppression of women because it reduced women's issues to class issues.[137]

This concern, that gender was not given prominence in the analysis of women's oppression, however, does not erase the fact that the article was generally feminist in nature. "The Women's Question Is a Class Question" stated:

The subjugation of women arose along with exploitative class relationships, as the direct result of the development of private property. The family became the economic unit of society. From that point in human history women and women's work were considered outside the economic life of society and were held in contempt. Home and child-rearing became a private burden and doom rather than a valued form of social labor.[138]

In the voice of the pseudonymous author Celia Sojourn, the WUO was addressing the oppression of women in this article but did so in a way that was derivative of the economic status of women. The article saw the family as a locus for women's oppression, but primarily in an economic sense. In this piece, then, an analysis of how and why women were treated as lower class citizens was present, as opposed to an analysis that addressed women's oppression in and of itself. The Sisters were correct to feel that the WUO took a reductionist position in this piece, though we should not be too quick to think that this position is dismissive and not at all feminist.

Although "The Women's Question Is a Class Question" contained the kind of reductionism that the Sisters were worried about, the paper also explained that the WUO would continue to "struggle fiercely against all forms of sexist behavior and always fight to root it out from among the people," and also would build coalitions in their effort to achieve their overall goals of building a "movement that reaches into every office, sweat-shop, household and high school to demand jobs, equal pay, adequate income, day care, the right to unionize, an end to every type of racial discrimination and equality for women."[139] Unlike the PL, which thought a concern with gender issues was divisive and did not merit attention, the WUO, even during times when there were similar concerns of reductionism, articulated recognizably feminist positions. So while it is true that the WUO is concerned with class, as the PL was before the SDS split, this concern is not akin to PL's dismissive view of feminism. That is, both the PL and the WUO, at least in part, engage in reductionism, it is only the PL's reductionism that is dismissive: they felt that since class was of primary importance, there was no need for feminism. For the PL's reductionism, we can safely ignore feminism because class consciousness would simply subsume feminist concerns and so feminism is unnecessary. Even when the WUO engaged in reductionism, it still recognized the importance of feminism. "The Women's Question Is a Class Question" clearly comes out strongly in favor of fighting against male supremacy and for increasing the power of women.

Hence, "The Women's Question Is a Class Question" emphasized class struggle (perhaps to the point of reductionism) but did so in alliance with feminist aims and with an understanding that a movement for female liberation must also account for class oppression, economic oppression, and racial oppression. The WUO was a politico organization. The "politico" label referred to feminist groups that were involved in political action, were not identifying gender-based oppression as the sole or even primary oppression and saw capitalism as oppressive in itself. The WUO also was against separatist feminism, a strand of feminism that held that women should leave whatever group they were involved with (such as a leftist one that prioritized political action) and join one that primarily fought gender based oppression and was woman centered.[140] Weatherwoman Cathy Wilkerson discusses the damaging conflict between separatist groups and the WUO. She explains that at the time, she couldn't understand the need for a separatist movement, as she felt committed to the needs of Vietnamese women and not just white women. But she concludes that all the women involved in factional struggles between politico and separatist groups would later see their work as interrelated.[141] Activist Roxanne Dunbar-Ortiz also discusses this conflict, referring to it as "a false dichotomy" presented to women. She envisioned a third option, one where a woman-centered platform, along with anti-imperialist agenda working for socialism existed side by side.[142] In a sense, the WUO already instantiated this third possibility. Furthermore, the WUO deeply believed that men and women struggling together against chauvinism was the best way to stamp out all oppression collectively. The WUO wove together all of these threads in its own brand of feminism.

Sixties historian Dan Berger adds to the criticism against "The Women's Question Is a Class Question" by pointing out that this article neither addressed the plight of female prisoners nor engaged in a discussion of the need of women to defend themselves against rape—concluding that, on this basis, the WUO was out of touch with mainstream feminism. Specifically, Berger states that the editorial made no mention of Joan Little's plight. Berger concludes that this absence shows that the article in particular, and the WUO in general, missed some of the key points of the feminist movement.[143] While it is true that the "The Women's Question Is a Class Question" did not focus on rape or the famous Joan Little case—where an imprisoned black woman had killed a guard who was forcing her to perform oral sex on him—which was unfolding during this time period, other *Osawatomie* articles did. Notably, the *Osawatomie* cover for the Autumn 1975 issue was dedicated to prisoners. Importantly, a special section titled "Women Locked Up" discussed sexual assaults against women, specifically referencing the Joan Little case and the special oppression of women in jail.[144] This article, and the issue of *Osawatomie* it was printed in, was from the Autumn 1975 issue and came immediately prior to the issue that carried "The Woman's Question Is a Class Question" ("The Women's Question Is a Class Question" was in the next issue, the Winter 1975-76 issue). Thus, the allegation that the WUO ignored discussions about rape and the plight of female prisoners, and consequently was not in touch with the heart of feminism, is heavily uncharitable.

An anti-sexism message is prominent in other WUO papers, indicating that the organization, in spite of its sexism, was attempting to locate and provide a feminist message. The "Weatherman" paper itself, previously discussed in this chapter, prescribed the smashing of sexism and the breaking out of restrictive gender norms for women.[145] Furthermore, another WUO piece, the summer 1975 "A Mighty Army: An Investigation of Women Workers" (note that the title of the piece suggested that women were thought of as a powerful source for fighters in the battle against imperialism), explained that most women at work suffered from a lack of daycare and maternity leave (and that these women were trying to unionize to attain help in alleviating these problems). The WUO identified this dearth as leading to women's everyday oppression.[146] These concerns were, in a sense, very much the domain of women and intrinsically constituted a feminist platform—the WUO's attempt to support working women in unionizing and solving these urgent issues was neither an exclusionary nor an anti-feminist position.

"A Mighty Army" further explained that working women also worked a second shift at home that was devalued and unappreciated. The piece added that working women "are last hired and first fired" and are paid the least, with the pay gap between men and women widening.[147] Additionally, the paper discussed the special gender bias against women workers, namely that they are treated in a paternalistic fashion and expected to fall in line easily, and are prey to the sexual advances of their bosses.[148] While the WUO, in its papers, could be interpreted as being overly preoccupied with class or economics (and thus interpreted as reductionist), these same WUO papers were attempting to provide substantial analyses and real solutions to women's oppression. Even though they might not have fit the feminist mold that is based on the other feminist groups from the time period, there was plenty of evidence of the WUO's hammering out their own brand of feminism.

Perhaps another reason as to why the WUO was not recognized as feminist by other feminist groups of its time period was that the WUO actually attacked those other groups as "bourgeois." Dohrn, in the same tape where she called herself a "token," stated, "I have attacked the women's movement as bourgeois, separatist, anti-communist, divisive, anti–Third World, and a grave danger to revolution."[149] Gilbert recognized that "we tended to have contempt for those who formed an independent women's movement."[150] Finally, the Sisters of the WUO, writing in 1976, argued that the WUO picked out bourgeois feminism as the main problem for women.[151]

In spite of these largely unfair attacks on other feminist groups, many women who were self-identified feminists joined the WUO. To understand why, one must keep in mind the choice that anti-imperialist feminists of the day had to make. Other feminist organizations of the day not only failed to take up anti-imperialist activities, but also took on some racist and classist positions. As Wilkerson puts it, "the women's movement at that early stage was very embedded in middle-class concerns ... we had different concerns than the rest of the women's movement."[152] On the other hand, anti-imperialist organizations, like the WUO, were sexist. Women who were both feminists and anti-imperialists had to choose between organizations that took on a singular focus that missed much of what they felt required fighting against, or organizations that were inherently sexist.[153] As Gilbert recalls,

> Only later did I learn from Naomi and others what a difficult, almost schizophrenic period it was for them: politically "at home" neither in the anti-imperialist Left, with its still rampant sexism, or the predominantly white women's movement, which distanced itself from frontline national liberation struggles and gravitated toward defining women's issues from a white and often middle class perspective.[154]

Wilkerson adds: "All of us women were in this hothouse environment where we like you had to participate in *either* radical politics *or* feminist and we were on both sides [italics in original]."[155]

This choice could not have been easy for women who were feminists but also race, class, and colonialism conscious. Instead of building a strong coalition with women's liberation groups, by attacking those groups, the WUO undercut any chance for an alliance, and isolated women who may have wanted to join both types of groups.

The fact that Weatherwomen had to make this choice did not mean that they were not also developing a feminist tradition within the WUO. For example, the six Weatherwomen of the Columbus collective were actively educating themselves on feminist issues, and forming feminist study groups to discuss women's liberation materials.[156] They worked together to analyze and identify how sexism and male supremacy worked as "tools of the ruling class."[157] They started learning feminist theory and "writing on the women's question."[158] They were also advancing a theory of feminism that blended anti-racism and anti-classism with anti-sexism, all within an analysis of the capitalist/imperialist system.

Dohrn was developing a feminist theory along the same lines, such as in her essay "Toward a Revolutionary Women's Movement." This piece attempted to explain that the problem with mainstream, second wave feminism was that it resulted in a "middle class single issue" type of activism that privileged gender as the locus of oppression at the cost of all other loci of oppression. Dohrn explained that the WUO's feminist vision was more inclusive and responsive than mainstream feminism:

> A revolutionary women's movement must be politically based on the most oppressed sectors—black, brown, and white working-class women. This does not mean that movement women are not a significant part of that movement, or that we must wait until there is a working class women's movement. It does mean that we must be conscious of our perspectives and the class interests which our demands represent. It means that our immediate job is to organize masses of women around the full scope of radical demands—including the destruction of male supremacy.[159]

Though the WUO should not have implied in their papers that the bourgeois traits of women's liberation groups were worse than patriarchy, this critique does not mean that bourgeois feminism was not problematic: women's groups at the time generally advocated a middle class, white female perspective. Historian Becky Thompson points out that the choice of joining a white women feminist organization was limiting to the activist women of that era: the radical feminists of the time denounced anything that was not primarily couched in gender oppression, and frowned on anti-war, anti-racist, militant women as being somehow duped by men into ignoring gender.[160]

Feminist theory has recognized that second wave feminism was strongly associated with a white, middle class point of view, which minimized or ignored the oppression experienced by other groups of women, and led to an elitist point of view—the very same qualities that the WUO critiqued.[161] Weatherwomen were largely middle class, white women. But they were choosing to use their class and race privilege to take action as allies on behalf of other marginalized women. Consequently, the WUO insisted that the voices and experiences of poor and Third World women be added to the mix. Additionally, as we have seen, the WUO's brand of feminism identified sexism and patriarchy as problems that must be defeated, and that were perpetuated (and taught to the populace) by the imperialist/capitalist system. Hence, the WUO advocated revolution as a way to gain true female liberation. Far from being anti-feminist, the WUO, unlike most feminist organizations of the period, insisted on a third wave type of feminism where the subjectivities of all women were respected. The WUO may have engaged in reductionist evaluations of women's oppression in some papers, and they did openly attack women's liberation groups. However, in many of their other papers, the WUO critiqued the oppression of women on its own terms; in almost all of their papers on the gender issues, they showed an appreciation for the importance of fighting women's oppression. Though they attacked women's liberation groups, their attacks pointed to legitimate concerns, and, thanks largely to the Weatherwomen, they were making important third wave advances beyond those groups. Though there is sexism in the WUO's papers, it is not nearly enough to declare the organization as a whole to be sexist.

Additionally, we should note that even the sexism at issue here is not what we normally think of when we say writings are sexist. The WUO papers neither express belief in the inferiority of women nor the superiority of men in any sense. They neither sexualize or objectify women nor make sexist jokes in their papers. Instead, much of the sexism at issue lies in the facts that they explain gender issues through the light of class analysis and they too enthusiastically point to the racism and classism of women's liberation groups of the time period. One of the key things to remember in analyzing these charges of sexism is that they are mostly addressed to the male leaders and members of WUO. Insofar as the Weather*women* responded within the organization to these same problems, the organization can be both sexist (with respect to what many of the men were doing) and feminist (with respect to what many of the women and some of the men were doing) at the same time.

Furthermore, feminism is not a zero-sum project. One can develop feminist theory and push for a feminist agenda and still not be thoroughly successful in the face of sexism. But the feminist project itself—the articulation of theory, the development of feminist stances, the raising of consciousness as to feminist themes that the Weatherwomen engaged in—needs to be recognized as a feminist effort. One hundred percent effectiveness should not be required to count as feminist.

Feminist to a Person: Finding Feminism in Spite of Sexism[162]

Based in large part on the instances of sexism discussed above, the secondary literature argues that the WUO cannot be feminist.[163] This conclusion clearly draws to a large extent from a focus on the men of the organization. The premises upon which this claim is based appear to be that almost all of the men were sexist, the men held more power than the women, and the women were completely unable to change Weathermen's sexist culture. While there was a good deal of sexism among the men, this does not mean that men held so much power that only the men's positions should count as the organization's positions or that the organization had a singular mission that flowed solely from the men. Rather, the positions, roles, and activities of the Weatherwomen ought to be recognized as significant in their own right.

Weather did not have a hierarchical, linear power structure with a single leader at the top. Though the Weather Bureau (Weather Bureau was the name used for those in national leadership positions) at times represented a central committee, there was no central leader for the Bureau. The Weather Bureau organized national actions, and local collectives were autonomous.[164] Hence, the local collectives could organize their own, local actions and make their own local decisions without needing any permission from the Weather Bureau. Instead, the Weather Bureau mainly held power when it came to putting together national actions. Further, the Weather Bureau always contained a significant number of women, whose number consistently approached or surpassed the majority of the leadership group. Given how fluid power was in the WUO and how much power women held, it would be inaccurate to reduce the organization to a unitary message that only comes from the men. The Weatherwomen's work played an essential role in the formation and statement of the WUO's mission and should not be liquidated by reducing that mission to a simplified, unitary, and male viewpoint.

Another common misperception is that the WUO was not a feminist group but rather *only* an anti-imperialist or politically motivated organization.[165] This view fails to recognize that there are many types of feminism, and therefore, the WUO's vision of coalescing sexism and women's oppression with concerns about the oppression of Third World individuals and people of color is a valid type of feminism.[166] Activist Judith Mirkinnson also offers an answer to this seeming dilemma, stating that it is not a question of the feminists working against the anti-imperialists, but rather of two movements working together, side by side, and challenging each other.[167] Weatherwoman Bernardine Dohrn states, rather succinctly, "The women of Weather were feminists to a person."[168] Their feminism, however, was blended with and inseparable from their other aims, such as the anti-war effort and anti-imperialism. Instead of not being a feminist group, the WUO's feminism was multi-layered and nuanced in ways that are easy to miss.

Most importantly, Weatherwomen found ways to assert themselves in the WUO, to challenge its sexism, and to contribute to the WUO's feminist mission. Focusing on their actions gives us a different perspective on the organization—one where Weatherwomen are recognized as active contributors and are not erased from the historical record. With that shift in focus, the Weatherwomen emerge as autonomous agents due to their involvement in the WUO. The Weatherwomen's continuing roles within the WUO are further investigated in the next chapter, which explores how these Weatherwomen found ways to autonomously express themselves and build their visions of feminism within, and because of, the WUO. As such, the next chapter illustrates how the WUO served as a locus of empowerment for some of these Weatherwomen, as it not only provided them with an arena in which to become politically active, but as it also served as a vehicle for these Weatherwomen to go against traditional gender norms and become leaders in their own right.

CHAPTER 3

Female Leadership and Authenticity

In the fall of 1969, a confrontation between Weatherman Terry Robbins and several women of the Chicago WUO collective exposed both the undercurrents of sexism within the organization and the members' efforts to identify and combat it. Cathy Wilkerson recalls:

> In one [Chicago collective] meeting, he responded to one of the women with a tone of voice that many women, including myself, found offensive. We immediately challenged him, angrily accusing him of sexism, of disrespecting a woman's opinion. While Weatherwomen were committed to fighting for those who suffered most, we could fight sexism within our own ranks along the way.... [W]hen Terry at first defended himself angrily, standing up aggressively to make a point, two or three of us stood up to challenge his stance and tried to push him back into the chair. As we all wrestled, a small lamp was knocked over. The shattering glass bulb brought a quick and rather foolish end to our dramatic posturing.
>
> Later, Terry, a few other women and I sat in the kitchen trying to resolve the conflict. The conversation evolved into an interesting discourse on what we really thought about the meaning of equality. We didn't agree, but I was conscious of the fact that this was one of the first times since joining the collective in which there had actually been a give and take of ideas, and not just people pontificating. I felt a kinship with the other woman who had stood up with me, sensing the same passion in her, and also a kinship with Terry, for holding his ground and following through, even if I thought he had been wrong.[1]

Wilkerson's remembrance highlights the multiple ways in which Weatherwomen fought—sometimes literally—against the sexism of some of the men of the WUO. Significantly, Wilkerson's story also illustrates how the Weatherwomen's direct challenge to this sexism could result in meaningful communication over a feminist issue. As Wilkerson notes, the discussion did not come to a final resolution, but it did signify progress toward gender equality, both ideologically and materially. Not only did passionate exchanges, such as this one, challenge personal outlooks and foster closer bonds among the members, but these moments also embodied the process through which women gained respect, became empowered, and found their autonomy both within and beyond the organization. For these Weatherwomen, the political was personal.

The women of the WUO were not simply victims of male chauvinism. Rather, they were empowered political ideologues and activists who worked to confront the sexism they observed or experienced. As a result, women in the WUO moved into leadership roles that were not otherwise readily available in other leftist organizations or in mainstream society in the 1960s and 1970s. In fact, Weatherwomen changed the overall leadership and style of the WUO, making it into a less sexist, more open, and more feminist organization.

This chapter excavates the important contributions of female leaders of the WUO that have been neglected in the historical record. These women established themselves as autonomous agents and respected leaders at a time in U.S. history when women were still expected to remain on the sidelines. By examining the struggles and accomplishments of individual women, specifically Bernardine Dohrn, Diana Oughton, and Susan Stern, who rose to leadership in the WUO, the autonomy and authenticity of women in roles of leadership comes to attention and casts new light on an organization that has been historically noted more for its sexism than its gender balance.

Women Wresting Leadership Away

For a political organization that was not mainly dedicated to women's liberation issues, the WUO had a large segment of women leading the organization, putting it at the forefront of American political organizations in terms of gender parity in leadership. Most activist or left-wing organizations, including the Student Nonviolent Coordinating Committee (SNCC), the Southern Christian Leadership Conference (SCLC), the Black Panther Party (BPP), and others, had male dominated leadership throughout the 1960s. While women were very active in these organizations, women were almost always placed in secondary positions, with males being associated with leadership and decision-making. For example, men like James Foreman, John Lewis, Julian Bond, Bob Moses, Charlie Cobb, and Stokely Carmichael were identified as the public leaders of SNCC; women such as Diana Nash (one of the founders), Daisy Bates, Jo Ann Robinson, and

Mary King, while active organizers, were for the most part in secondary positions (Mary King was communications assistant to Julian Bond, for example). Historian Ann Standley notes that "because they saw themselves as having to convince whites to support the movement, and because they identified so completely with the struggle for civil rights, Bates, Robinson, and Nash refrained from making critical judgments about the movement or their roles within in" and therefore "suppressed their differences with the male leadership."[2] While race played a role in this division in SNCC (in a famous position paper they published, titled "Sex and Caste," white women reported more of a sense of subservience, while black women felt they were active and respected), men still held control over the leadership positions and served as the public faces of the organization. For example, Ruby Doris Smith-Robinson worked in an administrative capacity in the Atlanta office of SNCC, and was the only woman who served as executive secretary for the organization; moreover, Kathleen Cleaver reported that "while working for SNCC, beginning in 1966, that women did most of the work but few women held positions of authority."[3]

For the SCLC, the most well-known leaders were Martin Luther King, Jr. (president of the organization until 1968) and Ralph Abernathy (president from 1968 to 1977). While Ella Baker was also a significant figure, she was not considered for the post of executive director of the SCLC as she was deemed to be inadequate (the position went to John Tilley). Baker also felt that men were limiting women in political actions.[4] As Baker put it, she also "knew from the beginning that having a woman be an executive of SCLC was not something that would go over with the male-dominated leadership."[5] Septima Clark, another activist in SCLC, also criticized the group's leadership for their sexism: "I was on the executive staff of the SCLC, but the men on it didn't listen to me too well ... those men didn't have any faith in women, none whatsoever. They just thought women were sex symbols and had no contributions to make."[6]

The BPP was founded in 1966 and developed feminist aims in conjunction with a self-defense agenda. Kathleen Cleaver, using her SNCC experience, fashioned the post of Communications Secretary for BPP, and stepped within it; Elaine Brown became the Minister of Information only in 1971, amidst a still male-dominated leadership. While, as mentioned previously, it is true that Brown became the Chairperson of the party in 1974, there were very few other female leaders on the national stage in the BPP. Significant BPP women whom we associate with being very active and having accomplished a great deal within the organization, such as Angela Davis or Assata Shakur, were not in fact part of the national leadership.[7]

Men also controlled the leadership of most mainstream organizations, including the federal government as well as political parties and various business groups (for example, there were only ten women in the Senate from 1922 to 1969; additionally, in 1969, the period we are interested in, there were no women in the President's Cabinet).[8] Many such organizations, especially those that were politically and socially conservative, would not integrate women into significant leadership positions for decades to come. As of the recent 115th Congress, women represent 20 percent of the 535 seats in Congress, 23 percent of the 100 seats in the Senate, and 19.3 percent of the 435 seats in the House of Representatives. There are six Republican women and 17 Democratic (or Democratic-Farmer-Labor) women in the Senate.[9] This long history of women's exclusion from high-profile leadership positions in American political organizations makes consideration of the ways in which women achieved gender equity in the WUO all the more vital.

Women were well represented within the WUO, at first in membership and then in leadership. As chronicler Harold Jacobs states, "If Weatherwomen occupied a secondary place within the typically male-dominated organization at its inception, less than six months later women were successfully challenging men for leadership, eventually coming to hold the majority of leadership positions."[10] As an anonymous Weatherwoman put it in 1970, "Much of the leadership of Weatherman throughout the country are women."[11] The FBI's infiltrator Larry Grathwohl also notes that women were present in leadership positions: he points out that Weatherwoman Diane Donghi was at one point a leader of his collective (among other women who were in charge), and he also recollects that in Cleveland it was Weatherwoman Linda Evans who was in charge.[12] Weatherman Bill Ayers notes that women were active in leadership positions throughout the WUO; he remembers a Weatherwoman named Gloria was the leader of the New York collective.[13] Further, David Gilbert remembers:

> I had a coleader [sic], a woman whose politics and organizing work I admired [in the Denver collective]. Our gender balance reflected the organization as a whole. Of the five CC [Central Committee] members, two were women, with Bernardine Dohrn identified as "first secretary" and primary spokesperson. On the next level, regional leadership was generally shared by a man and a woman. Such parity was almost unheard of in Left organizations of the day where men always heavily predominated. Our difference was more a tribute to the women's individual assertive efforts to build anti-imperialists politics than to any organized program against sexism.[14]

Weatherwomen were present, involved, and taking the reins of the WUO's leadership.

As they obtained positions of power, Weatherwomen were not afraid to push through a feminist agenda. For example, the previously mentioned War Council in December of 1969 (a national level meeting for the WUO organization held in Flint, Michigan, where the organization decided to go underground) included a panel discussion on women's liberation. There, those in attendance decided that the women in the film *The Battle of Algiers* were good role models for female empowerment. A popular 1966 film, *The Battle of Algiers* depicted guerrilla warfare against the French government in Algiers, providing images of combat in which women played a significant role.[15] Djamila Bouhired, Zohra Dift Bitat, and Hassiba Ben Bouali were three women who were real life revolutionary activists fighting for Algerian independence from colonial rule, as highlighted by *The Battle of Algiers*. Bouhired worked as an agent for the leader of the Algerian independence forces; Bitat set bombs as part of the opening volley of the war for Algerian independence; Bouali worked with a revolutionary cell and was killed by a bomb set by the French police. The movie played in the United States in 1967 and was nominated for three academy awards.[16]

Thus, the Weatherwomen upheld *The Battle of Algiers* as a good model for revolutionary activity and for the cultivation of more assertive norms for women. And they followed through with their planning: FBI informer Larry Grathwohl attested that his first prolonged contact with the WUO was at a recruitment meeting where *The Battle of Algiers* film was viewed. He opined that the film was a great tool for recruitment for revolutionary groups, as while watching it, "you had sympathy for the rebels."[17] Just as strong female leaders arose in the *Battle of Algiers* through an embrace of militancy, the Weatherwomen saw their own liberation as coming from taking leadership, becoming politically assertive, and not being squeamish about violence.[18]

As women obtained authority within the WUO, breaking out of limiting female gender norms and actively seeking power and influence, some men became uncomfortable in the face of female leadership. One male response to this increased female autonomy and agency came in the form of impotence:

> Actually, even promiscuity suffered a temporary setback. With the push for women's political leadership, there was an epidemic of male sexual impotence. Men withdrew politically and emotionally, as well as sexually. Then women had to struggle again to teach that passivity was not a form of accepting leadership but rather a way to undercut it, because everyone needs engagement and dialogue to grow.[19]

Women were breaking the passivity of their requisite gender roles, and as a response, some men were displaying fragility and a lack of sexual response.[20]

Men were also disengaging from political dialogue. Even though men were not responding favorably to women's changing roles, their negative responses underscored that women were becoming leaders, and that women's assertiveness was paying off. Weatherwomen were implementing their plan of achieving liberation through leadership and influence. Once they became leaders of collectives or at the national level, Weatherwomen fought against the male withdrawal response by showing the compatibility of anti-sexism, anti-racism, and anti-imperialism.

Eventually, the Weatherwomen's work would result, at least in some ways and in some circumstances, in the WUO becoming less sexist, as men often came to value the positive contributions women were making to the WUO. The experiences of the women in the Columbus collective illustrate this process well. Women's actions (such as confronting working women about their objectification or about the pay gap) resulted in the men of the collective, in the words of Weatherwoman Lorraine Rosal, "dealing with us [women] as a political people."[21] As Rosal explains it, the Columbus Weatherwomen, through their activism, were recognized for their political work. They were acknowledged as effective organizers and gained respect as agents of the revolution. Another effect of successfully organizing women-centered actions was that the women felt more empowered. This empowerment, in turn, led to leadership positions: "It served as a real impetus for all of us to form political collectives, go out into the streets and the parks, etc., do mass work around the national action, and do some heavy and consistent organizing. Because of the women's continuing practice, we began to really assume leadership positions."[22]

The Columbus Weatherwomen sincerely believed that their political work gained them respect from men, which eventually resulted in making the men less sexist as they realized that the women could perform the same organizing tasks as them. This work included both feminist, woman-centered work, and political activism that dealt with imperialism. For the Weatherwomen, the two were intertwined. As the Columbus Weatherwomen put it, "we began to see the caucus working within the larger collective as a place for women to share organizing experiences and to develop an analysis of male chauvinism and supremacy as tools of the ruling class, an analysis between white working-class women and the international proletariat."[23] Women's actions "forced guys we have been organizing to combat their chauvinism, to understand more clearly the right for women's liberation, and to begin to see their role in aiding that liberation."[24] In addition, the Columbus Weatherwomen reported that the fact that one of us, Elizabeth Stanley (no relation to the Stanly Company) was in jail on inciting to riot charge (felony, 1–3 years, $25,000 bail) because she aided the black struggle organize against racism, did more to combat male chauvinism and bring the idea of female revolutionary leadership home—both to the kids we were working with and to the men in our own project—than all the discussion, criticism sessions, etc., that we had had about racism and male chauvinism all summer.[25]

Concrete action, in other words, served as the women's "credentials" and allowed them to work alongside men in a collaborative manner, where they would be trusted and respected, without being challenged. According to one anonymous Weatherwoman, this sort of concrete action broke down paternalistic and chauvinist male attitudes that insisted that women were weak or stupid.[26] Moreover, the women were modeling alternative gender norms for males (young and old) who they came in contact with: "The kids we began organizing came in contact for the first time with strong women whose purpose in life was not to have a home and babies."[27] The Weatherwomen were modeling a new kind of womanhood—one that was aligned with the goals of female liberation and featured women accomplished at something other than being homemakers.

Leadership styles in the WUO also developed in new ways as women became leaders. As one anonymous Weatherwoman reflected in 1970, "Men can learn from women and become better leaders themselves."[28] Also, as the anonymously authored document "Weather Letter" attests, female leaders valued open communication, collaborative processes, honesty, and frankness. Women leaders saw strength as deriving from collaboration and pushed for open communication between members:

from this strength which we got from our honesty, particularly with each other, we were able to confront men and feel the power we had to change both ourselves and [the] men. A new kind of leadership began to emerge based on building each person to be strong rather than on reinforcing the power of the few at the expense of others.[29]

Frankness and collaboration built trust and a sense of unity, all of which empowered women to continue working together in their revolutionary roles. Furthermore, this basis of support nourished women in their anti-sexism work. This style of leadership and communication also aided men in their self-growth, as it allowed them to see that criticisms were meant to be constructive. Weatherman David Gilbert explained that this new dynamic, built on open communication and trust, made one feel as if one was worthy of love and was capable of change (when it came to realizing that one was a chauvinist pig, it was easier to change if one was mentored through that transformation). Gilbert explains that it's "an act of love to try to take the time to not just walk away from someone but to criticize someone in a constructive way."[30] This act of love made the WUO into a better organization, as it was "more attuned to relationships," and more committed to collectivity.[31] This new dynamic also made for more unity within a given WUO collective when collaboration was valued over competition. Hence, female leadership was leading to an embrace of feminist values, including a more collaborative environment, men confronting their sexism and growing from doing so, and, according to Gilbert, a sense of collegiality permeating the group.[32]

A Weatherwoman summed up how female leadership was translating, to a certain extent, into more female autonomy, female empowerment, and stronger feminist values:

> Women who previously were passive and sat quietly at meetings have become political leaders (thinkers as well as fighters). The myth of the exceptional political woman is breaking down. Generally what occurred in the past was that a few women in each organization were recognized as leaders by adopting male conceptions of leadership, aggressiveness, domination, and the whole ego trip. We've learned that all women can become political. Much of the leadership of Weatherman throughout the country are women.[33]

Thus, female gender norms were changing. Women were becoming active, outspoken, and seizing power, but they were doing so without taking on overly-masculine leadership styles, such as being egotistical, aggressive, and dominant, as mentioned in the above quotation. This promotion of new gender norms challenged men's beliefs that women were somehow inferior or weaker than men, and therefore aided in smashing sexism. Moreover, in the very act of becoming leaders, the women themselves came to see themselves as emboldened and capable agents who preferred the model of liberated womanhood they were creating.[34] And we can see this self-empowerment, which is intimately connected to their feminism, in a few examples: Bernardine Dohrn, Diana Oughton, and Susan Stern.

Bernardine Dohrn:
The WUO's High Priestess[35]

Bernardine Dohrn not only ascended to national leadership, but also was often the face of the organization. Not only was Dohrn an author of the "Weatherman" paper that accentuated the differences between the various factions within SDS and led to its eventual split in June 1969, but she also was the person who led the walk out against the Progressive Labor (PL) forces on the convention floor to actively initiate the split. As the PL was moving away from supporting a policy of self-determination for black nationalists and Third World revolutionaries, Dohrn grabbed the microphone from a wavering and confused Mark Rudd (who was thinking about asking for a break to figure things out), and, in no uncertain terms, Dohrn announced that the real SDS needed to decide for itself if it would stand for such a shameful position.[36] By taking that action, Dohrn precipitated the rupture of the organization. Further, Dohrn later gave the speech that convinced Revolutionary Youth Movement (RYM) members (many of whom would later become the WUO) to expel the PL faction. In what a reporter characterized as "obviously the outstanding political speech of the whole week," Dohrn—while standing on the stage front and center, "flanked by a dozen SDS delegates (chicks up front) who stood Panther-style on the podium"—argued convincingly that the real SDS stood for different values than the ones that the PL stood for, including a commitment to black and national liberation struggles.[37] Dohrn effectively convinced those present to expel the PL. Dohrn's leadership therefore facilitated the birth of the WUO.

After SDS split apart, Dohrn was voted in as a member of the leadership committee, called the "National Interim Committee."[38] As part of the committee, Dohrn planned and arranged actions, including trips to Cuba.[39] On one such trip in July 1969, which she organized along with Weatherwoman Julie Nichamin and where Dohrn dubbed herself "cruise director," Dohrn met with representatives of the Democratic Republic of North Vietnam and the Provisional Revolutionary Government of South Vietnam (PRG) who identified her as a leader of the Weatherman faction.[40] The point of this meeting was to find ways to stop the Vietnam War, to promote resistance to the war in the United States, and to build solidarity with the Vietnamese struggle. At these meetings, in order to build a fighting force in the United States, Dohrn was advised to "look for the man who fights the hardest" and recruit that person for the revolution.[41] Having adopted various strategies from those meetings, Dohrn was instrumental in mapping out the WUO's tactic for militant struggle, where radical action in the streets was supposed to result in political change (the idea of which was summed up through the "Bring the War Home" slogan later used at the Days of Rage).[42] In constant contact with Huynh Van Ba (the head of the PRG delegation) even after the July trip to Cuba, Dohrn not only was involved in all the Cuban meetings, but she also presented reports on her experiences to the rest of the Weatherman group and developed the WUO's position of solidarity with the Vietnamese. Dohrn not only communicated with Van Ba through telephone calls, but she even sent him a telegram on behalf of the women contingent of the SDS/WUO, signed by Bernardine Dohrn and 100 other women. The telegram was a condolence message on the passing of Ho Chi Minh.[43]

Dohrn also was one of the organizers of the Days of Rage, during which she was arrested.[44] At this October 1969 action in Chicago, Dohrn was instrumental in motivating and inspiring the WUO members to act in a revolutionary fashion—after all, engaging the police was scary work, especially when only hundreds, and not the anticipated thousands, of WUO members had shown up. WUO members had worked throughout the summer to recruit, but those who came to the Days of Rage numbered anywhere from 400 to 600, and not the thousands who were expected. Various reasons account for this low turnout, among them a fear of the police (Mayor Richard J. Daley had promised to retaliate with force, instructing his policemen to shoot at the crowds) and a sense of the WUO holding itself up as an exemplary fighting force, which led to other organizations distancing themselves from the WUO's outright aggression.[45]

At the first meet-up in Lincoln Park, leaders from the Weather Bureau gave speeches to the assembled crowd. Then Bernardine Dohrn stepped up to the microphone. Weatherman Bill Ayers describes the scene:

> The feverish revelry was at a peak when Bernardine Dohrn appeared on a slight rise to the left of the fire and the troops exploded into a chanting frenzy. HO, HO, HO CHI MINH, THE NLF IS GOING TO WIN! She was wearing a black leather jacket over a black turtleneck, her trademark short skirt and high stylish black boots, an eye-liner pencil peeking from her breast pocket. Her blazing eyes were allied with her elegance. She had earned her role as the voice and leader of the militants through practice, but she was also a stunning and seductive symbol of the Revolutionary Woman—J. Edgar Hoover had dubbed her "La Pasionaria of the Lunatic Left"—and as she stood in that frenzied park late that night, her dark hair whipped by the wind, her brilliant eyes flashing in answer to the fire, I would have followed her anywhere.[46]

"La Pasionaria" translates to "Passion Flower"; it also was the nickname of the Spanish Republican leader of the Spanish Civil War, Isidora Dolores Ibarruri Gomez. This nickname was given to Dohrn to signify her standing in the group—as a leader and effective role model. Informer Larry Grathwohl describes Dohrn in a similar fashion, noting: "She stood erect, like a high priestess waiting for her followers to quiet down."[47] As she took control of the masses, masterfully, Dohrn spoke to the crowd, engaging them and building up their self-confidence. Grathwohl also remembers that Dohrn

> radiated confidence and displayed a poise that can be acquired only from countless public appearances. She was one of the most traveled of the Weather people ... she was one of the founders of Weathermen ... she began talking; her words belied her

feminine appearance ... she criticized white revolutionaries for being afraid of fighting alongside blacks in the streets ... "we can't just stand around and talk about it; we have to get into armed struggle." She condemned our racist, chauvinistic society and urged the women to become more involved in all aspects of the movement.[48]

Even though Grathwohl makes what could be characterized as a sexist comment about Dohrn's "feminine appearance," he still clearly presents Dohrn as a leader and as the person motivating the protestors into action. After she spoke and inspired the crowd, Jeff Jones announced the night's target, and the marchers were off, fighting their way through police lines.[49]

The next day, October 9, an all-women's action against the Chicago Draft Board office was scheduled. Weatherwoman Susan Stern remembers that the women looked "too exhausted to move, blood-spattered and smeared with grime and sweat" from the previous night's protest—yet they had shown up to this scheduled rally, firm in their commitment.[50] To inspire and encourage, Dohrn addressed these battle weary Weatherwomen, and spoke about "the strength and courage of women."[51] She praised their efforts and valor, and led them into this new encounter with the police.[52] Even though they were outnumbered, the Weatherwomen charged the police lines, resolute and screaming, in two by two formation— yells and shrills were deemed to be part of a good strategy based on the *Battle of Algiers*.[53] Dohrn fought alongside these Weatherwomen, "with genuine rage," in the process injuring her leg and getting arrested.[54]

Once in jail, Dohrn again served as an inspiration to the other women arrested with her, as her self-assurance and quiet strength encouraged the other women not to feel defeated, even behind bars. In fact, while arrested, Dohrn kept the Weatherwomen active discussing political and feminist strategy and in a state of preparation; as she recalls, "I remember doing karate on the floors of the jail."[55] As such, she also recalls having to defend that position to the jail warden, by arguing with him that "having political discussions, and exercising, and having our meetings was not a violation of his law."[56] Due to this perseverance, Weatherman Shin'ya Ono explained that the WUO prisoners were able to hold strong: "In the Cook County Jail, we organized ourselves into affinity groups, chose our leadership, and carried on full, disciplined political lives: political education, karate and physical exercises, criticism sessions, general political meetings, doing the housekeeping chores in a collective way, carrying on political struggle in alliance with other inmates, etc."[57] Even in a scenario where their options were severely limited, Dohrn was still showing herself to be an active (and inspiring) leader.

Weatherwoman Susan Stern recalls that Dohrn's body language indicated contempt for her surroundings and an unyielding self-confidence.[58] Stern continues:

> [Dohrn] possessed a splendor all her own. Like a queen, her nobility set her apart from the other women.... There was something else, a type of authority, a sense of self that one had to have before one could lead other people, before they would follow.... Whatever she possessed, I wanted it. I wanted to be cherished and respected as Bernardine was.[59]

Dohrn's commanding presence was also a reason why the WUO moved away from a strategy of non-discriminate violence to a strategy of symbolic bombing. After her return from the Cuba trip in July of 1969, while organizing the Days of Rage in Chicago and other protests, Dohrn was careful to maintain a balance in the struggle so that outright violence would not overtake the organization. She counseled Weatherman John Jacobs (known as J.J. in WUO circles) to be careful in his actions: "Just because you can always win, doesn't mean you're always right."[60] Jacobs, an influential leader first with SDS and then later with WUO, had been involved in the protest at Columbia and was one of the authors of the Weatherman paper. Jacobs is also one of the Weatherpeople who advocated the creation of an underground revolutionary struggle at the Flint War Council in December 1969.[61] After making the decision to go underground at the War Council, a small contingent of Weathermen, including founding members Jacobs, Terry Robbins, and Teddy Gold, insisted on outright violence—alarmingly allowing for the possibility of human casualties. They formed a small, clandestine collective or cell in New York; Terry Robbins and John Jacobs came up with the idea of fire-bombing the home of John Murtagh, the judge in the New York Panther 21 conspiracy trial (the Black Panthers who had been indicted on charges of conspiracy to bomb police stations). This collective threw a bottle filled with gasoline at the front steps of the judge's house—the bottle broke and fizzled out, luckily without creating much damage.[62]

Unfortunately, the cell's next plan did not sputter out; Robbins and Gold introduced the idea of working with dynamite.[63] As a leader, Jacobs likewise advocated a policy of increasing indiscriminate violence. This strategy eventually led to the Townhouse explosion in March 1970 in which the New York collective blew themselves up while in the process of assembling a bomb meant for a dance at Fort Dix (people would have been injured if the plans had been successful, which marks a clear departure from the WUO's prior and later political actions).[64]

In contrast, Dohrn believed that the WUO needed to move away from the path of violent struggle. Dohrn viewed the future not as filled with explosives and attacks, but as a chance to take some time and develop "a more measured, coherent strategy" for the WUO.[65] This stance was not in keeping with what the remaining New York leadership was planning—the militant John Jacobs resented Dohrn's interference. After the Townhouse explosion, Jacobs was arguing that it was the inexperience of the Townhouse collective that resulted in their death—instead of seeing the moral wrong of the violence as illustrated through the death of his own comrades, Jacobs argued that the violence just needed to be refined and then put to fresh use.[66] Dohrn, on the other hand, saw the Townhouse as emblematic of the mistaken direction of the WUO.

Alongside Jeff Jones, another leader within the WUO, Dohrn called a meeting to map out a new strategy. At this meeting, held in Mendocino, California, in the late spring of 1970 (after the Townhouse incident), Dohrn and Jones argued that the WUO should back away from its open militancy. The location, Mendocino, was picked strategically: it was populated by hippies (and so Weather members descending on the town would not be out of place and draw unwanted attention to themselves or the WUO); importantly, both Jones and Dohrn hoped that the beach location would give these Weather members time to de-stress and return to a more rational mindset after the Townhouse explosion incident. In fact, the meeting had the rule that no group discussion would be held for the first few days, so as to first allow for a return to normalcy and rationality. As Thai Jones, the son of Weatherman Jeff Jones, puts it, "it was treatment by normalcy. A revolutionary laughing over a bowl of noodles was less likely to kill or be killed than one haunted and alone, eating scraps in a city cellar.... Jeff and Bernardine made converts and then threw open the discussion."[67] This self-care approach allowed for a clear-headed discussion of the proposal. WUO members were prescribed walks along the beach, fresh salad and pasta dinners, and general relaxation. Only after this atmosphere permeated their consciousness, did Dohrn begin the discussion of a move away from direct violence.[68]

Unsurprisingly, Jacobs resented it all, and insisted on the merits of a violent approach throughout the meeting. Jeff Jones's son adds that Jacobs was "eager to argue and looked everywhere for an audience."[69] Jacobs had envisioned the underground as a militarized space, filled with martyrs and cold blooded soldiers bent on indiscriminate violence; he now saw this "idea being taken away from him."[70]

The proposition was discussed for days, until "steadily, the opposition lessened until only Jacobs and a few others insisted on military action."[71] Dohrn's idea of moving away from direct violent action toward targeting mere symbols of American imperialism made Jacobs frantic and adamant that his plans were still the right path for the WUO. Dohrn told the group: "We're going to build a new political organization right here."[72] In spite of his influence and stature, Dohrn threw Jacobs out of the organization in a move that showcased her own clout: "Where we're going ... you're not welcome," she said to him.[73] As Thai Jones sums it up, "Bernardine, who had the ultimate authority to say it, told him he was out of the organization."[74] Acting as an empowered leader and clearly not as a token, Dohrn's authoritative decision moved the WUO away from the dangerous path it was on, and ensured that no human casualties would ever occur again as a result of a successful WUO bombing. David Gilbert explains that he was "profoundly grateful" to Bernardine Dohrn, Jeff Jones, and Bill Ayers (who had also been involved in the Mendocino meeting) for "leading us out of the volcano" of violence that the WUO would have otherwise become.[75]

Indeed, after the Mendocino meeting, the WUO, in May 1970, issued its Declaration of a State of War Communiqué, in Dohrn's voice and signed by her, announcing that attacks will now target "a symbol or institution of Amerikan [sic] injustice."[76] Outright violence had been repudiated due to Dohrn's vision and leadership.

Thanks to Dohrn, the group would not target civilians, or even people who could be seen as combatants, as Jacobs might have preferred.[77] Instead, they could see their symbolic violence as consistent with a feminist mission since it would be used to send messages of justice that did not physically harm people. Importantly, Dohrn was certainly no token woman: she not only removed one of the ostensibly highest male leaders from power, but also moved the entire national organization into alignment with her views and plans.

Dohrn's vision for the WUO was further illustrated in the "New Morning, Changing Weather Communiqué" that Dohrn drafted and released in December of 1970. The statement categorically explained that "the Townhouse forever destroyed our belief that armed struggle is the only real revolutionary struggle."[78] The communiqué explicated that the WUO had spent time in reflection and now understood its previous path as an error in ideology, since that road was not only violent but also led to a single mindedness of purpose that was alienated from, and was alienating to, potential supporters. Labeling the obsession with violence and the "glorification of the heavier [action] the better" as a "military error," Dohrn's communiqué outlined a new course.[79] Criticizing militarism as rash and misguided, the communiqué set forth a multi-pronged agenda of collaboration with other groups, the raising of collective consciousness as to U.S. injustices through symbolic actions, the adopting of collaborative, non-hierarchical leadership structures, and the propagating of feminist work for the empowerment of women. The communiqué also called for the creation of a world where men stopped being sexist and supported the liberation and leadership of women, noting that "men who are chauvinists can change and become revolutionaries who no longer embrace any part of the culture that stands in the way of the freedom of women."[80] Attacking rape as a weapon of war in Indochina (Vietnam) and praising revolutionary women as exemplars to be emulated, the communiqué called on feminist collectives to include this type of feminism in their conversations and educational outreach. Some of the specific revolutionary women included were Celia Sanchez, Heidi Santamaria (Moncada and Cuba), Lolita Lebron (Puerto Rico), Afeni Shakur (Harlem), and Vietnamese women such as Mme. Nguyen Thi Binh in Paris, and Pham Thi Quyen, a fighter in Saigon.[81]

Dohrn's leadership is also evident in her functioning as the voice of the WUO: it was her voice or signature that accompanied most of the WUO communiqués. As key examples, Dohrn signed or sent communiqué #1 ("A Declaration of a State of War," May 21, 1970), #3 ("Honk America," July 25, 1970), #4 ("Dr. Timothy Leary," September 15, 1970), #5 ("Fall Offensive," October 8, 1970), #6 (the aforementioned "New Morning, Changing Weather," December 6, 1970), "The Bombing of the Capitol" (February 28, 1971), "The Symbionese Liberation Army" (February 20, 1974). Other communiqués were sent/signed by "The Women of the Weather Underground" ("Collective Letter to the Women's Movement," July 24, 1973) or by the Women's Brigade ("Health, Education, and Welfare," March 6, 1974).[82] Jonah Raskin, the ex-husband of Weatherwoman Eleanor Raskin, noted in 1974,

> It is of historical significance that the leader of the organization is a young woman. Bernardine Dohrn's emergence is a clear sign of the crucial role that women have played in the radical movement. Many women have listened to her not simply as one angry, intelligent voice but because she has articulated the collective anger of sisters everywhere, the [cries] of women at home, in offices, factories, and schools, resisting illegitimate authority.[83]

Dohrn's leadership and collaborative style was tied into a narrative of collective work done by women who were looking for a female leader, one who would represent their interests in a political arena. Dohrn did just that as she was able to weave feminist aims through the WUO's agenda as a regular voice of the WUO, as evidenced in her contribution to so many of their communications.

Dohrn saw her fight against imperialism as intricately linked with the fight against male supremacy. As she stated in a 1976 interview for Emile de Antonio's documentary, *Underground*, "Imperialism has as one of its underpinnings: male supremacy. It is based on a system in which men are taught to think of themselves as superior. It is—uhhh—bred into all the institutions of society: into work, into the family, into the schools, into hospitals, into medical care, into education."[84] This imperialist political system allowed for male supremacy and for the exploitation of women. For example, Dohrn explained that women became sexual commodities in Third World nations, as well as Puerto Rico where women were trapped in the sex industry due to U.S. imperialism and economic policy.[85]

Moreover, Dohrn expounded that "a revolutionary women's movement must be politically based on the most oppressed sectors—black, brown and white working-class women."[86] She explained that "our immediate job is to organize masses of women around the full scope of radical demands—including the destruction of male supremacy."[87] Thus, Dohrn took the WUO in a decidedly feminist direction, placing the liberation of *all* women—regardless of class, race, or nation—at the forefront of the WUO agenda. Although she was the most visible female leader, Dohrn was not alone in her efforts to make the revolutionary mission of the WUO inclusive of women's liberation. Diana Oughton and Susan Stern joined her in this struggle.

Diana Oughton:
"My life is my values"[88]

Raised in Dwight, Illinois, Diana Oughton grew up in an affluent family, enjoying a privileged lifestyle that eventually took her overseas, where she studied for her B.A. abroad in Germany during her junior year.[89] Based on her experiences in Europe, Oughton realized that the United States was viewed critically overseas, especially with respect to U.S. imperialism.[90] Upon graduating from Bryn Mawr College, Oughton enlisted in the Voluntary International Service Assignments program and was assigned to Chichicastenango, in Guatemala.[91] There, as she taught Native American children how to read, Oughton quickly came to despair when faced with malnourished children, overworked women, and numerous baby-sized coffins (the result of what would have been, in the United States, preventable childhood diseases).[92]

Oughton also came to believe that U.S. imperialism was responsible for the poverty and despair she was witnessing in Guatemala. Oughton connected U.S. imperialism with the setting up of puppet governments that supported U.S. interests and policies instead of looking out for the interests of their own populace.[93] In response, she became a socialist, and upon her return to the United States at the end of her volunteer assignment, Oughton joined SDS. She also demonstrated against the Vietnam War, joining other SDS/WUO members in Washington, D.C. As Bill Ayers recalled, there were many methods of demonstrating. Some sang, or chanted, or burned draft cards. But Oughton took a different path:

> Her dream was to organize the soldiers to refuse to fight, and eventually that dream came true. She spent hours going down the line of troops, looking each in the eye, telling him a little bit about herself, and begging him to put down his gun. Others did the same as officers walked behind their troops repeating, Hold the line, Hold the line.[94]

She was aiming to get folks to realize the consequences of their actions in Vietnam. She wanted to speak to the moral conscience of the soldiers and hoped to change their minds about what they were doing. This approach both spoke to her dedication to taking direction actions (by talking to the very soldiers themselves) and her hope in the moral character of others.

    With Bill Ayers, who Diana met while working at the Children's Community School in Ann Arbor, Oughton worked to shape the SDS chapter at the University of Michigan into the "Jesse James faction," identified by the FBI as the "most militant faction" of SDS.[95] The Jesse James faction, so called because it believed that community organizing went hand-in-hand with radical protest, held that to achieve political change, SDS needed to become more confrontational, as other methods previously taken by the local SDS chapters were deemed too tame to bring about substantial political change. Future WUO leaders, Bill Ayers, Diana Oughton, Terry Robbins, and Jim Mellen, were all members. As such important WUO leaders populated the Jesse James faction, it would be intrinsic to shaping WUO policy, from the beginning with the Weatherman paper (several authors were members of the Jesse James faction) to the end of the organization.[96]

    Diana Oughton was actively involved in the Jesse James faction's actions, serving as a hard revolutionary worker and leader within this so called "action faction" (the label used for the most radical activists). For example, in September of 1968, she manned the bullhorn and addressed the crowds gathered at a protest confronting the University of Michigan's hawkish stance on the Vietnam War. This action resulted in the Jesse James faction taking over the SDS chapter at the University of Michigan, as the

Jesse James faction attacked the ineffectiveness of SDS's previous actions, ridiculing its polite protestations and non-involvement in the war protest. This opposition resulted in the Radical Caucus (the opposition to the Jesse James Gang) giving up its membership in the SDS chapter, leaving the Jesse James faction with majority control over the chapter. As a result, the Jesse James faction took control. In December 1968, the Radical Caucus tried to get its own chapter recognized at the SDS National Convention at the University of Michigan, but Oughton blocked their attempt by arguing that having separate chapters would lead to fragmentation. In this manner, she maintained control for the Jesse James faction.[97]

At the National Council meeting at the University of Colorado in October 1968, Oughton and other delegates discussed the concept of youth culture and how to tap into its alienation so as to use it to lead a revolution.[98] This conceptual undertaking would eventually result in the position paper "Toward a Revolutionary Youth Movement," written by Mike Klonsky in December 1968. This document signaled a turn toward militancy for SDS, and stated that youth, students, and workers could be radicalized based on their alienation with capitalism. This document also supported self-determination for oppressed groups and nations. Thus, it paved the way for the Weatherman document itself.[99] Oughton was also named SDS regional organizer for Michigan and served as a negotiator between the Jesse James faction and the University of Michigan administration.[100]

On the basis of all this work, by the December 1968 SDS National Convention meeting, held at the University of Michigan, Oughton had emerged as a recognized leader and as a "radical 'sister' in her own right."[101] The FBI characterized her as "having demonstrated leadership within New Left activities" and deemed her to be a danger to the security of the United States.[102]

After the SDS split, Oughton continued to lead and organize, but now for the WUO. Some of her actions include organizing "Cuba Month," a series of films on the Cuban revolution at the University of Michigan campus held in early 1969. In July, Oughton joined Dohrn as a delegate on the Cuba trip. Later that summer, she worked for the Days of Rage, even arranging travel for WUO groups to Chicago. The FBI had her under surveillance for all of these actions; the FBI file notes that an informant overheard Oughton state that at the Days of Rage, protesters would "confront the police," "bait the pigs," and "resist arrest."[103] Oughton was eventually arrested in the all women's action at the Days of Rage. Finally, in December 1969 she participated in the Flint War Council.[104]

Overall, Diana Oughton emerges from the historical record as being completely committed to her cause of socialist revolution, asking friends who shared her political outlook, "How can you think that way and then do nothing?"[105] In the face of injustice, Oughton believed that inaction was inexcusable—acting was morally required. The WUO offered Oughton a path toward making a real difference in the world—a path that she fully embraced as an autonomous agent in her own right.

Not only was Oughton committed to anti-imperialism, but she also was committed to women's liberation. As early as July 1967, Diana was involved with a women's caucus within SDS at the same convention where, according to Gilbert, women's liberation pierced SDS's sexism. There, as discussed in a previous chapter, SDS women put forth an agenda of stamping out male chauvinism and acknowledged women's leadership capabilities. Additionally, in March 1968, Oughton started her own women's liberation group in Ann Arbor. Discussions in the group focused on the subordinate role of women in the Movement, and on the problem of sexism within the Movement and society as a whole. Oughton also criticized the objectification of women in the media, particularly critiquing the 1968 film *Barbarella*. She viewed Jane Fonda's performance as being shaped by the patriarchy; in her view, *Barbarella* was essentializing Fonda as a commodity for male pleasure. This objectification severely impacted and limited the ways in which women were represented, in accordance to Oughton's analysis. Oughton's group not only applied feminist theory to popular culture, but also explored the idea of women's leadership within SDS.[106]

Moreover, Oughton and Ruthie Stein, another activist, had conversations with Bill Ayers about the male privilege imbedded in the concept of free love. As such, the women discussed the concept of free love with him, clarifying to Ayers that "free love only meant that movement men could screw any woman they could get, free of emotional encumbrances" and noting that relationships between men and women were not always equal.[107] Oughton elucidated these points to Ayers, making him aware of his own intrinsic sexism when it came to relationships.[108]

Oughton did not restrict her feminism to the Movement. In conversations with her sister, she tried to express her stance against conformist beauty norms and other restrictive gender norms.[109] Specifically, Oughton believed that women should be doers and helpers, and not be bound by their homes and babies to the bourgeois lifestyle. Oughton believed that the trappings of femininity encumbered women and forced them into spending money that could otherwise be used to fund the revolution or alleviate real social problems, such as poverty in black neighborhoods or Third World countries. She advocated a lifestyle that was based on gaining worth based on one's activities and one's commitment, not one's beauty.[110] Thus, when her sister Christina "simply stood titling away, mouth agape, eyes wide, holding her hand in troubled hands" and generally acted shocked at the fact that Diana had cut off her long, luxurious hair, Oughton explained that cutting her hair short was a way to achieve liberation and freedom. Oughton added that "this is a freedom cut—hassle free, carefree, convenient for street fighting. A kind of beauty all its own."[111]

Like Dohrn, Oughton also cautioned against the full valorization of violence. Believing that "we create a moral space when we cry out against harm," Oughton fully dedicated herself to changing society and bringing about a socialist revolution.[112] But she firmly believed that violence was a dangerous tool to employ to achieve this goal. Consequently, when Terry Robbins, a Weatherman and author of the original "Weatherman" paper, expressed that "a man of principled violence" had a place in the revolution, Oughton asked him, "How many innocents killed or hurt would be acceptable?"[113] She further counseled, "You know you can catch the very disease you're fighting, Terry—you want to stop the war, you become warlike. You want to fight inhumanity, and you become inhumane."[114]

Tragically, Oughton was one of the fatalities of the Townhouse explosion in March 1970, making her a victim of the inhumane violence that she cautioned against. Ayers indicates that Robbins convinced Oughton to travel to the New York clandestine collective (for a time led by John Jacobs and Robbins) and supposes that Oughton consented to go there to talk down Terry from using explosives indiscriminately.[115] Cathy Wilkerson additionally states that Oughton had misgivings about using explosives against human targets.[116] In any case, Robbins' vision prevailed, and Oughton's body was found next to his in the basement where he was single handedly assembling the bomb.[117] As best as it can be reconstructed, it seems that Robbins made a mistake with the circuit, killing himself, Ted Gold, and Oughton.[118] Even when warned by her concerned mother to leave the WUO so as to preserve her life, Oughton adamantly chose the revolution. "'Honey,' her mother had warned, 'you're only going to make things worse. You're only going to get yourself killed.'" Diana responded, "It's the only way, mummy. It's the only way." Diana Oughton lived—and died—for her beliefs.[119] After this incident, Bernardine Dohrn used Diana Oughton's tragic death (as well as the others') as an example of why this violent path should not be maintained.

Susan Stern: The Personal Journey of a Revolutionary Woman[120]

Like Diana Oughton, Susan Stern was a Weatherwoman who became a well-recognized, feminist leader. Stern began her radical journey in 1966, with the crossing of the country, east to west. She and her husband Robby Stern were relocating to Seattle, as Robby was going to start law school and Susan was going to pursue a master's degree at the School of Social Work. Stern remembers that she was very much a traditional wife back then, being very dependent on Robby's moods and happiness for her own.[121]

Slowly, Stern changed. She became involved with student groups at the University of Seattle, came into contact with hippies, and started questioning gender norms that the couple had taken for granted. As she explains:

> We fell into a routine. I went to school, held a job, cleaned the house, cooked, and helped Robby type his papers. Robby went to school. As time wore on I wore thin. It seemed to me grossly unfair that we should both go to school, and then I first had to do all the housework while he relaxed or watched the news or studied. We both considered housework shit work; why did I end up doing it all?[122]

As the couple explored these differences, they became enmeshed in the counterculture flourishing in Seattle's university district along University Avenue and Hippie Hill. By this point, it was the Summer of Love, and Stern was experimenting with drugs. She had "decided not to be straight anymore.... I threw most of my clothes into a valise.... I got my ears pierced and wore long, dangling, vividly colored earrings. I let my hair curl naturally. I went without make-up. I gave up shoes and underpants."[123] As she was experiencing this newfound personal freedom, Stern was also embracing a new political outlook, where she identified the System as preying on flower children and sending them off to fight its wars.[124]

As Stern became increasingly anti-war, she also developed a feminist outlook. In 1968, she read Betty Friedan's *The Feminine Mystique*. An influential work usually credited with sparking the second wave feminist movement (as defined historically) in the United States, *The Feminine Mystique* focused on the unhappiness and alienation of housewives and advocated the choosing of an autonomous life path for women, where they would not be restricted to, nor defined by, domesticity.

Similar to many of the women who read this influential book, Stern realized that she was not alone in her dissatisfaction within her marriage, and self-identified as one of the first "babies" of the Women's Liberation

Movement—she saw herself as a feminist spawn borne out of Friedan's work.[125] Stern, talking with other Movement women, set up a women's group, which came to be known as "Radical Women." They offered classes and lectures on women's liberation issues, and even staged a demonstration against a Playboy bunny appearance on campus. Stern was nourished by all these activities:

> I talked incessantly. And as I talked, I grew. And as I grew, I thought more. And as I thought more, I read more widely. As I read more widely, I felt more secure in my knowledge. As I felt more secure in my knowledge, I felt a new sense of pride ... off came the sloppy jeans and on went the miniskirt and knee high boots, and I developed my Style. Zip, zap, I was a new Susan Stern, and honey, when I walked, I threw back my head, and moved with determination. People moved out of my way as I strode through them. When I entered a room, I did so with a flourish, and people looked at me, and God damn it, when I talked, they listened, finally they listened.[126]

With this newfound confidence, Stern was picked to serve as the Chairwoman for the General Assembly meeting of the Seattle SDS. She then went to the Berkeley area to find a political platform that spoke to her more clearly. There she met SDSer and future Weatherman Mike Klonsky, who invited her to Chicago for the 1968 Democratic convention. In Chicago, she met SDSer and future Weatherman John Jacobs. Side-by-side, they marched in the streets, fighting with the police. Stern recalled, "we gobbled up the night in a singing roar, violent and wild, saying clearly that we were on the side of the Vietnamese, on the side of freedom."[127]

This experience left Stern shaken at the state's response to protest and she became thoroughly convinced that she was on the side of righteousness. As she replayed the events in her head at night, "A new feeling was struggling to be born in me. It had no name, but it made me want to reach beyond myself to others who were suffering. I felt real, as if suddenly I had found out something true about myself; that I was not helpless, that life meant enough to me to struggle for it ... now I would fight."[128] Just as Stern found empowerment through her political awakening, her autonomy was made clear through her political action: who she wanted to be as a person was an active agent who was changing what was wrong in the world.

Stern traveled to New York next, working for the SDS chapter there and for the SDS Regional Office, where she was organizing, passing out leaflets, and staging protests, including women's actions. Some of these actions included two demonstrations in January 1969, primarily planned and led by women, against Marine recruiters.[129] As she attended the June SDS National Convention in 1969, Stern identified with the Weatherman faction, stating that after Bernardine Dohrn's speech against the PL, she "believed in the revolution with every quivering bone in [her] body. I was prepared to take on America, to do no less than save the world. I felt that I was a warrior of the people and that I was fighting for freedom."[130]

On the wings of this conviction, Stern returned to Seattle and joined the Weatherman collective there. During the summer of 1969, she planned and organized for the Days of Rage, and engaged in criticism, self-criticism sessions. These meetings were required sessions where members of the group were supposed to criticize one another and reflect on their actions, whether they were personal or political. Of this process, Stern noted that "our aim was to make ourselves equal, men and women, practically inter-changeable ... the process of criticism, self-criticism, transformation was the tool by which we would forge ourselves into new human beings."[131] This process was by no means easy—people could feel personally attacked and targeted—as everyone attempted to strip themselves of their preconceived notions, and had their most mundane habits analyzed, from the way they dressed to the way they ate, all in an attempt to forge themselves into rev-olutionary warriors who were fair minded and bent on treating everyone equitably.[132]

Stern quickly immersed herself in Weather activities and rose to lead-ership within the collective. In criticism, self-criticism sessions, she wanted to set an example for others. As she recalled, "I grappled desperately with my past in an effort to change, hoping to set an example for other women and men to follow."[133] She organized at the high school levels, educating students about Vietnam and the upcoming Days of Rage in Chicago. She laid out leaflets and typed them up, then passed them out, often working to the point of exhaustion.[134]

Stern also planned numerous demonstrations and actions for the col-lective, including an all women's action against an ROTC building in Seat-tle. Working in collaboration with the Seattle SDS women, Stern suggested making the Air Force building their target, as "it's so small we can just run on one end, do our shit, and run out the other end."[135] With a quick getaway being key for avoiding arrest, the women agreed. Scheduled for September 30, 1969, the action was planned and executed entirely by women. Women made the stink bombs and paint bottles that were used to destroy draft papers and the contents of filing cabinets. By WUO standards, the action was a success, and the women were aware of the role their gender played in this. In the melee, one woman was grabbed by ROTC males, but "shriek-ing at the top of our lungs, we ran back toward her, and began smashing at the ROTC trainees. Because they were caught completely off guard by the violence of our attack, and by the fact that women would fight a group of men, it took just a second for us to get free."[136]

Stern's feminism became increasingly visible in her leadership. On October 2, 1969, she gave a rousing speech to students and SDSers that blended anti-imperialism with feminism:

> Stalking up and down in front of them, shaking my fist at them, reaching my open hands to them, begging for them to join me, crouching, bending, twisting and pacing, I urged them to action.... The time has come not merely to protest, but to fight for what we believe in. The war is going—we must join it now. I know you don't want to wait any longer. And in fighting, women will discover strengths they never knew they had. They will take leadership and, along with men, create a new world on the ashes of the old. Fighting is the key not only to the liberation of women, but to the liberation of all human beings.[137]

Stern's impassioned speech resulted in an impromptu attack on yet another ROTC office, this time in Clark Hall on the University of Washington campus. The roused masses followed Stern into the building, spray painting walls and engaging ROTC personnel in a scuffle, injuring two ROTC cadets.[138]

Stern also attended the Days of Rage in Chicago and continued developing as a Weatherwoman and an activist. She reports of her experience, "I felt that I had finally connected with my personal destiny; that I had a place, a function in life. That place was with the Weathermen, that function was to fight for the revolution to the best of my ability.... For the first time in my life that I could remember, I was happy."[139] Stern's revolutionary activity, her awakening to politics and feminism, had allowed her to develop as an autonomous woman: she had discovered that her agency did not lie in accepting a dependency on her husband, but instead involved an embrace of militancy. This example of autonomy widening through the embrace of militancy was not exclusive to the three Weatherwomen discussed here, but instead was spread through many of the women in the organization.

Autonomy through WUO Militancy

All Weatherwomen engaged in militancy, whether it happened as part of an ROTC building invasion, at the Days of Rage, or at a jailbreak. "Jailbreak" was the term used for high school demonstrations, where Weatherwomen would run through the halls, yelling "jailbreak" to the students: the idea was that the state treated schools as tools for social control, tracking students according to race and sex, teaching them the state's approved political and social narrative, jailing the minds and the limiting the futures of students.[140] Through their militancy and their involvement in the WUO, these women expressed their agency as they made difficult decisions for themselves and others. They reshaped their lives around WUO collectives, choosing to live an uncomfortable existence as they fought for their commitments to revolutionary change.

In *The Theory and Practice of Autonomy*, Gerald Dworkin defines "autonomy" as the "equivalent to self rule or sovereignty, sometimes identical with freedom of the will ... usually equated with dignity, integrity, individuality, independence, responsibility, and self-knowledge."[141] In this sense, the Weatherwomen acted autonomously as they chose the direction their lives would take as political activists. As the examples of Bernardine Dohrn, Diana Oughton, and Susan Stern demonstrate, when women joined the Weather Underground, they did so as a conscious rejection of mainstream political, economic, and gender values. Their political realignment both reflected and reinforced changes in their personal lives. They embraced this self-growth and development, seeing it as a crucial part of the making of what they saw as a new society that would be just and fair. These were not women who were duped into militancy through their relationships with men. Instead, their militant actions reflected their autonomously emerging ideology. For example, the Weatherwomen of the Columbus collective saw themselves not only as active agents and revolutionary fighters, but also as models for the society at large to follow. They said of their organizing activities that "the kids we began organizing came in contact for the first time with strong women whose purpose in life was not to have a home and babies, but to pick up the gun and fight in a communist revolution."[142] Thus, their militancy was linked with the breaking up of gender norms and liberation. They believed picking up a gun would achieve a new world, where gender parity was the norm.

At the WUO War Council, the document "Honky Tonk Women" expressed the view that women will achieve liberation through fighting:

> Our liberation as individuals and as women is possible when it is understood as a political process—part of the formation of an armed white fighting force. Political power grows out of the barrel of a gun, and the struggle to gain and use political power against the state is the armed struggle for our liberation.[143]

The message was once again one of liberation—liberation that was going to be achieved through a militant struggle in which women would actively fight to destroy the paternalistic chains that held them back as political agents.

Weatherwomen engaged in this struggle for liberation in various ways. In the summer of 1969, the women of the Motor City collective (Detroit) undertook an all-woman action at McComb Community College. This action constituted an example of female and feminist leadership in action as the aim of the women was to discuss anti-imperialism and how female liberation played an important role in the revolution. The nine Weatherwomen in the collective went to the community college to disrupt a sociology class; as it happened, the class was taking its final exams. As the women themselves reported in the *New Left Notes*, each had assigned roles for the action, and they were prepared for any eventuality:

> One woman distributed Chicago leaflets while the rest of us lined up in front of the classroom ... one woman began to address the class. She rapped about how American imperialism fucks over the people of the world, and about people's struggles for self-determination. Another woman spoke about how imperialism oppresses the black colony within America. When a third woman began to talk about the material oppression of women and the necessity to break out of subordinate roles and join the struggle, some men got uptight and tried to charge the door....[144]

Notice that the men listened while imperialism and racism were discussed but got up to interrupt the Weatherwomen when sexism was introduced in the discussion. While we will not know these men's motivations, this response is suggestive of an inability to listen to criticisms related to their own sexism. In any case, the Weatherwomen were prepared for this response, and another source explains how they dealt with the interruption:

> When they began to talk about how women are kept down in this country, two men got up to leave the room. It is reported that the Motor City Nine responded to such an exhibition of male chauvinism and general pig behavior by attacking the men with karate and prevented them from leaving the room. They then continued to discuss how women are used as slave labor in the household, exploited on the labor market, and turned into sexual objects.[145]

The Detroit Weatherwomen made sexist males listen, administering karate chops as a remedy to the males' misogyny.

The Weatherwomen were proud of their action and explained their rationale for engaging in it:

> It was women who made the situation happen. Organizing women through exemplary action is key to the way we work. It is necessary to struggle to raise consciousness of women's oppression and male supremacy in the context of world revolution. We do not just urge women to become fighters, nor do we just talk to them about taking sides.... The force needs fighters—both men and women.[146]

The Weatherwomen went on to explain that based on their experience at the McComb Community College, they gained more proficiency in leading other actions: they refined their methods and became more skilled in setting up demonstrations. Thus, they started having tactical leaders who scouted the area and developed a plan for action. They also used affinity groups, that is, groups of women who acted together and looked out for one another in the midst of an action. The Weatherwomen also learned to set and use signals so as to communicate more easily and efficiently with one another. All these measures were taken and implemented in the wake of the McComb action, as the women engaged in criticism sessions afterwards and realized that they did not have good escape routes away from the community college. As former Weatherwoman Laura Whitehorn remembers it, they had actually parked uphill from the college, so when they were trying to disperse, the incline worked against them and made it easier for the police to catch them.[147]

Additionally, the Motor City Weatherwomen's action brought women's efforts and leadership into focus. It drove home the point that women were capable revolutionaries. As the Motor City Nine themselves put it, the action "spoke to the new role that women have to play, and has helped bring women from McComb and around the city into our fighting movement."[148] It also resulted in yet another action, this time at Henry Ford Community College. Due to their enhanced preparation and practice, the Weatherwomen were able to raise the consciousness of college students for an entire afternoon.[149] Overall, the Motor City Nine exhibited agency, their commitment to feminism, and their skilled use of militancy in their activities.[150]

Similar processes took place within the Pittsburgh collective. Together with Weatherwomen from around the country, the Pittsburgh women conducted a major jailbreak to raise the consciousness of students at South Hills High School in Pittsburgh in September of 1969. This action was prefaced by marches and rallies throughout Pittsburgh the previous night, all conducted by dedicated Weatherwomen. The *New Left Notes* described the action, explaining that women carried the Vietnam flag throughout Pittsburgh, and even took part in "small guerrilla actions around the city in sections where kids usually hang out" and engaged in several "confrontations with the pigs" (pigs meant police personnel).[151] Then,

> on Thursday all the women went to South Hills High School, which was by then covered with writing on the walls and sidewalks such as "Vietnamese Women Carry Guns," "Ho Lives," and "Jail Breaks." ... The women marched together around the school, handing out leaflets about the National Action and rapping with the kids. They ran through the school yelling "jailbreak" and then held a rally outside the school.... The pigs attacked and the women fought back, protecting their sisters and the Viet Cong flag. They fought, liberating every sister that the pigs tried to arrest, and left the scene of the struggle chanting.[152]

These women autonomously chose to travel to Pittsburgh, engage in the multiple actions throughout the city, and fight back and protect one another once the police tried to stop their efforts. Mainstream media did not focus on this sort of dedication modeled by the women—instead reports negatively focused on the breaking of gender roles that the women embodied.[153] One report described the women as frenzied and unkempt, while another stated that they "bared their breasts as they rushed through corridors"— newspapers were casting the Weatherwomen as threats to the gender order.[154] After all, these women were active agents who rallied and even fought back against the police. They were not simpering females who needed protection. As such, they were threatening the status quo.

In fact, they were not bare-breasted at all, and Laura Whitehorn explains that the reports started due to the fact that Bernardine Dohrn happened to be wearing a low-buttoned top that day.[155] But the media went after what would inspire apprehension and titillate more. David Gilbert says of the bare-breasted report, "The fact that this was totally false didn't stop the mainstream media from reporting and the white Left from trumpeting this 'news' to discredit and dismiss us."[156] Equating female courage and militancy with lewd behavior, the media acted to discredit the Weatherwomen's actions, portraying them as frenzied and out of control.[157]

The Weatherwomen, though, saw their action in Pittsburgh as successful. They associated the action with both feminism and anti-imperialism, as they stated that "through the collective struggle of the women in Pittsburgh we took one more step in building a fighting force of women, the very existence of which attacks male chauvinism and male supremacy and strengthens the forces of fighting imperialism and racism."[158] According to Larry Grathwohl, the event inspired pride in the Weatherwomen of the Cincinnati WUO collective, as he remembers a Weatherwoman named Joyce speaking proudly of the action, "That was the women.... We had 60 women march in downtown Pittsburgh. White women supporting the black liberation struggle."[159] The Weatherwomen saw themselves as committed revolutionary feminists.

The Weatherwomen in the Cincinnati collective also were dedicated revolutionary feminists in their own right. When working to recruit students in either colleges or high schools, they not only informed these students about problematic U.S. policies in Vietnam, but also drew their attention to gender inequality at home, asking pointed questions to potential female recruits, such as "Why should you earn less when you graduate?"[160] These women worked to raise the consciousness of the general public as to the sexist nature of mainstream society, melding anti-imperialist work with their feminist aims.

According to FBI infiltrator Larry Grathwohl, Detroit Weatherwomen also planned bombings. Weatherwomen Marsha Brownstein, Naomi Jaffe, and Beth Wales planned the bombing of the Detroit Police Officers Association Building, alongside with Bill Ayers and Grathwohl himself in 1970.[161] Grathwohl explains that first Marsha Brownstein, then Beth Wales helped him case the building over several days. He also adds that in this and other actions (such as one planned on Wright Patterson Air Force Base in Dayton, Ohio), Naomi Jaffe came up with the strategy of using gender as a shield that would protect against possible detection: assuming a gender normative demeanor, revolutionary women could alleviate suspicion from male guards. Grathwohl remembers Jaffe saying, "Getting past those male chauvinist pig guards would be simple. Any woman can do it. All we need is a short skirt, make-up, and a flirtatious smile."[162] The idea was to "playoff [sic] their chauvinism."[163] The Weatherwomen's militant commitment was welded together to a very personal commitment to revolution.

Weatherman Bill Ayers explains that it was due to another Weatherwoman, simply known as Anna, that the bomb at the Pentagon went off. The Pentagon was targeted, in Ayers' words, because it was "the nerve center of American military might, the most hated symbol throughout the world, we thought, of America's bloody global mission."[164] Anna, supported by two other Weathermen, Aaron and Zeke, "scouted the Pentagon irregularly for months."[165] Eventually, after everything was mapped, Anna, "her fingertips painted with clear nail polish to obscure the identifying marks of her naked hand, and heavily disguised in suit and blouse and briefcase," entered the Pentagon.[166] As an innocuous, gender normative woman, "She was never challenged," Ayers remembers.[167] One morning she walked to the women's restroom and locked herself in the stall. By 9:10 a.m., she was unscrewing the drain cover and placing the bomb inside.[168] Anna's militant action was meant to uphold the revolution, and paradoxically was made possible because she was consciously aided by her performance of gender.

Another significant example of women's militant action occurred at the Days of Rage, already briefly discussed in this and previous chapters. The WUO linked women's activities here to personal liberation *qua* woman, and to discovering self-confidence, as posters appeared throughout Chicago proclaiming that "more and more women are fighting on the right side now. They are realizing the strength within themselves and in women who are free and complete human beings, fighting out of love for all the people."[169] Personal liberation and political liberation were the same for the WUO.

Not only did women participate in the general protests scheduled for the Days of Rage, but also they had their own, all-women's action planned. The Weatherwomen did not come from a single collective to participate in these actions, but rather from various collectives throughout the country. The Weatherwomen started gathering at 9:30 a.m. in Grant Park, already battle weary from the night before. "One woman had a bandage over her eye, where she had been cut with glass," Stern remembers. "Another had a bandage covering her scalp, where she had been clubbed, and had had stiches. Still another had bandages up and down her leg, and could walk only very slowly with the help of a cane."[170] Far from giving up, these women wanted to fight, the one with the cane pleading to come as others insisted that she was too injured to participate in the action. The woman with the bandage over her eye and the woman with the bandage over her scalp formed their own affinity group so as to not hold anybody else up.[171] These unnamed Weatherwomen were models of fortitude to the rest— injured, tired, yet autonomously choosing to enter the fray again.

The Weatherwomen were armed and ready for their encounter with the police. The Weatherwomen had helmets and clubs; some held Viet Cong flags.[172] When Dohrn arrived around 10:15 a.m., she gave a speech announcing herself as "Marion Delgado": Marion Delgado was the code word by which Jeff Jones had started the protest the night before. Delgado was a young Chicano boy and revolutionary fighter who had derailed a train by placing a concrete block on a train track in 1947; he was a symbol of revolutionary courage to the WUO. Dohrn then explained that through this action, "we are here to tell people that this is not a women's movement of self-indulgence. This is not a movement to make us feel good."[173] Dohrn was putting down mainstream feminism with this statement, but at the same time she was expressing a new kind of feminism, one that was about fighting and aligning with Third World peoples, one that was about class and race, well before it became the norm among third wave feminists (as historically picked out) to link class/race/gender under an intersectional analysis.

The Weatherwomen felt like the all-women's action at the Days of Rage allowed them to offer up an example of liberated womanhood. They saw themselves as achieving a feminist agenda through their militant struggle and through their breaking of gender roles; they were done with being lady like. They were fighting for worldwide liberation and to win respect for *all* women. Reporter Tom Thomas recalled that, as the women approached the police line, the Deputy Chief of Patrol James J. Riordan ordered them to stop, but they continued on anyway:

> Approximately ten women, led by Miss Dohrn, charged into the police line. The officers, using clubs and mace, quickly subdued the women after about a four-minute scuffle. One policeman, holding a demonstrator in a double armlock, asked: "Now are you going to behave like a nice lady?" She turned and spit in his face.[174]

The police presence was intimidating. In Susan Stern's words, the women were outnumbered "about five pigs to every woman," and the police "were holding their black clubs in one leather-gloved hand and tap-tap-tapping it steadily against the other."[175] But the women charged the police line anyway, with a shrill. Stern recalled:

> All around me women were fighting with pigs; I could hear the clubs smashing down on them.... I saw a woman from my affinity group wedged up against a park grounds shack. Two pigs were working her over with their clubs as she lay there, her arms wrapped around her head. Something in me clicked at the sight, something stronger than the danger all around me. I galloped like one possessed right toward the pigs, who were smearing the woman with her own blood. One of them was bent over administering his pounding. I stood behind him for a split second, and then I carefully lifted my pipe and brought it down with all the strength I had right at the base of that motherfucker's neck, right where it was exposed beneath his helmet. He fell forward. I turned to find another pig towering over me. He rammed me across the chest with his club, staring at me as I fell backward to the ground. Then he grabbed his club with both his hands, like a baseball bat, and he raised it as high as he could in the air, as I had just done, and he smiled, and I saw the scar on his nose wiggle—then he brought that club down on my face. My glasses shattered; then I was spun around as another pig kicked me hard in the shoulder. "They're killing me," I thought.[176]

David Gilbert explains that "with the police completely prepared, the women outnumbered, many felt disappointed that they did not prove to be more of a fighting force. But to me, that was a realistic result of the balance of forces. Simply having an all-women's action at all was a major advance."[177] The courage of these women was on display as they stood their ground even in the face of violence and personal danger out of a conviction in doing what they thought was right. Weatherman Shin'ya Ono explained that the women's determination and calm throughout *all* of the actions at the Days of Rage was an inspiration to all the Weatherpeople there.[178]

Weatherwomen repeatedly framed their militancy as a deliberate, conscious choice that they made for themselves. Weatherwoman Linda Evans explains that this acceptance of militancy was a choice she made: "Vietnamese women fighters and Black women in the struggle were role models for me—because they were dedicated to fighting until victory was won. Their courage and dedication, their willingness to risk everything for freedom, the fact that women were being empowered by the process of struggle—all were exemplary."[179] Evans autonomously chose militancy as a way to achieve social change.

Weatherwoman Naomi Jaffe tells much the same story. She saw the example of Vietnamese women fighters as empowering; importantly, Vietnamese women had also achieved equality.[180] To name just a few ways that, through their struggle, Vietnamese women had achieved equality, we should note that they obtained access to political power in the National Liberation Front and the Provisional Revolutionary Government, they attained greater gender equality in education, and they earned higher combat positions and military leadership positions in the Democratic Republic of Vietnam (DRV). Furthermore, day care and child care centers were built to support women in their individual pursuits, away from their families. Likewise, feminist education programs, emphasizing women's equality, educated males as to gender bias, taught them to share household responsibilities, and generally aided in dismantling the patriarchy.[181] As such, Vietnamese women were inspiring exemplars. In fact, Jaffe identified so much with these Vietnamese fighters that she wore a piece of a shot down American plane on a necklace around her neck—she had acquired the piece on a trip to Hanoi in 1968, after helping to shoot down the plane according to one FBI theory.[182] Larry Grathwohl, who testified before the Subcommittee and partly inspired the theory, remembers Jaffe discussing her Vietnam trip as such: "I met a girl who had shot down on of our war planes. Imagine. A 14 year old girl.... We have to have the spirit of that little Vietnamese girl. I was so proud of her. I had my picture taken with her."[183]

Additionally, the Weatherwomen of the Columbus collective saw themselves as fighters. They said of themselves, "we decided that women should train in self-defense, along with the rest of the project, but that the caucus would see itself as an affinity group, learning how to move well in the streets, and serving as an exemplary fighting unit."[184] These Weatherwomen were deciding to choose militancy, growing authentically in their roles as revolutionary fighters. When the Weatherwomen deliberately chose a path of militancy, which entailed going outside of prescribed social norms for women, they demonstrated their newfound autonomy.

The Weatherwomen were not only committed to changing the way women were viewed by society, they were committed to bringing justice and dignity to all the oppressed masses. This viewpoint is by no means inconsistent with feminism; nor is it inauthentic. It rather bespeaks a deep staunchness to the feminist, revolutionary cause the Weatherwomen believed in. As the following chapter will argue, the Weatherwomen's feminist ideology not only fit within the second wave, but also would fit within the third wave, as it is defined conceptually speaking. In other words, the Weatherwomen's brand of militant feminism was complex, attempted to address economic, social, and political oppressions for *all* women, and thusly shows the problematic nature of relying too much on the historical approach to the wave metaphor.

CHAPTER 4

As Women to the Cause of Women

The active and principled sisterhood of women is a crucial part of the struggle to free all people. Unity among women enables us to be vigilant and forceful against sexism, to encourage and strengthen each other, and to develop a culture of resistance. We have worked hard to build a women's community: developing programs around women's issues, growing as fighters, reclaiming the true history of the people, and developing an ideology that integrates women's experience with that of the people as a whole.

We have undertaken campaigns to identify and root out sexist behavior and ideas among comrades. Male supremacy poisons people's lives; where it is not vigorously opposed, it holds back the development of the revolutionary forces. This struggle is an ongoing one. It changes everyone, women and men, and makes it possible to be a united and insurgent force against the state. The revolutionary community needs to contain within it the seeds of a future society where people treat each other with respect and can see the possibilities of becoming new women and new men.[1]

In this introduction to their 1973 self-published book of poetry, *Sing a Battle Song*, anonymous Weatherwomen self-identified as feminists and reached out to the mainstream feminist movement. The Weatherwomen explicitly stated that this book was "one more way to share with you our thoughts and our growth" and that "during these years we have been part of the righteous struggles for the liberation of women."[2] This explicit commitment to a full feminist revolution stands in stark contrast to the representation of the Weather Underground in the historical record thus far. While the organization itself and its female members have been dismissed by activists of the time period, as well as by scholars since, as lacking feminist credentials or as not fitting within the scope of the historical second wave feminist movement, a closer perusal of the Weatherwomen's writings and actions reveals that many of their positions on feminist issues fit well within the discourse that second wave feminists, as defined conceptually speaking (as well as historically since the WUO was active during the historical second wave period), were shaping in the late 1960s and early 1970s.[3] Committing themselves "as women to the cause of women," the Weatherwomen believed that patriarchy was oppressive, that women were experiencing sexual harassment and prejudicial treatment at work, that female gender norms were constraining and limiting, and that objectification and sexualization were methods of commodifying and appropriating women's bodies for male pleasure.[4] These concerns, as they revolved around the various ways gender oppression played out, constituted the platform of what is, conceptually speaking, the second wave. As noted, the WUO is also active during the historical period of the second wave, and so the point here is that, contrary to any claims to the contrary, part of the WUO's feminism was conceptually consistent with the feminism of their own time period.

As previously discussed, scholars have employed the wave metaphor to delineate and categorize the specific feminist concerns of different historical time periods. In this chapter, the wave terminology is used to demonstrate that the WUO's brand of feminism fits in what conceptually counts as second wave feminism. While this chapter establishes that the WUO fits within the second wave both historically and conceptually, the next chapter demonstrates that the WUO's feminism effectively disrupts the historical wave metaphor by blurring the sharp historical lines that scholars have constructed between the waves. Overall, the WUO's feminism is complex and multi-faceted in a way that requires a move to a conceptual approach to the wave motif. This chapter continues the work of unearthing their complex feminism.[5]

Despite their clear articulation of feminist aims, some feminists of the era attacked the authenticity of the Weatherwomen on the grounds that their embrace of militancy was inherently anti-feminist. A well-known example of this dismissal is Robin Morgan's 1970 essay "Goodbye to All That." Morgan accused the women of the Weather Underground of "run[ning] hand in hand with your oppressors," calling them out for being inauthentic revolutionaries and for "reject[ing] their own radical feminism for that last desperate grab at male approval that we all know so well, for claiming that the machismo style and gratuitous violence is their own style by 'free choice' and for believing that this is the way for a woman to make her revolution."[6] Morgan excluded the Weatherwomen from feminism by arguing that their militancy appeared to have been foisted upon them by the sexist, oppressive men of the WUO. True feminist organizations, Morgan insisted, eschewed male membership.[7]

In contrast, the Weatherwomen argued that real feminist work happened only when men and women worked *together*.[8] Furthermore, they saw militancy not as oppressive, but rather as a potential path for liberating them from gender roles that defined women as passive and meek. Indeed, in the later 1973 packet "Mountain Moving Day," the Weatherwomen recognized that "the women's movement does not see us as women, who have also gone through many years of struggle around being women, and whose lives have been shaped by the same kind of experience as theirs" but even in the face of this refusal to be acknowledged, the Weatherwomen claimed for themselves their roles as "white revolutionary feminists."[9] As "Mountain Moving Day" further explicated, Weatherwomen saw themselves as involved in feminist activity "since our inception," and viewed feminism as "one of our foundations we have built upon."[10]

Previous chapters have established the efforts of the WUO to address internal sexism, the important leadership roles played by women, and the personal significance women placed on their involvement in the organization's militant actions. This chapter furthers the discussion by exploring the complex feminist ideology crafted by the Weatherwomen. The Weatherwomen, as they put it, spoke "in many voices," using everything from traditional outlets, such as letters, leaflets and posters, to armed actions, to demonstrate their commitment to a broader revolution.[11] This chapter excavates the varied strands of the WUO's militant feminist platform that would fit within the second wave historically and conceptually. Based on the material presented here, it will be illustrated that, despite their exclusion from the historical narrative, the women and men of the Weather Underground were ideologically aligned with the women's liberation movement of their time period.

Chained to Family and Labor Structures That Allow Us No Freedom[12]

One of the key issues facing women in the 1960s and 1970s was that social expectations and customs drove women towards restrictive gender roles both at home and in the workplace. One way that the second wave can be conceptually distinguished from the first wave is based on the second wave's understanding that sexism and patriarchy could not be overcome simply through greater political rights. As long as women were still oppressed in the home, at work, and elsewhere, they would not be able to achieve their full autonomy. This point, which largely defined the concep-

tual second wave movement, can also be found throughout the Weatherwomen's writings.

Like other second wave feminist groups, Weatherwomen saw the gendered roles women were expected to perform both in the home and at
work as intrinsically oppressive. The Weatherwomen identified domesticity, motherhood, and traditionally feminine careers (such as secretarial
jobs) as part of the patriarchal structure of society. In their analysis, society
prescribed and emphasized these gender norms at the expense of women's
agency. Just as Betty Friedan's 1963 bestseller *The Feminine Mystique*
linked the "problem that has no name" to the special oppression of housewives who were restricted in their authentic self-development by domesticity, the Weatherwomen also saw housework as limiting women's well-
being. Moreover, Friedan criticized the idea that a woman's self-identity
"rested on necessary work and achievement in the home." Friedan also
wrote that patriarchy "does not permit women to accept or gratify their
basic need to grow and fulfill their potential as human beings."[13] In this
feminist analysis, gender normative behavior for women meant that women
did not develop on their own terms.

This second wave analysis of the restrictive and burdensome nature
of domesticity is present throughout many of the WUO's writings. As
early as 1969, a month after the WUO was born, Weatherwoman Cathy
Wilkerson published a piece targeting family-based oppression, which
stated that "women identify primarily with the home and family. In their
roles as provider, wife, and mother they are pushed by even more forces
than men to ally with their oppressors. They feel more immediately the
need to maintain stability so as to keep stomachs full, children clothed;
they feel the threat to the stability of their position ever more acutely."[14]
Weatherwomen continued to refine this position. For example, in an
anonymous 1973 poem, titled "Riding the Subways," a Weatherwoman
provided an assessment akin to Friedan's critique of homemaking and
housework, while also critiquing the second shift that many working
women experienced daily:

> What I wanted to ask you:
> Is someone at home
> your husband
> your teenage son...
> making dinner
> getting things ready
> so you can just unlock the door,
> drop your packages,
> say hello,

take a minute or two
without rushing...
never mind time-clocks
never mind rush-orders
never mind good manners...
Eat good
enjoy it
make a feast of it...
because
you sure look tired now.[15]

"Riding the Subways" presents a feminist critique of women's unpaid labor in the home, and appeals to a shared experience of drudgery, which the poem depicts as identifiable with a single glance, from one female passenger to the next, in the subway. Asking whether a male helper existed at home to lighten the woman's burden after a long day at work, a day that had already been lengthened by necessary household shopping in the afternoon, the poem tries to evaluate whether the woman could finally take a rest. In other words, this poem zeroes in on the problematic nature of the second shift for women (where the second shift refers to women's additional work in the home, over and above their jobs outside the home, which would be their first shift).[16] Like other second-wavers, the Weatherwomen were critical of women's extensive, unpaid labor in the home.[17] An additional point that we must make here is that that the Weatherwomen are making this theoretical distinction of extra work (after a full day of work at one's employment) before the second shift label was coined in 1989 by Arlie Russel Hocschild and Anne Machung.[18] In other words, the Weatherwomen are employing a conceptual third wave term in the historical second wave, again supporting my point that we need to rethink the waves and employ them conceptually.

The 1973 packet "Six Sisters" also provided a feminist analysis of women's domestic roles. The packet, which dates to the summer of that year, is made up of several pages of writing having to do with feminist practice and feminist study for Weatherwomen.[19] Weatherwomen wrote that women's unpaid labor in the home was a product of sexism and akin to imperialism, in that it colonized women (in their relationship to men) and reduced them to second class citizens, similar to other oppressed populations across the globe.[20] The Weatherwomen further explicated that sexism and male chauvinism also enforced a hierarchy within the home, one where women performed "unpaid labor, necessary to capitalism—raising, feeding, socializing children and men."[21] Paradoxically but purposefully, this important work—of maintaining a much needed labor pool for a capitalist society through housework—went unrewarded, thus signaling women's inferior status not only to the men in their lives, but also within the overarching societal power structure.

The Weatherwomen's feminist analysis of homemaking continued in the 1975 pamphlet *Prairie Fire: The Politics of Revolutionary Anti-Imperialism*. In *Prairie Fire*, the Weatherwomen offered a complex evaluation of women's domesticity. Explaining that the family was the basic unit of capitalist society, Weatherwomen argued that women not only reproduce the labor force and "bear the major responsibility for the nurturing, health and education of families," but they also complete housework.[22] The Weatherwomen noted that "housework is hard work, done alone, but it is denied any social value and it is not paid for in any formal way."[23] Furthermore, in "A Mighty Army: An Investigation of Women Workers," the WUO espoused much of the same point, critiquing the trend that devalued women's labor in the home, and made it "invisible" and "lonely."[24] Additionally underscoring this same point, in "The Women's Question is a Class Question," the WUO explained that "home and child rearing became a private burden and doom rather than a valued form of social labor."[25] Moreover, as Cathy Wilkerson indicated as early as 1969 in "Toward a Revolutionary Women's Militia," this unpaid labor that women performed in the home paradoxically contributed to their own oppression, as it made them dependent on the very men for whom they cooked, cleaned, and bore children.[26] Weatherwomen developed these feminist critiques for years.

The Weatherwomen's analysis fit within second wave assessments of housework, which held that women's labor was undervalued, burdensome, and inimical to women's self-development. For example, the Redstockings, a feminist group from New York, also critiqued women's home labor and held that women are exploited as "domestic labor, and cheap labor" in their manifesto.[27] Even Robin Morgan, who made clear that she saw herself quite opposed to the work of the Weatherwomen, espoused these same views, as she wrote that "the nuclear family is oppressive to women." Morgan further argued that it is through the family structure that a woman is kept in a dependent position, is not valued for her much needed in-home labor, and not paid a real wage if employed.[28] Echoing this general analysis, in their previously mentioned article "The Women's Question Is a Class Question," the WUO argued that the family held women back when they sought employment, noting that there are many women "who want a job now but aren't looking because of household responsibilities."[29] Women, to fit into society, married and exchanged freedom for a "sense of economic security, status," competing with each other for the approval of males.[30] Therefore, in the WUO analysis, the socio-cultural gender norms associated with domesticity held women back from gaining meaningful and enriching employment.

Furthermore, in *Prairie Fire*, the WUO pointed out their concerns with the patriarchal structure of the common family unit. Here, the WUO argued that the modern family unit was "male-run" and that "male supremacy is given concrete form in the family."[31] So, even though women performed the majority of the work in the home, the family was still structured as another environment in which men were treated as the true leaders. The emphasis on domesticity, according to the WUO, became a "trap for women."[32] Hence, women's domestic labor provided them no real domestic power; in the home, women did the work while men retained control to dictate women's lives.

To escape the oppression of enforced domesticity within the family unit, the WUO argued that women needed to be allowed to develop autonomously, which required an end to sexism and gender-based oppression. In "Toward a Revolutionary Woman's Militia," Wilkerson wrote:

> In high schools, for instance, we must organize girls to fight along with men against the tracking system in general, as well as the way it affects girls in particular. Girls will also struggle against pigs and against the war. At the same time we can form women's militias of high school girls which directly attack male supremacy and the broader set of bourgeois values upon which it rests. We have seen that one of the greatest oppressions of young working-class women is the restriction and surveillance of parents. "The family" is constantly trying to define their identity as submissive, mateable, and skilled in family tasks.[33]

This particular paragraph, per Cathy Wilkerson, in an earlier edit was also going to have sections on how these women groups "could respond to men who were abusive or to parents who kept their daughters locked up at home."[34] It was a vision Wilkerson had that these neighborhood women's groups could make men accountable for their actions or protect the women who needed it, through the spread of information—naming the abusers publically would ensure women's safety. This part was edited when the piece was published, but it is unclear why or by whom.[35] In any case, the WUO had a vision of female autonomy and independence that would range from education—where women would be encouraged to study whatever interested them instead of being tracked into traditionally female jobs—to dating—where women were encouraged to love whomever they fancied.[36] The WUO, in other words, advocated a break from traditional gender norms, and fashioned a feminist vision rooted in autonomous womanhood.

In addition to these ideological critiques, the WUO also took up more practical considerations, such as the wage gap. In 1966, the newly formed National Organization for Women (NOW) cited statistics showing that women were paid less than men:

> full-time women workers today earn on the average only 60% of what men earn, and that wage gap has been increasing over the past twenty-five years in every major industry group. In 1964, of all women with a yearly income, 89% earned under $5,000 a year; half of all full-time year round women workers earned less than $3,690; only 1.4% of full-time year round women workers had an annual income of $10,000 or more.[37]

Akin to NOW, many second wave organizations tackled the ways in which patriarchy discriminated against women in the economic sphere. The WUO was no exception.

The WUO advocated women's rights at work by targeting the wage gap and gender bias in employment as specific problems that needed to be addressed so as to improve the lives of working women. As such, the National War Council packet "Honky Tonk Women" stated that "some parts of our oppression are concrete—imperialist schools track us into jobs as secretaries and housewives; we get lower wages than men, and fewer job opportunities; we are chained to a family structure that allows us no freedom. Amerika's [sic] rules use us as surplus and domestic labor to contribute to their pile of profits."[38] Thus, the Weatherwomen did not see sexism within economic roles to be merely incidental. Instead, the patriarchy, for them, was essentially interwoven into the American economic system: American capitalism depended on women's free labor as housewives and cheap labor in service positions to maximize profits for the rich.

Importantly, second wave feminists of the time period, who denied the WUO's feminism, were in clear agreement with WUO's analysis on this economic point. Robin Morgan wrote that women worked outside of the capitalist economy, and that their unpaid labor within the family went unrewarded, "since the employer pays only the husband" and "gets the rest of the family's services for free."[39] Bread and Roses, another feminist group of the time period that was founded by Meredith Tax and Linda Gordon in Boston in 1969, were a radical feminist organization that lasted until 1973.[40] Bread and Roses also attacked the WUO for not being feminist, in spite of the two groups holding similar views on women's roles and their labor.[41] Bread and Roses held that the family unit stifled women's development and that women were unable to procure employment due to family obligations. Furthermore, Bread and Roses noted gender bias in hiring and levels of pay, advocating that women should be paid the same as men for equal work.[42]

Expanding on their earlier analysis, in "The Women's Question Is a Class Question," the WUO advocated fair pay for women and supported female unionization. The WUO stated that women were "caught between rising prices and dwindling checks" and were already in a disadvantaged position in the market since they earned less pay due to gender bias.[43] The WUO explained, in agreement with other second wave feminists, that women traditionally were offered lower pay since the male wage was culturally assumed to be sustaining the family.[44]

Moreover, women were seen as "secondary breadwinners," the WUO pointed out.[45] Not only was this system grossly unfair and a "myth" in the WUO's estimation, but it was further complicated by the fact that women were kept in traditionally feminine, unskilled jobs, most of which were not unionized.[46] This same point is also made in "A Mighty Army: An Investigation of Women Workers," where the WUO argued that women were paid less than men, were "last hired and first fired," and not unionized. In this piece, the WUO also pointed out that working women were subjected to sexual harassment from bosses and supervisors and had no recourse if they wanted to keep their jobs.[47] Seen as unskilled or untrained expendable labor, women were therefore open to economic and even sexual exploitation from their bosses. The WUO argued that economic subjugation was made worse since "there are no maternity-leave benefits and no daycare facilities."[48] As such, the WUO was offering a complex feminist analysis of women's secondary status in the workplace while raising consciousness of women's oppression. Through its emphasis on collective action through unionization—a tactic recommended by women's groups of the era—the WUO also attempted to formulate a real-life solution to major problems in women's lives.[49]

We Can't Get No Satisfaction from Gender Norms[50]

Even as the Weatherwomen explored these practical solutions to women's oppression, they also continued to tackle restrictive gender norms, including ones that defined women as passive and compliant, and others that sexualized women. Like other second wave organizations, the Weatherwomen argued that social expectations encouraged women to give up their autonomy: if women were only passive, sexualized creatures, they were left little room to explore their own individualities.[51] Firstly, the WUO saw these gender norms as undermining women's power by defining their personalities in a weakened fashion that placed them in an inferior position to men. Secondly, the WUO argued that women needed to break free of the patriarchal social expectation that women be sexually available objects whose existence revolved around fulfilling male fantasies.

Numerous second wave feminists linked patriarchy to the propagation of restrictive gender stereotypes for women. For example, the Bread and Roses feminist collective held that women were socially "defined as docile, helpless, and inferior."[52] The Redstockings was another prominent feminist group from New York. Ellen Willis and Shulamith Firestone founded the Redstockings in 1969, and they were active in New York until the fall of 1970.[53] In the Redstockings' founding Manifesto, they also addressed this issue by stating that, on a daily basis and in myriad ways, women were pressured to be submissive to men.[54] Also, Robin Morgan identified the color pink as emblematic of women's gendered socialization.[55]

In spite of the dominant position that they were not considered to be feminists, the Weatherwomen were making many of these same points. In "Toward a Revolutionary Women's Militia," Wilkerson explained that women were taught to be passive and compliant. These qualities made them open to manipulation by the capitalist imperialist system and its apparatuses, such as the media and consumerism. Wilkerson explained: "Having been taught to feel passive and defenseless, especially in physical ways, they [women] are more threatened by the specter of black struggles as defined by the mass media, the ruling class through the PTA, women's magazines, etc."[56] In other words, not only did these gender norms hold women back from developing authentically, but they also propped up various social oppressions, such as racism, middle class materialism, and a bourgeoisie lifestyle that emphasized adherence to traditional values. Since these stereotypes resulted in a tightening noose, one that was "especially tight against the necks of women," Wilkerson advocated a program that focused on smashing sexism and fixing social problems for women, through revolutionary activity.[57]

Further, "Honky Tonk Women" explained that "imperialism has colonized our minds," producing a "false consciousness of what women should be," so that women internalized these stereotypical personality traits:

> Men believe that we are stupid, inferior to them, and that the only way they can be
> strong is to dominate and possess a woman. Their strength comes from making and

keeping us weak—by defining what we should look like, how we should act, and what we should think and feel. We are made into and kept half people, dependent and passive by definition.[58]

In other words, women lost independence due to internalized gender norms because these gender norms defined men as strong and in charge of men while women are defined as weak and under men's control. As the WUO noted, "The organization of society teaches and reinforces the inferiority of women."[59] The WUO held that breaking out of these gender norms was essential for the autonomous development and human flourishing of women.

This idea of being groomed through gender norm adherence was also taken up in the packet "Mountain Moving Day." Here, the Weatherwomen wrote, that as white women, they "have grown up thinking of ourselves as objects, love objects, listening objects, understanding objects, sexual objects. Weak. Passive. America tries to keep us this way, making life near impossible for a woman to be an independent and full person, culturally, economically, psychologically."[60] In this analysis, social norms kept women back from developing autonomously; as a result, women were groomed to be meek, compliant, and to not express themselves authentically. However, breaking through these shackles, Weatherwomen believed they could eventually come to "define our present" in a way that was empowering to women.[61]

The WUO summed it up by saying that "women are taught to think of ourselves as weak in body and mind, passive, second rate dependent objects. The organization of society teaches and reinforces the inferiority of women…. The media portrays women as empty-headed, sexy and addicted consumers."[62] The media, in other words, propagated and reinforced stereotypes of women. Not only did the media push the view that women were passive and weak, but also that they were sexual objects without thoughts of their own. The WUO joined the second wave critique of the patriarchal idea that women's worth was based in their beauty and sexuality. Seeing the objectification and sexualization of women's bodies as inherently limiting to women's development, feminists rebelled against beauty norms and against the commodification of women's bodies for male pleasure.[63]

Moreover, the WUO's "Honky Tonk Women" packet argued that women were alienated from themselves and their own self-interests by the U.S. culture that propagated these social norms. Thus, "Honky Tonk Women" stated that

we [women] are objectified and used sexually—the Amerikan [sic] culture had totally dehumanized us, destroying the possibility for satisfying sexual relationships between men and women. We are taught to see other women as our enemies and to compete with them, wiping out any chance for strong, revolutionary human relationships between us women....

We [women] are taught that we should not want or expect or care about sexual satisfaction—and men are taught that sex can only be a physical encounter with an object made solely for his satisfaction. Imperialist Amerika [*sic*] teaches its children that this is love....[64]

The WUO argued that women were socialized to seek male approval, to define themselves through their relationships with men, and to not pursue collaborative efforts with other women (whom they are taught to see as competitors for male approval) or their own sexual satisfaction. Women were commodified for the consumption of males, who, in turn, were taught that they were entitled to women's bodies. Concluding that "we have been taught, well-taught by Amerikan [*sic*] society that women are weak—that thinking, struggling, and fighting are unfeminine," "Honky Tonk Women" advised that women's self-empowerment came from breaking through these restrictive beliefs.[65]

The Weatherwomen saw women's bodies as further appropriated by the social demand that women live up to unrealistic and stifling beauty norms. The Weatherwomen, and the WUO in general, noted that these beauty ideals held women back, and diverted their attention from feminist revolution to a concern with self-surveillance and fitting into beauty culture. Thus, *Prairie Fire* held that "we are conditioned to look and act within narrow confines to fulfill our primary role as sexual partners and reproducers. Distorted and competitive standards of beauty are the surface over a whole system of sexual objectification.... Men are taught to use women."[66] The WUO held that the quest for beauty propped up the commodification of women's bodies by men. Moreover, "Honky Tonk Women" linked this commodification of women and imperialism:

... This is an imperialist view of women—a Miss America standard of beauty, desirability, success, and docility. She is a pig woman. We all still believe in her, although her power grows less every day. Her image was imbedded deep within us—who among us could think she was beautiful or desirable or strong, measured against such a standard?[67]

The position paper also noted that beauty ideals were internalized and led to self-doubt for women.[68]

Feminist groups of the time period, such as the New York Radical Women (a women's liberation group founded by Shulamith Firestone and Pam Allen in fall 1967), likewise actively fought against beauty ideals in protests, such as one against the 1968 Miss America Pageant. This protest occurred in Atlantic City, and was organized by women's activists from all over the nation; the activists picketed against the pageant and engaged in guerrilla theater, such as parading sheep on the boardwalk to parody how women are judged at beauty contests.[69] The New York Radical Women produced a position paper, the "No More Miss America Manifesto," which included a Ten Points analysis of women's objectification through beauty contests. For example, this document explained that women were "enslaved by ludicrous 'beauty' standards we ourselves are conditioned to take seriously."[70] *Prairie Fire* echoed the New York Radical Women's analysis. *Prairie Fire* explained that "we are taught to hate our bodies, mistrust our minds, fear ourselves and everybody else."[71] Thus, the WUO clarified that women's bodies were used against them: women were alienated from their bodies, which became enemies to them since their figures did not sufficiently conform to male fantasies.[72] To the WUO, destroying the "pig woman" that epitomized beauty ideals and gender norms was the only way for women to gain their self-sovereignty. In doing so, they were very much in step with the second wave, which shared this agenda.

Women's Autonomy Over Their Bodies

Not only was the WUO forging a feminist platform against the objectification of women, it also shaped a positive agenda for women to seize control of their bodies, starting with fighting for reproductive freedom. This position was also very much in agreement with that of the second wavers, as the issues of abortion and women's reproductive control was at the forefront of the women's liberation movement.[73]

Weatherwomen believed that women ought to control their bodies and their destinies, and they advocated for the practical application of those beliefs—for a woman's right to choose—in everyday life in the United States. As such, a Venceremos Brigade member and WUO affiliate named simply Cathy (no last name), discussing her trip to Cuba, explained that women's rights to their bodies were respected there. The Venceremos Brigade was a group of young women and men who went to Cuba starting in February 1970 to show solidarity with the Cuban Revolution (they had been invited by Fidel Castro in a speech given January 2, 1969). Weatherpeople were members and planners of the first and second Venceremos brigades.[74] Comparing her experience in obtaining an abortion in Cuba to obtaining one in the United States, Cathy noted that in the United States, a woman was made to feel as if there was something wrong with her for not wanting a baby, as well as ashamed and embarrassed for not wanting to keep the pregnancy. She stated:

> ... a nurse asked me if I wanted a baby. My simple "no" sufficed, and by nine the next morning, after spending the night in the hospital, I was waking up from sodium pentathol [*sic*], the D-and-C operation completed.
>
> At no time in the hospital or afterwards in the Brigade did anyone, Cuban or North American, imply that there was anything wrong with my not wanting a baby, even though I was a married woman. I felt completely free to explain why I had been in the hospital. This is such a contrast to my feeling previously in the U.S. When I had an abortion there, out of embarrassment and shame for not wanting a child, I told no one....
>
> This experience has liberated me, because it has given me my first complete understanding of my rights—not privileges or special favors, but rights regarding my body and my life.[75]

Weatherwomen believed that a woman should choose what to do with her body. In her memoir, Wilkerson bemoaned the fact that prior to *Roe v. Wade* (the 1973 Supreme Court decision that made abortion legal in the United States), women had difficulty obtaining an abortion.[76] Wilkerson defended a woman's right to choose, explaining that women obtained abortions even though they feared being "mutilated or even raped" in a back alley abortion.[77]

This respect for women's innate rights over their own bodies was something that came up again and again in the WUO's writings. In "Six Sisters," Weatherwomen supported the idea of a right to access to abortion centers.[78] In *Prairie Fire*, the Weatherwomen stated clearly that women wanted birth control and determination over their reproductive choices.[79] They advocated a cultural change in the way society viewed women. They wrote, "We live in an anti-life culture, where women are denied control of our bodies, where sexual repression and taboos go hand in hand with prostitution and exploitation. Men are taught to use women."[80] A move away from this schema was imperative in the Weatherwomen's estimation. The stance of the Weatherwomen on this issue fit in rather snugly with the standard positions of the second wave, which was that male control of women's reproductive capacities was an outright obscenity.[81]

In the Weatherwomen's analysis, sexism and imperialism were also responsible for sustaining rape culture. Defining rape and sexual abuse against women as "the prerogative of the conqueror, a means of undermining women's resistance, a murderous assault, part of the arsenal of control and domination" of women, the Weatherwomen explained that women as a whole needed to rise against this type of oppression.[82] The Weatherwomen saw rape in the United States as part of mainstream culture and as an increasingly significant problem for women's lives.[83] They wrote: "Rape—a massive, brutal system of terror perpetrated on women by men. Most rapes are not reported so the statistics are far lower than the reality, but attacks on women constitute the fastest growing category of crime in the U.S."[84] Seeing rape as a tool of repression against women and as a systematized apparatus ensuring women's subjugation, both the Weatherwomen and the WUO held that a revolutionary women's movement would lead the way to creating a woman-oriented culture where rape would be minimized. Similarly, the second wave feminist movement also was organizing around issues of rape. Eminent second wave feminist, Susan Brownmiller, wrote in "The Mass Psychology of Rape," that rape was "not only a male prerogative, but man's basic weapon of choice against woman."[85] Rape, in other words, kept women subordinate and was used to prop up male supremacy.[86] Therefore, there are clear links between the Weatherwomen and second wave feminists of their time period, especially as seen in their shared recognition of the importance of women's rights to bodily autonomy.

Empowering Women through Action and Theory

The WUO not only critiqued the problems that arose due to patriarchy, but it also posed solutions. Some of these remedies were hotly contested by other women's liberation groups of the time period. This most especially was the case with the group's advocacy of militancy. Nevertheless, other solutions reflected mainstream feminist approaches to patriarchal problems.

Interpreting the embrace of violence or the taking on of qualities generally associated with masculinity (such as aggressiveness) as inauthentic and non-feminist, second wavers, such as Morgan, attacked the Weatherwomen's feminist credentials. However, as Benita Roth explains in *Separate Roads to Feminism*, feminist groups of the era had different approaches and epistemologies—each had a distinct ethos and "idea about what constituted good politics"—but a difference in judgment did not preclude the fact that they were all feminists.[87]

Whereas some feminist groups categorized violent action as masculine and chauvinist by its very nature, the Weatherwomen saw an embrace of militant, aggressive action as liberating and as necessary for smashing male privilege. As previously noted, Morgan, in her 1970 essay "Goodbye to All That," accused the Weatherwomen of running hand in hand with their oppressors, "for claiming that the machismo style and gratuitous violence is their own style by 'free choice' and for believing that this is the way for a woman to make her revolution."[88] The Bread and Roses collective also objected to the Weatherwomen along the same lines, noting that "a woman becomes a heroine in Weatherman circles when she is a tougher, better fighter than the men."[89]

Weatherwomen fought back against these attacks. In "Inside the Weather Machine," a Weatherwoman explained that at a conference in September of 1969, men and women became committed to the politics of the WUO because they identified strongly with the need to support black and Third World liberation struggles; the way to demonstrate that support, they believed, was to actually help in their fight for independence.[90] Thus, she explained, "We had to pick up the gun."[91] This "we" included women on an equal basis with men; Weatherwomen made the choice to act militantly. As Weatherwoman Susan Stern put it, "With every pore of my body I wanted to be part of the solution," even if that solution meant outright attack.[92] Furthermore, Weatherwoman Kathy Boudin noted that "one of the things that the government tries to separate the most is that you can't be a strong person and also a gentle person at the same time...."[93] As such, she was warning against setting up or replicating a binary that would limit women's behavior. *Prairie Fire* also warned against this binary, warning that "our movement will be self-defeating if we reject militancy as 'male' and 'macho.'"[94] *Prairie Fire* went on to explain that doing so—perpetuating this false binary—would take away from the struggles and active resistance of women to effect change, minimizing or erasing their contributions.[95]

Moreover, the Weatherwomen believed that their commitment to militancy did not preclude feminism. On the contrary, as an anonymous Weatherwoman explained, militancy actually helped women break free of the restricting gender norms and gender roles that they had been taught. Since internalized gender norms and male supremacy kept women back, as it "prevented us from assuming any real kind of role in the revolution because most of us felt there was very little we could do," the embrace of militancy broke down those gender norms.[96] Becoming a political force, and picking up the gun, broke women free of their internalized inferiority. As *Prairie Fire* put it, militancy was "a rejection of the passivity and acceptance for which we are bred."[97] Militancy was empowering in that it gave concrete expression to women's agency. The WUO's militancy program included learning karate and jogging, which were seen as enabling women and men to gain self-confidence and to learn to defend themselves in fights and encounters with police.[98] Interestingly, other feminist groups of the time period advocated that women learn karate specifically for these same reasons: to gain a sense of empowerment and self-reliance in confrontations. Historians Rosalyn Baxandall and Linda Gordon note that "although it is doubtful that karate expertise or any kind of physical resistance is the best defense against attack, women nevertheless benefited mentally and physically from the confidence, strength, agility, and discipline of these [karate] skills."[99] Robin Morgan also learned karate as part of her transformation into "a 'feminist' committed to a Women's Revolution."[100]

The Weatherwomen also employed other tactics to address sexism that other second wave groups used, such as bringing women together to create a common power base from which to act. Second wave groups believed that women working together, collectively, would help one another overcome their oppression. For example, the New York Radical Women, in their founding principles, held this position, seeing collaboration—"collective wisdom" and "collective strength"—as the root of female liberation.[101] Putting women in positions of power was another accepted second wave prescription for the liberation of women. For example, the Redstockings held that women needed to develop politically, to the best of their abilities, through participation and leadership in activist endeavors.[102] Similarly, Cell 16, another feminist group formed in Boston by Roxanne Dunbar-Ortiz in 1968, was developed specifically to allow women to experience leadership, as a sophisticated vanguard of women that would lead theoretically and through direct action.[103] The WUO supported and practiced both of these methods for liberating women.

As discussed earlier, female caucuses were a basis of power for women within the WUO.[104] These caucuses allowed Weatherwomen to discuss and develop feminist themes, to provide a united front against male chauvinism, and they served as a foundation for female leadership within WUO collectives.[105] Indeed, collectives such as the one in Columbus applied this strategy to their group. Weatherwoman Lorraine Rosal wrote that the female caucus within the collective, "took responsibility for researching and writing on the women's question.... The caucus will also be responsible for collecting study material on women's liberation for the study sessions."[106] This mission was part of the later 1973 "Six Sisters" summer study, feminist WUO collective. This collective investigated women's history, studied feminist theory, sought connections with other liberation groups, and generally planned a feminist agenda for the WUO. Among some of their explorations is their study of women's history, from the Grimke sisters and the Seneca Falls Convention to Eisenhower's and Nixon's platforms toward women.[107] The group met twice a week to discuss feminist themes focused around the area of health, education, and welfare. They had a feminist reading list with such titles as the famous *Our Bodies, Ourselves* or *Women, Midwives and Healers.*[108]

The anonymous Weatherwomen's 1973 poem "For L." can be interpreted as explaining the strengths of female caucuses within the WUO or, at least, as celebrating bonds between women:

> Many times
> We have talked, laughed, shared.
> A flash of recognition in your eyes
> Told me
> Whether you smiled in agreement
> Or wrinkle your brow in disagreement
> That you never question me, or my right
> to speak up, to explore
> what I think.
> There is the warmth of sisterhood
> And the keen eye of politics,
> Watching.[109]

The poem presents a milieu where Weatherwomen felt that they could agree, disagree, and freely speak their minds, without fear of reprisal; it represents an environment where they always supported each other and saw each other as sisters working together. These types of arrangements nourished Weatherwomen and were generally supported specifically because they allowed women to build deep abiding bonds that sustained both personal and political growth.

When it came to the choice that far-left feminists had to make at the time—to work within an all female, separatist group only on women's issues or to get involved in other work, such as anti-war or anti-racist activism—the Weatherwomen saw the benefits (but also the drawbacks) of the separatist plan. Weatherwomen agreed that separateness was good in part, so they advocated the creation of women caucuses within WUO. However, the WUO also believed that too much separatism would weaken the revolution itself. Thus, while the WUO accepted some amount of separatism in the caucuses that would fit with a second wave methodology, they did not completely accept these methods that would have women working alone solely on women's issues.

Their 1973 poem "Sisterhood Is Not Magic" can be taken to reflect this awareness that multiple feminist viewpoints can exist and become a root of disagreement:

Whatever did the witches do
They must have quarreled beneath the stars
About how to ease the pain of wound
With ergot,
Belladonna or
Nasturtium.
And argued
Taking long moonlight walks arm in arm,
About how to save the "devil's party"
Where to meet most safely
And best serve the peasants' needs.

...

To some
Their magic
Seemed easy
Be we
Who often walk
In their footsteps
Know better.[110]

This poem can be interpreted as recognizing that multiple feminist subjectivities are often at odds, that feminism itself is not static, and that quarrels might be had while trying to work for the same cause. Likewise, while trying to advance women's liberation, some feminists felt separatism was necessary, but the WUO did not. As an anonymous Weatherwoman explained, in "Inside the Weather Machine," fighting alongside men was thought to be necessary for several reasons. First, women needed to be there with the men they were trying to change so as to ensure that the men actually reformed, as "the fight against male chauvinism can only be carried out together by people struggling against their chauvinism. Separatism can only lead to a continuation of chauvinism...."[111] As this Weatherwoman explained it in 1970, as revolutionary women and men, all WUO members needed to work together to create new ways of addressing and relating to one another in the new society they were envisioning. They needed to put into practice the ideals of gender equity they were espousing. Women needed to be there to model and explain appropriate behavior, and actively create the non-sexist society they were envisioning, alongside the men. As she noted, "While the struggle with men is hard, there is no other way to do it. We have to start learning how to build this new society where people don't destroy one another but build each other. Otherwise our revolution is bullshit and we become like the Man."[112] It is interesting to note that Robin Morgan, in her 1970 "Goodbye to All That," advocated an all women's movement. This difference—separatist vs. working with men—is possibly another reason why she attacked the WUO.[113] But separatism was firmly rejected by the WUO. Later, in a 1973 collective letter to the Women's Movement, Weatherwomen still came back to this point, defending their choice to work alongside men. They wrote: "We realize that many women distrust us because we work with men.... We claim the integrity of our choice to work with them, and do not intend to either defend or reject them."[114] Rather, the point was to model behavior and teach through the struggle.

The poem "Straight Talk" from 1973 could be interpreted as an imagining of what that struggle would be like. The Weatherwomen wrote:

Hey—just a minute
Now what was that you said?
Oh. You really got guts
to say it again—
Well—let me be plain
No mincing words
Stick
Yes, stick—I mean stick
stickety stick
stick stack stuck
stick it up
Your ass
That's right—
That's just what I said
Yes—
you got it
now you can close your mouth
you actually understood
what I said
Rude?
Now really—
So I am rude
no manners to use
such language
such foul language—
no woman
should use
such foul language—
Foul!
Did you say foul,
while fouling me?
What a way
what a long way
yes quite a long way
still to go for us
even in these small
not particularly

revolutionary
as you might say
rude
little
details.[115]

This poem embraces the model of a woman who stands up for her beliefs
as an active interlocutor and who does not mince words when it comes
to defending herself and her views. This woman calls out her attacker, takes
on an aggressive posture, and claims it as her own. Importantly, she cau-
tions that the politics of respectability can be used to the detriment of
women through policing their behavior so as to keep them in line to a male
model of meek femininity, which would further work to silence their
voices. The poem acknowledges that there is plenty of work to do in
unlearning gender norms that declare women should be polite and quiet.
Even these "little details" betray how culture is imbued with male supremacy and is patriarchal in nature. The Weatherwomen's poetry is not revolutionary in the militant sense, but revolutionary specifically in the
feminist sense.

The 1974 poem "For a Troubled Sister" takes up the same idea, namely
that women's voices should not be silenced and should be listened to in
conversations:

Make your need known
need is human
pain is woman
You are precious
to me
to the circle
to the people.
Becoming resigned to
a life without need
without silence or rest
is incorrect. A bad example
A short sighted way.
Is this a cycle?
If so where is its door?
How do we break it,
shatter on to some new plane?
The others of us must hear your voice
and add ours
plan strategy to defeat this
thing sapping you
and others, too...[116]

Encouraging a troubled sister to speak up as to what her needs are, to lift
her voice and become part of the conversation, this poem upholds a vision

of an inclusive space where women's voices are part and parcel of figuring out solutions and creating strategies. Whether fighting for liberation or carving out a space for self-care, the point made is about incorporating women's needs and viewpoints in the process of solution making. Thus, the limits imposed on women—limits proscribing them to background, passive observer roles—could be shattered and progress could be made.

This point leads to another fashion in which the Weatherwomen's views were consistent with and related to second wave views: both Weatherwomen and other second wave feminists of their time period agreed that feminism required not just the advancement and empowerment of women, but also a change in how men viewed women. Men and women both needed to accept the equality of the sexes and the need to fight patriarchy, which meant that men had to renounce their male privilege.

Second wave feminist groups advocated the position that for sexism to be curbed, men needed to renounce male privilege and accept the equality of women. The Bread and Roses collective stated in their paper "A Declaration of Women's Independence" that "all men and women are created equal and made unequal only by socialization" and that therefore, this arrangement must be "dissolved."[117] Similarly, noted feminist Roxanne Dunbar-Ortiz, in her 1970 "Female Liberation as the Basis for Social Revolution," wrote that as feminists, women "demand the development of maternal skills and consciousness in men," as well as a change in how men viewed and cared about women.[118]

The WUO similarly believed that revolution would only happen when women and men broke out of the norms they had been taught to accept as putatively natural parts of their lives in a patriarchal and imperialist system. Patriarchy flourished by setting up false binaries, such as setting up men against women—with men in the dominant position. Just as women needed to throw off the shackles of their internalized oppression and needed to function as the autonomous, strong individuals that they were capable of being, men needed to stop identifying with their male privilege.

Early on, Weatherwoman Cathy Wilkerson stated that "men who claim to be fighting imperialism in any form must fight against their own supremacist practices and notions. Not to do so undercuts their own legitimacy as revolutionaries."[119] In other words, revolutionary males had to be feminist males. Furthermore, Wilkerson stated that the plan for revolution was to "initiate an attack on male supremacy as an essential part of our attack on those forces which push mother country working people to ally with the ruling class."[120] In the imperialist system, men felt as if they were better than women out of a false sense of superiority. This sense of superiority allowed men to dominate women and therefore to self-identify as members of the ruling class. Breaking down males' sense of privilege then was not simply feminist work—it was revolutionary work.

Breaking men of their sexist behavior sometimes happened through "criticism, self-criticism sessions."[121] At a criticism, self-criticism session in the New York collective, Teddy Gold, one of the founding members of the WUO, got attacked for his sexism. Gilbert remembers:

> Somehow the session with Teddy became a super-marathon. He wasn't any more male chauvinist than the rest of us, but as a leader he was the first one challenged to change—fully and immediately! The main sticking points all involved his resistance to accepting woman [sic] as equals. The session was intense and grueling. I could hear the clucking in Teddy's dry throat as he tried to speak, but he didn't bolt; he stuck with this excruciating process because he wanted to be a revolutionary and he knew that a full-hearted embracing of women's equality was an essential component.[122]

Here was a criticism, self-criticism session that could have been interrupted or called off, but instead continued because both Weatherwomen and Weathermen were attempting to stay committed to the feminist message of gender equality.[123] Such a session, which was meant to challenge and assist the men with being more feminist and less sexist, was only possible because the WUO was a group that included men. Thus, by not going the separatist route, the feminist women of the WUO were working their hardest to directly produce feminist ideals in the men around them.

A Total Change

While various connections between second wave feminist views and the views of the WUO existed, these similarities do not tell the whole story of the WUO's feminism. The WUO was not just fighting for the smashing of gender norms and for the establishment of gender equality. Weatherwomen and the WUO, according to Wilkerson, were fighting for a new way of relating to one another in a new kind of society: "women are not in particular demanding equality with men under the current conditions, but are demanding a whole new set of values—socialist values—by which people relate to each other in all forms of individual and collective relationships."[124] People were supposed to think of themselves collectively, not simply copy and reproduce old, gendered privileges. In the WUO's vision, society was supposed to be recreated in a socialist mold, where individuals would relate to one another collaboratively, with a new egalitarian and humanitarian consciousness permeating their everyday activities. In the 1969 article "National War Council," the WUO members similarly wrote that "creating new forms for living—collectives, communist relationships—and destroying the bourgeois consciousness in ourselves that keeps us from being able to touch, love, and struggle with each other against the Man is part of and necessary to destroying imperialism."[125] Consequentially, recreating society required developing a new way of looking at the world—one that involved loving each other and struggling with each other to make these significant changes.

The world the WUO envisioned was a socialist realm based in feminist, egalitarian principles. "Inside the Weather Machine" explained that destroying the imperialist system meant destroying domination and male supremacy: "male supremacy means dominating and Amerika [*sic*] is about dominating and controlling…. The system we live under is the oppressor and uses men to carry out its policies. By destroying this system we must destroy the relationships we had based on domination."[126] Getting rid of the imperialist system opened up the way to embrace socialism, and to relate to one another with respect to each other's humanity. Respecting individuals for who they were, for their intrinsic worth, and treating them fairly and equally was not only socialist, but also essentially feminist.

The WUO further drew out its feminist/socialist vision for a new world in its newspaper, *Osawatomie*. Here, the WUO laid out a multi-step program of what it stood for; the program was based in a stance against sexism, a commitment to the freedom of women, and support for class struggle and socialism in general. The group's program consisted of five key areas:

1. U.S. imperialism out of the Third World.
2. Peace. Opposes imperialist war and U.S. intervention.
3. Fight racism. Build an anti-racist base among white people. Support self-determination for oppressed people.
4. Struggle against sexism and for the freedom of women. Wage the class struggle. Fight for socialism. Power to the people.[127]

With the fourth point, the WUO was staking out for itself a feminist agenda. The WUO was openly aligning itself with feminist aims—such as the fight against sexism and freedom for women, akin to the second wave—while it was also proclaiming that it would fight for the rights of all peoples, and for socialism. This concern with the welfare of all peoples, whether minorities, Third World inhabitants, or women, bespoke an inclusive mindset, and set the WUO apart from some feminist groups of the time period. While the most visible second wave groups were concerned with the needs of women *qua* women, and implicitly embraced a white, middle class point of view, the WUO was dedicating itself to work for the interests of *all* peoples, in a conceptually third wave mold, which is the subject of the next chapter.

CHAPTER 5

The WUO's
Third Wave Approach

Writing on the topic of female liberation in a collective letter to the Women's Movement in 1973, the Weatherwomen penned these words:

> We are formalizing the beginning of an ongoing women's community in the underground. We live in many ways, mothers, lesbians, with men, with older women or alone, and are as varied as women anywhere. We look at each other in amazement, realizing how much it is possible for each one of us to grow, and that together we are part of giving birth to a new women's culture....[1]

They added:

> We cannot liberate ourselves in some vacuum of our own self-conception. The great majority of women in the world are bowed down by the questions of survival for themselves and their children, self-determination in their daily lives. The liberation of women cannot be realized while the United States empire [sic] remains the main consumer of the world's food, resources and energy. That is why our movement will have to take on the question of state power. And that is why our future is tied to the liberation of the Third World.[2]

Moreover, and by way of explaining their efforts to organize around feminist issues, the Weatherwomen's feminist summer study group from 1973 wrote in the packet "Six Sisters" that they worked in different groupings: one-on-one, study groups, collectives, front groups, underground and above ground women, etc. Through widespread collaboration and while on the run from the police, these women were deeply committed to creating an international revolution that was feminist, as they put it, "to build a program and actions that fought specifically for women."[3]

After nearly four years of deliberate feminist action, the Weatherwomen finally offered to other feminists a clear articulation of their ideology and intent. As the previous chapter indicated, there were some in the

mainstream women's liberation movement who denounced the Weatherwomen as inauthentic in their feminism. In their collective letter, the
Weatherwomen not only responded to those critiques, but also demonstrated how their feminist ideology, in fact, went much further than mainstream women's liberation, pushing the movement towards a more inclusive,
more expansive, and more revolutionary vision of feminism that was more
closely aligned to what conceptually speaking is the third wave.[4] This chapter explores the philosophy behind the WUO's brand of militant feminism,
paying particular attention to its alliance with Third World women and
its openness to a broader array of sexual desires, practices, and arrangements. In doing so, this chapter illustrates how the WUO's feminist platform disturbs the historical feminist wave motif previously established by
scholars, in that the WUO is temporally situated within the second wave
but contains third wave elements conceptually speaking. While the style
of feminism that the Weatherwomen espoused overlapped with the second
wave tradition, it also identified and developed third wave conceptual aims,
such as the inclusion and recognition of *all* women's subjectivities and an
unrestricted vision of the sexual liberation of women.

Firstly, this chapter explores how the WUO's brand of feminism was
all-encompassing and meant to be responsive to all kinds of oppressions,
weaving together the needs of *all* women, regardless of class, race, or
nationality. It also was a kind of feminism that fused personal context and
experience with a demand to oppose imperialist oppression. As such, the
Weatherwomen believed in aligning themselves with the struggles of Third
World women—and not just with the white middle class women generally
associated with the second wave. The Weatherwomen stated that they
wanted to forge an "international sisterhood" that would work to address
the needs and experiences of all women.[5]

Secondly, this chapter examines the WUO's openness to alternative
sexual identities and unfettered sexual experimentation—feminist positions that are usually recognized as being conceptually part of the third
wave.[6] The WUO, at times unsuccessfully, attempted to encourage sexual
experimentation as a norm within collectives. Their smash monogamy
campaign was designed to break up monogamous relationships. Origi-
nating with the Weatherwomen themselves, this campaign was intended
to be empowering for women, as it was meant to allow them to self-
identify as their own women, as opposed to only locating their identities
through associations with male partners. While there were instances where
this policy led to the sexual exploitation of female members, it also allowed
for a certain amount of sexual experimentation through which some

Weather members cast aside hetero-normativity and came out as gay or lesbian to their collectives. While there were obstacles and outright failures within the smash monogamy program, Weatherwomen and the WUO were advancing a theory of sexual freedom that would preview the more nuanced theories of sex positive feminists of the third wave.

The Limits of Bourgeois Feminism: Universal Sisterhood

The WUO's brand of feminism was multi-layered and complex. It fit closely within the second wave feminist agenda, but also contained third wave conceptual elements. It was a feminism based on the intersectionalities of gender, class, race, and imperialist oppression. While the WUO praised the achievements of the women's movement (such as women building and finding solidarity with other women, reclaiming their heritage and embracing a women's culture, and fighting sexism), it also set new goals for revolutionary women.[7] These goals would incorporate the perspectives and needs of poor, minority, and Third World women within the feminist movement.

This inclusive approach is a defining element of third wave feminism. As feminist theorist bell hooks explained in 1984, in "Feminism: A Movement to End Sexist Oppression," the second wave lacked the inclusion of all experiences and all subjectivities—instead, focusing more exclusively on the experiences of middle-class white women. hooks called for inclusivity and an avoidance of giving one group primacy in the fight for female liberation.[8] She wrote that "broader perspectives can only emerge when we examine both the personal that is political, the politics of society as a whole, and global revolutionary politics."[9] Third wave feminists took up hook's call for inclusivity and broadness of scope, as they fashioned a multiracial, multicultural, and multisexual style of feminism.[10] From this inclusive basis, third wave feminists saw themselves as being able to achieve significant social change that was responsive to multiple subjectivities.[11]

The WUO previewed both the inclusivity of the third wave and bell hooks' call for a broader perspective that included multiple experiences and blended politics with female liberation and revolution. In 1973, in the position paper "Mountain Moving Day," the Weatherwomen demonstrated this inclusive feminist stance. Writing that "we should view our feminist struggle in a world wide context," they expressed that feminism needed to be responsive to the needs of all women.[12] The Weatherwomen also warned that "we can't afford to put blinders on our faces, letting us see only the lot of American women. Women live in every country, are oppressed in many places."[13] Global alliances and inclusivity for all women was part of the WUO's feminist agenda.[14] In 1974, the WUO's *Prairie Fire* articulated that female liberation was predicated both on inclusivity and on building a coalition with Third World and poor women, not just with the so called bourgeois feminism of the second wave (which, through its middle class focus, was limited in its scope and point of view).[15] The WUO also saw a continued opposition to racism as part of its mission.[16]

More than a decade before bell hooks wrote about inclusivity, the WUO criticized their contemporary feminist activists as not being responsive enough to the needs of all women. As early as 1969, Bernardine Dohrn, in "Toward a Revolutionary Women's Movement," pointed to this shortcoming in the mainstream women's liberation movement. Starting out with a concern that separatist women's groups "promote a pop personality, individualistic view of the struggle and are based on an unstated white middle class consciousness and perspective," Dohrn articulated that the women's movement, as it operated at the time, was not integrating the needs and contexts of *all* women within its vision of equality.[17] Building on this concern, Dohrn further explained: "Most of the women's groups are bourgeois, unconscious or unconcerned with class struggle and the exploitation of working class women, and chauvinists concerning the oppression of black and brown women."[18] In Dohrn's analysis, these groups were failing to account for class or race, and the oppressions—such as poverty or racism—that these categories resulted in (and compounded). By implication, Dohrn was claiming that the WUO was not making this same mistake.

Previewing but also echoing hooks' and Dohrn's concern with a false sense of equality (that of middle-class white women to middle class white men), was Cathy Wilkerson's "Toward a Revolutionary Women's Militia." This piece argued that the feminist struggle should not just be about equality to men, as that simple focus could be dangerous and even racist. Rather, the feminist struggle needed to encompass anti-racism and self-determination struggles as an intrinsic component to female liberation. The WUO's brand of feminism, according to Wilkerson, addressed women's oppression *qua* women, but it was also politically informed: "White women workers who voted for Wallace could easily wage a national chauvinist struggle for equal wages with men, without understanding the relationship between their oppression and the oppression of Third World people, and therefore without understanding the relationship between their struggle and the struggles for national self-determination."[19] Just fighting for women's rights *qua* middle class, privileged women, without considering racism or classism, was not enough. Furthermore, in this manner, the WUO advocated intersectionality (a concern with how someone's class, race, sex, sexual orientation, gender, etc., produced interlocking oppressions, based on each aspect of that person's identity) before the term intersectionality was even coined.

Indeed, the WUO's feminist action was rooted in alliances with people of color and with those living in poverty. Moreover, the WUO rejected any compromising of this commitment to serve larger political ends. For example, the WUO criticized New York feminist groups, who, in the fight to promote the Equal Rights Amendment, allied themselves with a white conservative Republican assemblywoman from Queens who had a platform "against busing and for white control of the NYC school system" instead of "turning to the millions of Black and Puerto Rican women in the city for support."[20] In the WUO's analysis, supporting the Equal Rights Amendment did not need to come at the expense of poor, minority women (and that of their children). Not only was inclusiveness the right, moral thing to do out of a respect for each woman's experience, but in the WUO's estimation, it was also the strategic thing to do: feminist groups needed to align themselves with the female majority, not with racist politicians. Feminist groups needed to be aware of racism, needed to work with poor and minority women, and needed to focus on issues that affected *all* women.[21]

The WUO believed that it was imperative for feminists not to emphasize a uniform "sisterhood of everywoman," but rather to focus on the real life, varied challenges women experienced, within their various contexts, as these were defined based on their class, race, and other sociological statuses.[22] An awareness of intersectionality needed to be the foundational basis for any action—as even a feminist action could negatively impact women. The WUO noted that inequalities in power had real life consequences, such as when the pharmaceutical industry experimented on Third World women living in Puerto Rico, Haiti, and within the United States to develop the birth control pill. The birth control pill Enovid, to gain FDA approval, conducted trials in Puerto Rico—as such, Puerto Rican women were experimented on (and their complaints of headaches, rashes, weight gain, etc., were dismissed as hysterical when they were in fact caused by the high percentage of hormones present in the pill).[23] Procreative control for one group of women translated into loss of life or injuries for another group of women—this model, in the WUO's estimation was problematic and unfair, because *all* women deserved and needed to be awarded the same dignity and respect within society. An awareness of the privileges of class and race was therefore needed so as to ensure that minority, poor, or Third World women were not marginalized or exploited.

To respond to these issues, Dohrn proposed a new kind of feminism: "A revolutionary women's movement must be politically based on the most oppressed sectors—black, brown and white working-class women."[24] This feminism—aware of the injustices, oppressions, and varied experiences of all women based on their own, unique contexts—had a better chance to achieve real change that would benefit all women's lives. Dohrn was quick to explain that this revolutionary feminism did not mean that middle class women should not organize to address their own needs, but rather that, to achieve real, overall social change, "our immediate job is to organize masses of women around the full scope of radical demands—including the destruction of male supremacy."[25]

This point, that women needed to be organized so as to respond to various needs (including the need to eradicate sexism) within their lives, was also present in the WUO's 1975-1976 article "The Women's Question Is a Class Question."[26] Here the WUO argued that women needed a "movement that reaches into every office, sweatshop, household and high school to demand jobs, equal pay, adequate income, day care, the right to unionize, an end to every type of racial discrimination and equality for women."[27] Acting from a basis of solidarity, women would be able to support each other as they worked to achieve change for one another through organized action. The article categorically stated that this effort should not be just a bourgeois movement, but should reach out to poor women and working women—to do any less, it added, would perpetuate "a false notion of women's liberation as the property of a small and precious group of women."[28] Clearly, the WUO was embracing a sense of inclusiveness that was emblematic of the third wave and that moved beyond second wave demands for equal pay and employment and educational opportunities discussed in the previous chapter.

Further underscoring the importance of inclusiveness, cooperation, and solidarity with women's real-life problems, the Weatherwomen crafted poems that aligned them with the goal of liberation for all women in their book *Sing a Battle Song*. With "Revolution is our way of liberation!" proudly inscribed as the epigraph for the volume's introduction, the Weatherwomen explained that their feminism espoused a rhetoric that allied them with the needs and struggles of women everywhere, from the United States to the Third World.[29] As they put it in the introduction to the poems, "we are joining our lives with the needs and aspirations of poor and working class women; we are learning our strengths as women fighting for liberation alongside our sisters here and around the world."[30] Thus, their poems made references to the individual subjectivities, needs, and experiences of women from various backgrounds.

One poem in which the Weatherwomen attempt to show sympathy for real women's issues is "Spider Poem":

> spider, spin me a world web
> touch women far away
> I go slide down the strands
> subway spider strands
> to other lands
> touch other hands
> spider, spider a world web
> a meeting place to share a meal...
> warm baths and back rubs
> shared children
> shared fire
> shared burdens...
> we will meet
> all of us
> women of every land
> children on backs, in
> arms, in shopping carts...
> to discuss
> to simply discuss
> to simply discuss amongst
> ourselves
> our lives
> and what is to be done
> and with our fine spidernet
> we intend
> to entangle
> the powers
> that bury
> our children.[31]

Here, the Weatherwomen linked women's experiences to the possibility of political, social change from shared oppression and burdens. The Weatherwomen recognized that women from other countries and from various economic classes would have different experiences from each other ("children on backs, in arms, children in shopping carts"), but still tapped into a shared experience that helped provide a basis for female unity: motherhood and a devout interest in the welfare of children. The concentration on shared experiences still allowed for a recognition of individualized subjectivities, as the poem referred to "other lands" and insisted on a frank discussion of all "our lives."

The use of a spider's web is a perfect metaphor for this purpose. On the one hand, it is sprawling ("a world web") and it unites women who are both separated across the planet ("touch women far away") and suffer under oppressive patriarchy in their own ways ("shared fire, shared burden"). On the other hand, the spider web represents a shared response against this oppression ("we intend to entangle the powers that bury our children"). What was once a fragile and weak web almost becomes a reinforced net—a transformation nourished by the collaboration of women working across the globe—that remediates female suffering. Therefore, this poem both fits second wave feminism in its sisterhood motif and in its aim to resolve issues that touch on child raising, but it also clearly fits into a third wave feminist narrative by recognizing the vast differences of women across nations.

Another poem that also fits this motif is "Women's Lament," dating from 1971. The poem laments the death of children due to war and culminates by calling on all women to "let us wail and weep together/so that our lament/becomes—also—a weapon/which we direct against the vicious demons/who haunt our world today."[32] The demons described are war strategists and the White House. It goes on:

> Let us wail at the gates of the White House
> night and day
> Let us wail at air force and navy bases
> to give solace to young men who are resisting
> and to send in the echoes of the ages
> to arrogant men who think
> they are the torch bearers of "civilization."
> And let us wail at the homes of the strategists
> who masquerade
> as ordinary citizens, determining the values
> by which we live.
>
> These men
> must not conduct war
> in peace.
> Our grieving
> will become a cancer within ourselves
> if we do not turn it into
> vengeance.[33]

This poem finds commonality in the shared experiences of women across the globe—women who have their kids killed by "bombs [diving] into the children's bed" or women who have the privilege to live in the imperialist motherland—and calls on them all to come together to resist the war makers (the "demons").[34] The Weatherwomen's poem envisions fruitful collaboration across the globe for the shared goal of ending suffering and death. It is also important to note that the some of the lines could also be interpreted as an endorsement toward militant action. In this case, the Weatherwomen could be interpreted as saying that for women whose children were dying across the globe, militant and aggressive protest ("let us wail and weep together.... Our grieving will become a cancer within ourselves/if we do not turn it into/vengeance") might be justified as a means of preventing further loss of life.[35]

Importantly, both "Spider Poem" and "Women's Lament" suggest that these Weatherwomen were looking for an active response to these problems. The active response for the Weatherwomen included cohesion as a basis of action: solidarity across class and race. A 1973 poem titled "For Assata Shakur" further underlined this ideal of collaboration and solidarity with women of color. From its inception, the WUO saw itself as a supporter of the Black Panther Party. Assata Shakur was a member of the Black Panther Party and then became a member of the Black Liberation Army. She was arrested by New Jersey state troopers on May 2, 1973 (the same that year the poem was written) on charges of murder, assault, and armed robbery.[36] With this poem, the WUO once again advertised its inclusive stance, even when it meant that it was forging a coalition with individuals hunted by the police:

> And during those last months
> when they hunted you hard
> I was an invisible supporter,
> working another front...
> And when you were captured, sister,
> I wept
> for all of us.[37]

The WUO's active response to oppression and injustice also included a commitment to militancy, which would be used to protect the interests of *all* women. The 1974 poem "Foodlines in Oakland" took up this point:

> People are standing in lines, women mostly;
> folded shopping bags, hats against the sun
> swaying crowd
> somber chatting glad...
> the vultures, cameramen,
> descend to record the defiant dignity
> the disorder
> the human and ordinary need for food
> Crumbs and raw anger now hurled back.

Hungry hands
empty yet
can hold a rock, clench a furious fist,
as they have held hoes and brooms and babies
for generations.[38]

Through this poem, not only did the Weatherwomen shine a light on the insensitive and disrespectful portrayal of poor, minority women in the media, but they intrinsically claimed solidarity with these women, in a third wave fashion. The Weatherwomen expressed outrage on these impoverished women's behalf.

In "Foodlines in Oakland," the Weatherwomen also implied that shared need and poverty were a legitimization for militant action; severe, systematic poverty reflected a need for immediate social change through militant feminism. After all, the fact that there were people, children included, starving in America, a land where there was plenty of food available in any grocery store, was in itself a kind of violence against those hungry individuals. It was a further attack on the hungry people to put their pain and suffering on display, as if they had no dignity by virtue of being poor. If these people were starving, and if there were people who could help but instead let people starve, then it would seem like those people would have rights of self-defense to protect themselves and their children. This poem also points to the communalism of socialism. As discussed in the previous chapter, the WUO had a vision of a socialist society where all members would help one another and live aligned with feminist principles. Under such a system, they believed that injustices such as the ones described in this poem would not happen, as the entire community would eradicate hunger and ensure that needy individuals were helped. The Weatherwomen were pointing out that for starving women, violence ("hold a rock, clench a furious fist") may be justified as a means of self-defense. All of these poems, then, exhibit the idea that the WUO's brand of feminism was therefore action-oriented and inclined towards employing militant tactics for goals that would help improve *all* women's lives.

Imperialism and Inclusive Feminism

The WUO's full sense of inclusiveness integrated Third World women, but this addition would lack substance if it did not come along with an understanding of the specific nature of those women's unique experiences—with a comprehending, that is, of what incidents they endured and what life obstacles they faced while living under imperialism. Both the Weatherwomen and later third wave feminists agree upon this point. In 1997, J. Ann Tickner explained that under imperialism, state apparati tend to ignore and marginalize women's issues in favor of upholding state interests.[39] In 2000, Cynthia Enloe expounded that imperialism and capitalism victimized women in colonized states.[40] For example, women suffer under imperialism by being forced into the sex tourism industry, by suffering economically (being employed in low paying/unskilled jobs), or are affected by economic sanctions, militarization, rape, etc.[41] Decades prior to these critiques, the WUO showed a similar concern with how imperialism affected women's lives.

In *Prairie Fire*, the WUO articulated the following analysis concerning the connections between sexism and imperialism:

> Under imperialism, the organization and fabric of society—the family, production, reproduction, and all social relations—keep women dependent and powerless. Sexism is this institutionalized and encouraged system of control. In the Third World, imperialism imposes the most brutal forms of modern sexism. Women are murdered/tortured, sterilized/raped, stifled/crippled, owned/exploited under the banner of male supremacy.[42]

The way the WUO saw it, imperialist control of other countries translated into controlling the population of those countries—keeping the people docile and unresisting to colonial rule. This control extended to women, as colonized women were trained to be passive, taught that they were weak, and were generally kept in subordinate positions both in relation to their colonizers and to colonized men. Colonized men might have propagated sexist attitudes so as to maintain a sense of superiority—at least over colonized women—in the face of imperialism, but they were also pushed to adopt sexist attitudes by the imperialist system.[43] This point also was previously developed in the meetings of the feminist summer program conducted by Weatherwomen in the summer of 1973. Weatherwomen analyzed the hierarchy created by the capitalist/imperialist state, noting that women (and children) were at the bottom of the ladder.[44]

Prairie Fire explained that the root of sexism under imperialism was premised in possession and stated, "Imperialism lays claim to all the natural resources of the colonized society, including the women. They are valued and controlled as laborers, breeders, and sexual commodities."[45] This schema positioned women in undervalued, precarious situations that further constrained their lives: the WUO argued that imperialism forced urbanization that resulted in the displacement of women and in their increased dependency on men or on factory jobs.[46] Furthermore, factory jobs devalued women's labor, as women were paid the worst, just at subsistence level.[47]

Both third wave feminists and the WUO pointed out that one of the most heinous mechanisms of imperialist control was rape. In the year 2000, third wave feminist Cynthia Enloe, in her *Maneuvers: The International Politics of Militarizing Women's Lives*, discussed rape as a weapon of war against women in militarized zones.[48] Used to intimidate, control, degrade, coerce, or humiliate, Enloe explains that state governments or troops widely employ rape to "guarantee that authority is so crystal clear that it is always—and quickly—obeyed."[49]

Previewing Enloe's analysis, the WUO argued that soldiers or male invaders could adopt a sexist attitude and feel more emboldened to act unjustly or cruelly in war or invasions from an allegedly privileged position against inferior humans (that is, colonized women). As a vivid instance of this point, the WUO noted that rape was often used as a weapon of colonial wars, such as in the Vietnam War, stating: "Rape and sexual abuse is the prerogative of the conqueror, a means of undermining women's resistance, a murderous assault, part of the arsenal of control and domination."[50] Oppression through imperialism and sexism led to a culture that valued women as sexual commodities to be used and discarded at will.

Another oppression that the WUO pointed out when it came to Third World women related to the issues of sterilization and the loss of bodily integrity. The WUO noted that as part of population control, U.S. imperialism sterilized Third World Women; missionaries, along with various foundations and family planning clinics were limiting potentially dangerous populations through sterilizations.[51] The WUO also pointed out that sterilizations were attempted against allegedly dangerous populations within the United States, noting that Congress tried to sterilize Japanese women in internment camps during World War II.[52] Simply put, imperialism required the control of the subjugated populace, or, as the WUO stated, "it is easier to kill a guerrilla in the womb than in the mountains."[53] The WUO pointed out that often times, when it came to Third World countries, mandatory birth control was a condition for receiving foreign aid.[54]

A few years later, and still consistent with their inclusive feminism, in the article "Puerto Rico Is the Test of Fire of Anti-Imperialism," the WUO focused on the economic plight of women in Puerto Rico, also noting that Puerto Rican women were sterilized without genuine consent.[55] The WUO also noted that Puerto Rican families survived on less than $200 per year. Additionally, in this article, the WUO discussed the plight of Puerto Rican women living on welfare in New York.[56] In "An Open Letter to the U.S. Workers" in the same issue of *Osawatomie*, Bernardine Dohrn explained that solidarity was needed with Puerto Ricans, and highlighted that Puerto Rican women were suffering oppression from "the lowest-paying dangerous jobs; malnutrition and hunger for their children because 70% of the people must depend on food stamps; and a 40 year U.S. program of forced sterilization."[57] By bringing forward all of these issues, the WUO was weaving together an intersectional feminism, one that was aware of the interrelated oppressions experienced by Puerto Rican women living under imperialism.

Taking up another critique of imperialism—the control of the economy and the food supply by powerful global economies to the detriment of Third World, developing nations—the Weatherwomen's "Malthusian Mythologies" poem wove these issues of imperialism and bodily integrity together:

—'There are too many people in the world
and not enough food.'
—No, we said, a few control the world's food.
Food as weapon Food as profit
—'Well, the poor in Latin America
would have to come here then,
where there is plenty.'
—They are forced to grow, we said,
tobacco and coffee for the Yankees.
You can't feed children cash crops.
—'Too many mouths, too much suffering, not enough corn,
better to lessen the burden.'
—Give back the land, the ore the copper the tin,
we cried.
Don't take away the babies!

...

Can you imagine the head of HEW
announcing support for more
Black babies
and Puertorriquenos and Eskimos?
"There's no space for all those brown babies here."
It's a child-beating society,
Divided against selfsame blood,
eager to export the solutions:
U.S. prime sterilizations
of the life processes;
A death culture
carried by missionaries and Rockefeller agents:
the peddlers of chains that tie the tubes.
They come wrapped in signs saying: Free the Women.

Mirror of history
mirror of war, fear of the fast-breeding poor.
"it is cheaper to kill a guerrilla in the womb
than in the mountains."
Genocide.
Women, sisters,
We must discover uncover
ways to bear and ways to not bear;
birth and death are sacred rights of people.
These men confound them:
they war on wombs.
Upside down planning from the rich...[58]

Here, the Weatherwomen point out U.S. imperialist policy and attempted to mobilize against it, by calling on women to take up their "sacred rights"— their human rights—in deciding for themselves whether to have children, how to live their lives, and how to resist imperialist pressure.

Calling out white feminist groups for ignoring the plight of their sisters of color in and outside the continental United States, the WUO embraced an inclusive brand of feminism. Addressing mainstream, white feminist groups, the WUO asked pointedly, "Do they attack the criminal fact that 34% of women of child bearing age in Puerto Rico, a U.S. colony, have been sterilized?"[59] Sterilization concerns were noted also in "Six Sisters," where Weatherwomen drew attention to the problematic sterilization of poor, minority women, women seeking welfare benefits, and the infamous sterilization case of the Relf sisters in Alabama.[60] The WUO forcefully argued that poor women and Third World women needed to not be "used for medical experimentation and profit, subject to forced sterilization, and unsafe 'family planning.'"[61] In other position papers, the WUO also noted the plight of Native American women and identified Native Americans as a group to also be supported in their struggle for liberation.[62] Marginalized women at home and Third World women, in the WUO's estimation, needed the support of allies to assert their authentic desires and autonomously choose their own life plans.

Though the Weatherwomen were pointing to problems in the lives of Third World women, they were not doing so from a false perspective of superiority. Instead, the WUO saw Third World women as aspirational models of revolutionary feminism. "Honky Tonk Women" explained that women in Vietnam and Cuba were active agents and leaders in their own right and were "winning formal equality in a process that began when they picked up the gun to destroy the U.S. These revolutionary women are liberating themselves in a national struggle."[63]

The motif of Third World women as exemplars is also seen in the poem "People's War," in *Sing a Battle Song*. Alluding to the example of "women warriors" who held back the "Mongol invaders" for "two thousand years of war," this poem states that the Weatherwomen look up to these models of strength. In fact, the poem states that "we honor those who went before" and goes on to acknowledges that the tenacity of Vietnamese women fighters is a model the Weatherwomen strive to follow:

> Still you persevere,
> tired faces, with a subtle and quiet confidence
> the leaders in their worn clothes
> gather in a semi-circle
> at a meeting in the forest
> The eyes of your children
> The smile of Ho
> A woman's laughter before a song begins.
> Your faces are all in our dreams.[64]

Notice that in this poem, the female exemplars are active fighters, but they still laugh, sing, and are there for their children. These women are complex, multi-dimensional beings who are politically aware, active agents fighting for political change—they inhabit a space where leadership and mother-hood intertwine seamlessly. This imagining dismantles gender norms and re-envisions the world in a new vein.

"Mountain Moving Day" likewise reasserted the view that Third World women were models for the Weatherwomen. Here, Weatherwomen wrote that "we have learned so much from our Vietnam sisters in the recent years"; they also explained that they have much to learn "from Cuban sisters."[65] The Weatherwomen also allowed that the process of learning was a give and take, where all parties taught/learned/reflected on their practices. This document also added that the white women's movement should not be threatened by these international perspectives.[66]

Accordingly, the WUO's militant feminism derived from the examples they saw in the Third World, such as in Cuba or Vietnam. As the Weatherwomen put it, "The women of Vietnam were our model. We had met with them ... heard their battle stories, and saw them gaining freedom in the process of their people's war for independence."[67] Learning from the revolutionary examples of minority and Third World Women would make for effective, social change and achieve real equality. More concretely, Weatherwoman Laura Whitehorn explained that members of the Vietnam Women's Union advised the WUO to work cooperatively and use strategic planning, as these tools would result in successful armed actions.[68] And Whitehorn also adds, "We were organized and inspired by the examples of Vietnam and other national liberation movements, where women played leading roles."[69] The WUO was clearly open to learning from international exemplars.

Following the lead they saw in Third World women fighting for their freedom, the WUO felt the fight for a new society must be worldwide. In "Inside the Weather Machine," the WUO stated: "Women must pick up the gun and kill the pig. Our liberation depends on this fight as well as seeing this fight as part of a worldwide struggle with all the people of the world."[70] In the WUO's estimation, this worldwide focus was the key to creating meaningful change; doing any less was racist and irresponsible. As "Honky Tonk Women" indicated, if white middle class women did not realize that imperialism was problematic for the well being of the women (and men) of the world, then these white women were replicating the problem of imperialism, all the while winning false victories as part of their feminist struggle. Their victories would count as hollow, in the WUO's analysis, because the imperialist system would give in to these women's demands, while setting them up as a privileged class of women, at the expense of all the other women of the world, all in an effort to maintain the imperialist system. As the WUO explained, "recent history shows us that imperialist pigs are willing to make great sacrifices, grant huge demands, to keep white people on their side."[71]

White women therefore needed to realize that "U.S. imperialism is our common enemy, and white women must join in this fight before they can win anything but empty transitional demands."[72] Furthermore, the WUO charged that if white women ignored what was happening in the Third World, that behavior was racist: "For white women to fight for 'equal rights or right to work, right to organize for equal pay, promotions, better conditions...' while the rest of the world is trying to destroy imperialism, is racist."[73] Rather, they argued that the responsible choice for all feminists was to adopt the WUO's brand of feminism because it deliberately incorporated all subjectivities and identified imperialism and sexism as equal threats. Thus, "Honky Tonk Women" explained, "a real strategy for victory is not to get masses of people to fight with you for a few more crumbs—day-care centers for white women, equal pay with white men—but to fight with them against the source of our real oppression—pig Amerika [sic]."[74] Interestingly, the Bread and Roses collective noted that this WUO analysis (that imperialism was problematic and an inclusive focus was needed for feminism) was correct, noting that "some of Weatherman's criticism is well-founded. Our internationalism has been sporadic and apologetic."[75]

The WUO's feminism was multi-ethnic, multi-national, and attempted to incorporate all women, especially Third World women, in its scope.

"Mountain Moving Day" also defined the WUO's commitment to a feminism based on intersectionality and inclusivity. It explained that the WUO's perspective saw anti-imperialism, anti-racism, and anti-sexism as interlocked, and advised that "race, class, sexual orientation, age" needed to be accounted for when conceiving of feminist action with a world-wide outlook.[76] As Weatherman chronicler Harold Jacobs stated, the WUO did not want to limit itself to "demands for material improvements in the lives of white women" because those were "not only readily co-optable, but avoid the most profound source of women's oppression."[77] Solidarity with all oppressed groups, especially the Third World, was a priority for the WUO. Thus, in a way that was more consistent with the third wave's movement against globalization from above, the WUO supported a position where all oppressed persons, including all women, joined together to fight against the imperialist system.

Incorporating Different Sexual Identities

In keeping with its third wave approach, the WUO's brand of feminism was also inclusive of non-heterosexual relationships, at least in theory—the Weathermen certainly did not completely overcome their homophobia and heterosexism. Harold Jacobs explained that "weatherman looks favorably on women developing 'full sexual and political relationships with women' alongside their relationships with men."[78] This sexual openness fits well within the third wave model, as third wavers embrace not only multiple identities but also encourage and support all types of consensual sexual relations. As Mimi Marinucci, in her 2010 book *Feminism Is Queer: The Intimate Connection between Queer and Feminist Theory*, stated: "this solidarity [between feminists and queer theorists] seems born of a deep understanding that the oppression of women and the suppression of lesbian, gay, bisexual, and transgender existence are deeply intertwined. Feminist identity, like LGBT identity, stretches the boundaries of established categories of gender, sex, and sexuality."[79] The WUO's feminism at least attempted to capture this sense of solidarity by including lesbian women in its feminist positions.

As Harold Jacobs noted above, the WUO encouraged alternative sexual arrangements between adults, supporting alternative sexual expression without judgment. Bernardine Dohrn, in a conversation with non–Weatherwoman Jane Alpert, referred to this open acceptance within the WUO:

"Some of our women are lesbians and are active in the gay rights movement. A few are living in an all-women collective."[80] Dohrn indicates not only that WUO members were forging alliances with the gay rights movement, but also that the organization was creating space, quite literally, for women to explore alternative living arrangements and lifestyles.

Some bonds between non-heterosexual members were celebrated—and seem to have inspired WUO members—as the poem "For Two Sisters" indicates:

i [*sic*] think of you often
womanlove(rs)
sound of your steps
up the cellar stairs
emerging from the basement
in the mornings
still drowsy with sleep
lovemaking on your breath
on your bodies
aura of smells and warmth enveloped you then
it wasn't the words we spoke
or the things we did together
that have stayed with/in me these years
but the touch of your closeness and
womandepth [*sic*] of your loving
that have become for me
a time worn mirror
into which i've [*sic*] often looked
seeking my reflection there[81]

Describing the intimacy between two women—lovers and revolutionaries—this poem illustrates the acceptance of lesbian relationships within the WUO. The closeness and intimacy of the two women ("drowsy with sleep," "lovemaking on your breath") emerge as respected and even cherished by the author ("the touch of your closeness and womandepth [*sic*] of your loving that have become for me a time worn mirror"). This poem can also be interpreted as a coming out poem, as the author concludes that the love shared by the two women created a "time worn mirror" into which the author seeks her own reflection ("i've [*sic*] often looked seeking my reflection there"), perhaps as she embraces her own sexuality.

FBI infiltrator Larry Grathwohl reported on the open minded sexual attitudes of the WUO, stating that some of the women within the organization wanted to be completely independent from men, even when it came to sex: "Some of them even said that men were unnecessary for sex."[82] Moreover, he added that WUO members believed that "sex for pleasure could be enjoyed between two women just a much as between a man and a woman...."[83] According to Grathwohl, the WUO also felt that a liberated man could "enjoy sex with other men."[84]

Furthermore, the Weatherwomen's letter to the Women's Movement stated, "We live in many ways, mothers, lesbians, with men..." alluding to acceptance and unity within the WUO.[85] Weatherwoman Laura White- horn adds, "Most of our group's members were women, and lots of us were lesbian."[86] In some collectives, this supportive and open atmosphere enabled lesbian and gay members to come out to their peers. As Weath- erman David Gilbert remembers, that's exactly what happened in the Colorado WUO collective, where two gay men came out to the rest of the group.[87]

However, there were difficulties when it came to fostering this sup- portive, inclusive attitude in regard to sexual orientation. The open atti- tude did not extend to all the collectives: in San Francisco, Michael Novick did not feel enough support from his collective to come out with respect to his sexual orientation or to experiment sexually with other men.[88] Gilbert explains that in his collective, in 1972-1973, WUO members tack- led issues relating to sexual orientation, attempting to address concerns and to foster inclusiveness: "Our collective also held our first group dis- cussions of the politics of sexual orientation, as lesbian and gay members explained that they felt little support inside the organization for lesbian/ gay culture and politics."[89] While the having of this conversation bespeaks the reality that gay and lesbian members did not feel perfectly accepted, it nevertheless underlines the fact that heterosexual members were attempting to be sympathetic and worked on fostering inclusiveness when it came to sexual orientation.

The WUO's attempts, while not entirely successful, to promote sexual openness were linked to their view that sexual experimentation or non- heterosexual sexual acts were revolutionary. "Honky Tonk Women" equated same-sex affairs with breaking down bourgeois values: "Women sleeping with other women, developing full sexual and political relationships with each other, indicates that we are beginning to really destroy the bourgeois values we have believed in for such a long time."[90] Evidence that sexual experimentation through same-sex encounters were viewed positively also comes from the fact that some members thought these interactions may have been required to be revolutionaries. As Gilbert explained, "I remem- ber guiltily confessing to the Bureau member visiting Denver, and feeling my local leadership role was in question: 'I don't know why, but I just can't get myself into having sex with a man.' He responded with a laugh and said, 'There's absolutely no requirement that you do so.'"[91] Though same-sex encounters were not required, they were thought to be positive experiences for revolutionaries, at least in some collectives.

In *Prairie Fire*, the WUO's stance on sexual orientation was clarified. Writing on the achievements of the women's movement, the WUO explained its own position when it came to sexual identity and orientation:

> Lesbianism has been an affirmation of unity and a challenge to the partnership of sexuality and domination. Women have opposed the dominant culture's treatment of homosexuals—people who are harassed and assaulted, denied employment and housing, raped and even murdered because they don't conform to standard sexual roles and morality. Not all gay culture transcends the sexism of U.S. life, but the independence of gay people to live according to their own definitions represent an attack on sexist ideology which subjugates women. We support the right of all people to live according to their sexual preferences without discrimination or fear of reprisals.[92]

The WUO's support and solidarity with non-heteronormative sexual orientations or arrangements was clear. The WUO was inclusive of these identities and held the view that discrimination based on sexual orientation was wrong. Hence, while some members of the WUO definitely struggled with their own homophobia or heterosexism, the closest assessment as to an official position of the organization was that it was in favor of gay rights and supported same-sex acts as inherently revolutionary. The WUO's view on sexual orientation then was not only about being inclusive, but about a new way of thinking of sexual acts: the Weatherwomen saw the potential for sex to be transformative and empowering, which places them within the sex positive movement of third wave feminism.

Sex Positive Weather

In the 1990s, sex positive feminists argued that sexuality was a positive value in women's lives, and that sexual pleasure and sexual autonomy were to be embraced and feted. Third wave feminists such as Linda LeMoncheck held that feminism should promote "the kind of sexual agency and self-definition for women that will maximize sexual pleasure and satisfaction," especially when sexual activity "deviates from the acceptable norm."[93] In third wave analysis, sexuality was "a means of transforming the repressive sexual climate of patriarchy."[94] As long as sexual encounters were based on respect and mutual desire, instances of sexual expression were to be respected and embraced.[95] Furthermore, as Neeru Tandon put it, "sex positive feminism centers on the idea that sexual freedom is an essential component of women's freedom."[96] In a third wave vein, the WUO also viewed sexuality as something to be recognized, welcomed, and celebrated; sexuality was a part of a full, meaningful existence, and a necessary component of a revolutionary life. Weather members advocated openness toward sexual experimentation and toward relationships that were based on respect and equality.

Sex positivism infused the writing of the Weatherwomen. Cathy Wilkerson, in "Toward a Revolutionary Women's Militia," argued that men and women needed to change from the way they related to one another, and to break down the entrenched gender patterns that defined male/female relationships. She wrote,

> Within the Movement it is crucial that men and women both begin to fight against the vestiges of bourgeois ideology within themselves, to break down existing forms of social relationships. Only by developing forms in which we can express love in non-exploitative and non-competitive ways will men and women develop their full human and revolutionary potential for struggle.[97]

The WUO's aim was to restructure relationships so that these connections would result in gender equality and mutual admiration; sexual partners were not there for exploitation but were to be respected fully, as individuals with authentic desires.

This aim was not empty rhetoric, as Weather members practiced openness and embraced various lifestyles within their collectives or affinity groups. As Harold Jacobs explains, WUO affinity groups—made up of collective members who knew each other and had strong bonds of friendship or activism—practiced, respected, and incorporated a variety of lifestyles within their revolutionary practice.[98] Sometimes an affinity group was the core group of a collective; sometimes it was the entire collective. Affinity groups usually participated in actions together, looking out for one another during these actions (running together through police lines, helping one another if injured, etc.). These affinity groups were formed on the basis of "friendship and trust."[99] As Jacob states, the WUO embraced "a plethora of life styles: some involved communal living, some are made up exclusively of women or men, and sexual and personal relationships within groups run the gamut from fairly straight to highly experimental."[100] In spite of this position, David Gilbert notes that while WUO collectives would be supportive of various sexual orientations, homophobia was not necessarily eradicated in *all* members.[101] Laura Whitehorn supports this point, also noting that the WUO could have done even more to programmatically and concretely support gay and lesbian liberation.[102]

An anonymous Weatherwoman explained that the sexually liberated attitude of the WUO lead to increased sexual experimentation: "Women who never saw themselves making it with other women began digging each other sexually. People who live together and fight together fuck together. What Weatherman [WUO] is doing is creating new standards for men and women to relate to. We are trying to make sex non-exploitative as we don't use our bodies to control situations."[103] In other words, the WUO respected sexual autonomy in a way that inspired the formation of other sexual bonds, based on mutual respect and mutual enjoyment. Sex was supposed to be liberating and empowering, and not to be used as a weapon, at least in WUO's theorizing. Note that this approach supports female autonomy and theoretically shifts the background framework in a way that prioritizes women's agency and independence. When Diana Ougthon was criticizing Bill Ayers for his practice of free love, it was based on a situation where Ayers had power and the women were relegated to disposable objects of his desire. This new approach is trying to create egalitarian bonds where men and women approached their sexual interactions in ways that were liberating and not constrained by hierarchal power relations.

Smash monogamy was an important element of the WUO's sexual agenda that was intended to further this idea that sexuality should be kept separate from hierarchy in a liberating fashion. Smash monogamy was a practice that aimed to dismantle monogamous relationships between collective members based on the idea that a couple's exclusivity could have a controlling effect on the woman in the relationship while giving too much authority to the man. "Honky Tonk Women" advocated that "monogamous relationships must be broken up—so that the people involved, but especially the women, can become whole people, self-reliant and independent, able to carry out whatever is necessary to the revolution."[104] Hence, smash monogamy was intended to support women's autonomy by eliminating the hindrances to that autonomy that were often occasioned by exclusive, heteronormative relationships that were often marked by a gendered power relation within a patriarchal society.

The idea of doing away with traditional monogamy—and the conservative gender norms it entailed—was the result of a women's caucus meeting in Cleveland, Ohio, over the 1969 Labor Day weekend. An anonymous Weatherwomen reported in "Inside the Weather Machine" that

> women spoke about the need to break up monogamous relationships. These relationships are built around weakness and dependency. They're usually one man/one woman, although varieties spring up. Women identify themselves through their men and usually get introduced as someone's girl. Monogamous relationships are set up because people see them as the only way to feel secure and loved ... both members are into

trying to make each other feel safe ... they can always hide in each other when the reality becomes too heavy; they can always protect each other from having to fight oppression.[105]

Continuing the assessment that relationships defined women as men's property, this Weatherwoman equated the breaking up of monogamy with liberation.[106] She also stated that women were socially trained to seek out relationships and to measure their self-worth according to their relationship status. Women "clung to men because they had no other identity."[107] Breaking out of this pattern was supposed to encourage women to define themselves as their own persons. Through smash monogamy, women would grow into autonomous individuals who developed their own life plans and inclinations according to their own beliefs and perspectives. An anonymous Weatherwoman gave evidence from her own collective as to these positive results of the program: "Destroying the one man/one woman relationship was perhaps the most liberating thing that happened to us. We could speak up at meetings without being uptight ... we became self-reliant and don't have to protect anyone."[108] There was then evidence of positive results from the smash monogamy initiative.

Georgia, a Weatherwoman from the Seattle Collective—and a participant of the Cleveland meeting where the smash monogamy concept was introduced—also commented on the positives she had noted while in Cleveland: "Some couples broke up right there, and the women who had been real quiet before, you know, like women generally are, suddenly they were different. They looked different, talked different. They began to talk up more at meetings, and many of the men were surprised; the women had their own ideas and opinions."[109] In Georgia's estimation, smash monogamy had immediate positive results, as women began to act as their own individuals and to assert their agencies. Smash monogamy, then, appealed to some Weather members and served them as a viable tool for self-empowerment.

While there were these positive stories that resulted from smash monogamy, the overall results appeared to be less favorable. As WUO chronicler Ron Jacobs put it, "Doing away with traditional forms of monogamy was not necessarily a bad idea and formed part of a strategy to end male supremacist attitudes in the organization, but the authoritarian manner in which it was undertaken caused much useless dissension and emotional stress."[110] According to Weatherwoman Susan Stern, throughout WUO collectives during the summer of 1969, some couples separated in accordance with the policy, but others refused to put their love on the line for the sake of the revolution and instead left the WUO. In her own

Seattle collective, Stern noted that two WUO members named Jay and Beverly refused to give up their relationship in spite of the smash monogamy line, and stuck to their exclusivity in spite of pressure to separate.[111] Weatherman David Gilbert makes the same assessment as Stern, noting that smash monogamy placed undue pressure on couples to separate.[112] The paper "Weather Letter" noted a related concern, namely that smash monogamy, in its demand to separate couples, actually hurt the revolution and diminished the membership of the WUO. Thus, this 1970 document explained that the WUO reworked its smash monogamy platform, recognizing that "there are great possibilities for love between two people struggling to be revolutionaries."[113] The Weatherwomen writing the collective letter to the women's movement also noted this outcome: they write that while it was a "battle" to instantiate the smash monogamy policy so as to ensure that "we could be free of the 'couple form,' [to] be our own persons," this policy was fraught by a "lack of realism about what it meant for most women as a demand."[114] In this sense, then, the Weatherwomen recognized that members' sexual subjectivities should be respected and that their prior, over-eager prescription of the smash monogamy campaign might not suit everyone.

Even though smash monogamy did not work out as a viable policy for the WUO, its goals may have been valuable in and of themselves. Smash monogamy was supposed to encourage sexual liberation and break people free from their sexual repression. Like sex positive feminists of the third wave, the WUO felt that sexual liberation could derive from sexual experimentation. For instance, in 2008, sex positive feminist Heather Corinna wrote, "there are no barriers beyond the limits of our own imagination when it comes to rewriting the scripts of our sexual ideals, our individual sexual lives, and what we present to ourselves, our sisters, our daughters."[115] Weatherwoman Stern recalled that "group gropes, homosexuality, autosexuality, or asexuality" were all viewed as viable replacements for "antiquated monogamous relationships."[116] In both cases, these feminists (the WUO and Corinna) are calling for an opening of our minds to a variety of new ways to think about sex and women's sexuality that are not limited to just monogamy; both believe that such a rethinking would lead to sexual liberation for women.

Weatherman David Gilbert noted that even though this sexual experimentation was often contrived, it created a low affective environment in which people were at ease with non-normative sexual expression:

> The new line was that being liberated meant enjoying sex with both women and men and with multiple partners as well…. But even if our attempts to be "polysexual" were

artificial and often crude, they did help people break through the prevailing sexual repression. It was in that context that two of the men in our collective came out as gay, and it was a pleasure to see their sense of themselves open up and blossom.[117]

As such, the WUO allowed for sexual expression and encouraged people to value sex as an integral part of their lives. In "Inside the Weather Machine," an anonymous Weatherwomen stated that "sex isn't something to happen isolated from daily work"; WUO members saw sexuality as an integral part of the revolution.[118] Similarly, feminist theorist Carole Vance in writing on the need to move away from the second wave's condemnation of sex as patriarchal in practice, in an early sex positive paper in 1984, stated, "Feminism must put forward a politics that resists deprivation and supports pleasure.... It must understand that the women to whom it speaks, and those it hopes to each, care deeply about sexual pleasure and displeasure in their daily lives."[119] Both the WUO and the sex positive movement recognize that sex was not only a key part of women's regular lives, but also a likely locus of female pleasure and possible female empowerment.[120]

Conclusion: A Vibrant Part of the Women's Movement[121]

If one idea could best represent some of the key trends of the third wave feminist movement, it may in fact be inclusivity. Building on the flaw of bigoted restrictions found in much of the second wave, the third wave of feminism opens its arms to provide access and support to women of color, lower class women, working women, Third World women, lesbian women, and all other women who did not fit into the typically narrow viewpoint that was predominant, even in the feminist movement, in the 1960s and 1970s among the white, straight, middle and upper class American feminist left.

The Weather Underground embodied this inclusive attitude well before the historical period typically associated with the third wave. Though the WUO was flawed in many ways, it did not present itself as an exclusive organization. A commitment to inclusivity was one of the WUO's most commendable assets, and this commitment is perhaps clearest in the WUO's approach to feminism. The feminists of the WUO felt that feminism could not exist if it were limited to the concerns of middle and upper class, white, straight women from the United States. The WUO was concerned with the needs of almost *all* women (we should note that the WUO did not address the needs or oppressions of trans women and so they did not actually speak to the concerns of all women).

Previewing major movements that would come years later in the historically recognized years of the third wave, the WUO also had open minds about sexuality. The WUO attempted to include gay and lesbian members without bigoted judgment, even if they could not always overcome their own heterosexism. The WUO also attempted to create a sexual environment that would be liberating, especially as compared to male-dominated monogamous relationships that existed in the patriarchal society of the United States in the 1960s and 1970s. This effort, known as "smash monogamy," was mostly a failure as it did not produce female sexual liberation, but, instead, resulted in frequent break ups and even led to some men using the unattached women to meet their own sexual fantasies, as for example, Mark Rudd admits he did.[122] Nevertheless, the all-encompassing impulse was there, rooted firmly in the WUO's ideology, as the organizations staked for itself a position that was accepting of all sexualities and was interested in furthering personal autonomy for its members.

This inclusivity is perhaps best understood through Weatherman Bill Ayers' words on how to achieve meaningful social and political change in the world. Reflecting on what the crucial element is when attempting reform, Ayers stated the importance of remembering that "we are all in this together, all passengers and crew on the same global spaceship."[123] Embedded in Ayers' statement is the same inclusive spirit that set the WUO apart from other mainstream feminist groups of the time period. It is the recognition of the idea that accepting one another, celebrating each other's differences, and treasuring each one's subjectivities results in a deep abiding unity, which in turn informs and shapes the agenda of what needs to be changed in the world. This solidarity forms the basis of meaningful revolution that addresses the needs of *all* identity types, because it is predicated on, and responsive to, *all* of these multiple identities. This all-encompassing attitude is emblematic of the WUO, and it is the quality what sets the WUO apart as a third wave feminist organization.

Finally, in seeing the WUO as a 1960s/1970s third wave feminist organization, we have seen that the historical approach to the wave metaphor is in serious peril. Firstly, the instantiation of one organization in the wrong time period (roughly speaking, the WUO is a third wave organization approximately two decades prior to the historically recognized start of the third wave) at least shows that the historical wave motif is far from perfect. Perhaps, we could simply recognize this exception as an outlier.

However, the inclusivity of the WUO was not unique to them. As we saw at the start, it is fairly clear that women of color, LGBTQ women, women of excluded classes, and international women were all striking out their own feminist positions long before third wave feminism was historically considered to become inclusive. That is, it is a narrow historical perspective to think feminism suddenly became inclusive in the historically designated third wave, as opposed to thinking that white, mainstream feminism should not be thought to make up all of feminism prior to the putative advent of the third wave.

The WUO neither invented inclusivity nor would they wish to take credit for it. They are simply one clear example of an organization that should be thought of as feminist and that was representing what we conceptually think of the third wave long before the third wave is supposed to have historically begun. Thus, the WUO is just one example of why it is important to distinguish the waves based on conceptual perspectives. In this way, an organization, like the WUO, can in different ways represent more than one wave, just as they can represent a wave that is typically taken to exist in a different historical period. The WUO then is a conceptually third wave organization during the historical second wave, which thus proves the need for the conceptual approach to the wave motif.

Conclusion

As the explosive blast shook the four-story town house on West Eleventh Street in Greenwich, New York, on March 6, 1970, Weatherwoman Cathy Wilkerson recalled, "my bare feet felt the old, wood floor vibrating with escalating intensity.... I began to sink down, my feet still planted on the thin carpet as it stretched and slid across widening, disjointed gaps."[1] As she literally dropped through the floors disintegrating around her still upright body, Wilkerson was engulfed in a "noisy, moving, three-dimensional swirl" of dislodged "timber and bricks."[2]

Wilkerson survived the blast; it had been set off by accident. In the absolute darkness of dust and debris that ensued, Wilkerson cried out to her friends who had been inside the house. The bodies of WUO members Terry Gold and Diana Oughton, who had been in the basement, were blown to pieces. Wilkerson made her way to the edge of the crater, toward the middle of what was once a house. Calculating that Kathy Boudin, who had been taking a shower, would be within hearing distance if she had survived, Wilkerson called her name. As Boudin emerged naked from the remnants of the bathroom, the two Weatherwomen held hands and blindly groped through the haze and debris, making their way barefooted toward the light filtering from the outside.[3]

The spectacle created by the explosion, coupled with media reports that characterized the WUO as a violent organization filled with misguided, spoiled rich kids merely acting out their frustrations in a political tantrum, effectively distorted the complex message of the WUO. Moreover, as the WUO became memorialized as a macho, misguided organization, the contributions of its female members were erased from the historical record.[4] Like Wilkerson's and Boudin's escape from the destroyed home, the women of the Weather Underground have been portrayed as

160

naked, vulnerable, and even traumatized, barely able to see or speak for themselves.

The preceding chapters have revealed that nothing could have been further from the truth. These Weatherwomen were strong agents of change: they knew their own minds, had a clear vision of what society could and should become, and knowingly crafted for themselves a destiny that included political protest and militant action. When this action became violent, the Weatherwoman were cognizant of the risks that they were taking. As Diana Oughton told her mother shortly before her death, "It's the only way, mummy. It's the only way."[5]

This book also has shown that, despite efforts to reduce the WUO to its violent end, in reality, the WUO was a multifaceted organization, peopled by committed activists—women and men—who felt that they needed to act in an unjust world. As Weatherman Bill Ayers put it,

> I knew in my heart that the greater crime would be to do nothing, or not enough, as our country attacked, occupied, bombed, and slaughtered.... Inaction was not an option. Stepping into history, we would make errors; staying aloof from history would be its own choice and error. And so, believing in the immense power of people to challenge fate and accomplish the unthinkable, we plunged ahead.[6]

The WUO indeed charged ahead, and was active underground until the late seventies, fighting for an intricate anti-imperialist and anti-sexist agenda that was responsive to the needs of *all* peoples. WUO poems, leaflets, public actions, and symbolic bombings all pointed out social injustices, as based in sexism, racism, or imperialism. Moreover, the WUO saw imperialism as intricately linked with sexism and male privilege, as imperialism fostered a system that upheld patriarchal values and commodified women. As the WUO put it, "imperialism is sexism."[7]

The WUO was active underground until the late seventies, as during that time members started to turn themselves in. For example, Mark Rudd turned himself in to New York City authorities in September of 1970. Other members waited longer, for example, Cathy Wilkerson turned herself in to the authorities in New York City in July of 1980, while Bill Ayers and Bernardine Dohrn turned themselves in to authorities in December of 1980.[8] Usually, as WUO members turned themselves in, charges were dropped or reduced. Rudd explains that

> I easily settled both my criminal cases. In New York I copped a plea to a misdemeanor charge of criminal trespass stemming from the occupation of one of the buildings at Columbia in May 1968. In return, all the other charges were dropped.... The Chicago [Days of Rage] charges were also reduced to misdemeanors, and I pleaded guilty to two counts of aggravated battery, for which the other charges were dismissed. Even

though I was the one jumped by the cops, the deal was so good that I figured I had
nothing to argue about....[9]

As for Dohrn, "most of the charges against her and her cohorts had been
dropped due to the FBI's illegal methods of their pursuit."[10]

During this period, as underground members were considering turning themselves in or decided to stay hidden, the WUO's work nevertheless
persisted and the revolution continued above ground for at least a few more
years. WUO supporters and those members who had chosen not to go
underground formed the Prairie Fire Organizing Committee (PFOC) in
1975 (and underground WUO members were in contact with the PFOC).
The PFOC was made up of various organizing committees throughout the
country, in places such as San Francisco, New York, Boston, Seattle and
Chicago.[11] Like its predecessor, the PFOC was dedicated to gender equality
and to addressing the problems of oppression brought about by imperialism and racism. Eventually, this group unraveled, as members intensely
disagreed over ideology and action. At a November 1976 San Francisco
conference, things finally came to a head. As former member Diana Block
recalled, "at every workshop, in every caucus meeting, during every plenary, what might have been simple differences of opinion, developed into
angry, personalized fights."[12] Members of the PFOC were already highly
stressed and not predisposed to trust one another. This state was due to
the fallout from the previous January 1976 conference, the Hard Times
Conference set up by the PFOC, where the WUO (which had called the
conference but was still underground and not present at the conference)
was criticized as a racist organization because conference organizers "had
denied a request by the Black caucus to make a formal presentation at a
plenary session."[13] The other reproach was that the PFOC was trying to
"incorporate labor issues into the conference agenda," thus giving primacy
to labor, instead of race and gender issues.[14] In the wake of these criticisms,
the PFOC conducted a series of investigations as part of a so called "rec-
tification process," during which members were inaccurately attacked (for
examples, the efforts of the WUO to support unionization for unskilled
workers was interpreted wrongly as support for the persecution of undoc-
umented workers), thrown out of the organization, and generally speaking,
"paranoia swirled and people were isolated from all but their closest
friends."[15] Historian Jeremy Varon characterizes this period as "acrimo-
nious, even hysterical."[16] As such, instead of serving as a tool to bring the
activists into harmonious accord, the San Francisco conference was tense
and folks were on edge; Block remembers that after three days of bickering,
"it became impossible to continue working together."[17]

As a result, the group eventually splintered: one faction formed the Revolutionary Committee of the WUO (RC) and pledged itself to a renewed armed struggle, while another faction became the May 19th Communist Organization (May 19th). Named to honor the birthdays of both Malcolm X and Ho Chi Minh, May 19th forged alliances with revolutionary African and African American liberation groups. As Ron Jacobs explains it, the "raison d'etre lay in supporting the BLA."[18] May 19th also saw themselves as a white, feminist group "under the leadership of the Black liberation struggle."[19] May 19th most notably helped Black Liberation Army (BLA) member Assata Shakur escape from prison on November 2, 1979. Former WUO members and now May 19th members Kathy Boudin and David Gilbert were also involved in the October 20, 1981, Brinks robbery, the purpose of which was to steal money to finance the BLA. In the course of the robbery, two policemen were killed and Boudin and Gilbert were tried and sentenced to 75 years to life and 20 years to life, respectively.[20] The May 19th group was active until 1985, by which time most group members had been arrested.[21]

The leadership of the RC would also be arrested for conspiracy to use explosives against Senator John Briggs of California. Senator John Briggs was considering legislation that would have made it illegal for gay and lesbian individuals to teach in public schools. The RC was retaliating against this proposed initiative. The FBI had infiltrated the RC, as Clayton Van Lydegraf, the leader of the RC, had invited into the organization his supposed best friend, an FBI agent. Previously, Van Lydegraf insisted on violence and had seen the WUO's move away from unrestrained violence as a sell out of the revolutionary spirit. RC leadership was arrested on November 20, 1977.[22] Nevertheless, the RC did recover, and returned to the PFOC moniker. This PFOC organized around solidarity with South America, Puerto Rican independence, gay liberation, and feminism, and lasted until the mid 1990s, with a website devoted to its platform still active as recently as 2014.[23]

Indeed, former WUO members remain politically active, although without their previous militancy. For example, Bernadine Dohrn self identifies as an activist and child advocate and works as Clinical Associate Professor of Law at Northwestern University School of Law.[24] Bill Ayers likewise still self identifies as an activist working on the issues of social justice and peace and is a Distinguished Professor of Education and Senior University Scholar at the University of Illinois at Chicago.[25] They both organized protests against the War in Iraq and more recently participated in the Women's March against the Trump administration. Dohrn is also critical of the U.S. interventions in Iraq and Afghanistan in terms of what they mean for women's rights. Furthermore, both Dohrn and Ayers actively work in support of gay rights and prison reform.[26]

Some Weather members today recant their militancy but remain committed to social change. For example, Kathy Boudin regrets the crime she committed in the Brinks robbery. Released in 2003, Boudin now works as a law professor at Columbia, lecturing on the intersectionality of race, gender, and class within the law.[27] On the other hand, Weatherwoman Laura Whitehorn does not regret any of her militancy, stating, "I believe that all kinds of resistance are necessary to oppose the consolidation of reactionary forces."[28] Released in 1999, she has worked as an activist for human rights, prison reform, and healthcare, especially AIDS.[29] Importantly, Laura Whitehorn remains committed to anti-racist work.[30] Likewise, reflecting on the question of violence and militancy, Dohrn explains, "I think we have a myth about the good movements and the bad movements, and that's naïve.... I think violence is a tactic, and a tactic of last resort."[31] She remains committed to social change, and to fighting for women's rights, noting that women's work is still invisible and taken for granted, when in reality "Women hold up half the sky."[32]

Other former revolutionaries and WUO members remain active and are organizing for social, political, and economic change. For example, Naomi Jaffe operates a feminist community group and foundation (*Holding Our Own*) and has worked on the Free Mumia campaign.[33] Mike Klonsky is a professor in education and a dedicated community activist at DePaul University in Chicago.[34] Released in 1981, Jeff Jones worked as a reporter for *The Guardian*, focusing on, among other topics, the AIDS crisis and political movements. He also worked as an environmental activist.[35] Judy Clark was just recently released in April of 2019; while imprisoned she worked on AIDS education and to train service dogs for disabled war veterans.[36] While still incarcerated, David Gilbert remains a dedicated activist, and holds that the "building of a strong anti-imperialist movement" is still of critical importance.[37] He continues his anti-racist work, has authored many political writings while behind bars, founded an AIDS counseling program, and tutors fellow prisoners trying to earn their GED's.[38] For these Weather members and others, the legacy of the WUO remains firm. After all, as Ayers states, the WUO acted earnestly and "rose hot and angry, to—in our own terms—smite the warmongers and strike against the race-haters."[39]

In excavating the history of the Weather Underground, this book has demonstrated that the organization was more than just an anti-war, anti-racism group: it was also a militant feminist group, one with a varied and complex type of feminism that has been ignored in the literature up to now. As Weatherman Jeff Jones stated in 1984, the Weatherwomen "were very much a part of [the women's movement], reading, writing, struggling."[40] The Weatherwomen fashioned the feminist program of the WUO; they worked alongside supportive male members in doing so. Like second wave groups of their time period, the WUO critiqued male privilege, attacked sexism, agitated against female gender norms, and condemned the objectification and sexualization of women's bodies as commodities for male pleasure. Furthermore, the WUO denounced rape as a system of oppression for women and articulated a vision of a world in which women could live in safety and dignity. The WUO staked out a feminist agenda that aimed to respond to the needs of *all* women, regardless of class, race, or other social identities. Unlike some second wave feminist organizations that seemed to be concerned only with the needs of the nation's most privileged women, the WUO advocated inclusivity and an all-encompassing attitude as part of its feminist, political ideology.

Whereas previous scholars have focused on the male leaders of the WUO and their seeming descent into a violent madness, this work has examined the feminist inclinations of the Weatherwomen in particular and of the WUO in general. By placing the Weatherwomen's efforts at the center of the story, this book has made visible the organization's dedication to feminism. This manuscript has shown that the Weatherwomen, joined by many male members of the WUO, fashioned a feminist agenda that resembled that of second wave groups, and also took on the inclusive positions of third wave feminists. As such, the WUO's feminism disrupts the historical wave metaphor used for the feminist movement, as it embodies elements from each wave. The WUO then, as a feminist organization, shows the need for using the conceptual, and not the historical, approach to the wave metaphor. The WUO's third wave feminism was inclusive, intersectional, and sex positive; it was melded to a political ideology that viewed imperialism, racism, and sexism as interlocked oppressions.

Moreover, the preceding chapters have highlighted the importance Weatherwoman placed on militancy, including violent action, as the appropriate recourse for feminist revolution. They conceived of their feminism as a "gathering together as a thunder cloud—our voice will be heard far and wide, our doings will help cleanse the earth."[41] Highly critical of the gender norms that proscribed the lives of women, the WUO also was dedicated to using militancy to break through them, and the organization was firmly committed to leading a revolution to create a socialist, feminist world. Not unlike the move from non-violence towards a more militant Black Power Movement, the Weatherwomen did not think that the fundamental problems of oppression, including but not limited to patriarchy, were being addressed by non-militant methods. For the WUO, change required concrete action. Oppression, in the WUO's estimation, especially when looking at the hardest hit persons (which were often lower class women of color or Third World women), was so harsh and so violent that to not address it immediately and effectively amounted to allowing vast and severe suffering to continue unchecked among innocent people. In coming to this realization, the WUO was, as Bernardine Dohrn put it, "waking up."[42] This awakening out of complacency demanded direct action. This was no less true for anti-sexist campaigns as it was for anything else. To do nothing was the true act of violence. There was no choice but to fight. Being a feminist, bringing an end to sexism and imperialism, required being militant as well.

The Weatherwomen fought for a new world during the turbulent sixties and seventies. Their vision would not permit them to pick out one wrong to address at the expense of another; as militant feminists, the "Weatherwomen wanted it all."[43] They acted earnestly and were dedicated to their aims. Visionary revolutionaries, the Weatherwomen were essentially feminists as they imagined a world that recognized women's innate right to define themselves and shape their own life plans autonomously. As they put it, "Women can be everything we want this time around."[44]

Chapter Notes

Introduction

1. Lucinda Franks and Thomas Powers, "The Making of a Terrorist: Part 3," *United Press International*, 1970.

2. In addition to the term Weatherwomen, I use WUO as an umbrella term to refer to the organization itself, throughout its many instantiations over the years. Chapter 1 outlines the history of the group's name changes, as the organization existed as Weatherman (or Weather for short) until 1970, then as the WUO after 1970. See David Gilbert, *Love and Struggle: My Life in SDS, the Weather Underground, and Beyond* (Oakland: PM Press, 2012), 166. Additionally, when attributing authorship to various WUO publications, I employ the names listed on the documents themselves, which range from Weather, Weatherman, WUO, Weatherwomen, the Proud Eagle Tribe (a name given to the Weatherwomen acting together as a unit) or the Women's Brigade (another name given to the Weatherwomen's unit, as they later determined that the "tribe" label was offensive to Native Americans), to pseudonyms designated to signal collaborative efforts. It is also important to note that while the Weatherwomen authored some documents, other documents were written collaboratively, with men and women writing/editing together. As such, there are instances where WUO members fashioned a feminist vision together for the WUO.

3. Anonymous Weatherwomen, *Sing a Battle Song* (Red Dragon Print, 1975).

4. For more on the history of the women's movement and important positions held throughout it, see Leslie B. Tanner, ed., *Voices From Women's Liberation* (New York: Signet Books, 1970); Ruth Rosen, *The World Split Open: How the Modern Women's Movement Changed America* (New York: Penguin Books, 2001).

5. See Kimberlé Crenshaw, "Mapping the Margins: Intersectionality, Identity Politics, and Violence Against Women of Color," *Stanford Law Review*, Vol. 43, No. 6 (July 1991), 1241–1299.

6. For more on the fourth wave, see Kira Cochrane, "The Fourth Wave of Feminism: Meet the Rebel Women," *The Guardian*, 10 December 2013; Kira Cochrane, *All the Rebel Women: The Rise of the Fourth Wave of Feminism* (London: Guardian Books, 2013); Laura Bates, *Everyday Sexism* (London: Simon & Schuster, 2014).

7. I am here using the phrase "female liberation groups" in a non-technical way, as a simple way to address groups active within the second wave. For more on how female liberation was a specific strand within the second wave, see Sara Evans, "Re-viewing the Second Wave," *Feminist Studies* Vol. 28, No. 2 (Summer 2002): 258–267. As discussed, and broadly speaking, the second wave focused on achieving equality for women in the home, the workplace, and the legal arena. However, second wave feminists tended to operate mainly from a white, middle class point of view. The third wave focused on broadening that point of view to be inclusive. For more on second wave issues see Linda Nicholson, ed., *The Second Wave: A Reader in Feminist Theory* (New York: Routledge, 1997); Robin Morgan, ed.,

Sisterhood Is Powerful: An Anthology of Writings from the Women's Liberation Movement (New York: Random House, 1970); Rachel Blau Duplessis and Ann Snitow, eds., *The Feminist Memoir Project: Voices From Women's Liberation* (New Brunswick: Rutgers University Press, 2007); Nancy MacLean, *The American Women's Movement: 1945–2000* (Boston: Bedford Press, 2009). For more on the third wave, see Claire Snyder, "What Is Third Wave Feminism? A New Directions Essay," *Signs*, Vol. 34, No. 1 (Autumn 2008): 175–196; Naomi Zack, *Inclusive Feminism: A Third Wave Theory of Women's Commonality* (Oxford: Rowman & Littlefield, 2005); Stacy Gillis, Gillian Howie, and Rebecca Munford, *Third Wave Feminism: A Critical Exploration* (New York: Palgrave Macmillan, 2007). Some scholars identity a fourth wave, which is about continuing the work of the previous waves from an intersectional perspective (as the third wave) and is aided through the use of the internet. For more on the fourth wave, see Kira Cochrane, "The Fourth Wave of Feminism: Meet the Rebel Women,"; Kira Cochrane, *All the Rebel Women: The Rise of the Fourth Wave of Feminism*; Laura Bates, *Everyday Sexism*.

8. For additional critiques on the wave motif, see Becky Thompson, "Multiracial Feminism: Recasting the Chronology of Second Wave Feminism," *Feminist Studies*, Vol. 28, No. 2 (Summer 2002), 336–360; Kimberly Springer, *Living for the Revolution: Black Feminist Organizations, 1968–1980* (Durham: Duke University Press, 2005); Wini Breines, "What's Love Got to Do with It? White Women, Black Women, and Feminism in the Movement Years," *Signs: Journal of Women in Culture and Society*, Vol. 27, No. 4 (Summer 2002): 1095–1133. My use of the waves is thus practical and should not be taken as an endorsement of them.

9. Cherrie Moraga and Gloria Anzaldua, eds., *This Bridge Called My Back* (Third Woman Press, 2002); Kimberly Springer, *Living for the Revolution: Black Feminist Organizations*; Rebecca Walker, "Becoming the Third Wave," *Ms.*, January/February 1992, 39–41.

10. James Rocha and Mona Rocha, "Love, Sex, and Social Justice: The Anarcha-Feminist Free Love Debate," *Anarchist Studies*, Vol.

27, No. 1 (2019), 63–82. For a brief look at similarities between anarcha-feminists and third wavers in terms of sex positivity, see J. H. Morris, "Free Sex Relations," *The Firebrand*, 3 May 1896; Lucy Parsons, "Objections to Variety," *The Firebrand*, 27 September 1896; A.E.K., "It Depends on the Woman," *The Firebrand*, 24 April 1897; Emma Goldman, "Marriage," *The Firebrand*, 18 July 1897; Voltairine de Cleyre, "They Who Marry Do Ill," reprinted in A.J. Brigati, ed., *The Voltairine de Cleyre Reader* (Oakland: AK Press, 2004), 13.

11. Benita Roth, *Separate Roads to Feminism: Black, Chicana, and White Feminist Movements in America's Second Wave* (Cambridge: Cambridge University Press, 2004), 88.

12. *Ibid.*, 91.

13. *Ibid.*, 104. Also see The Black Panther Party, "The Black Panther Party: Platform and Program," reprinted in Judith Clavir Albert and Stewart Edward Albert, eds., *The Sixties Papers: Documents of a Rebellious Decade* (London: Praeger Press, 1984), 159–164.

14. Bobby Seale, "The Women of the Original Black Panther Party," *Facebook*, 24 May 2019 at 10:53 p.m., accessed 25 May 2019.

15. Anonymous Weatherwomen, *Sing a Battle Song*.

16. Huey P. Newton, "Huey Newton Talks to *The Movement*," *The Movement*, August 1968, printed by Students for a Democratic Society, August 1968. Available at https://archive.lib.msu.edu/DMC/AmRad/hueyne wtontalks.pdf (accessed 12 May 2018).

17. Though no one seems to have previously used the term "militant feminism" to describe this particular type of feminist group, there is work on women using militant means for their ends. For more on militant women, see Donatella Della Porta, *Social Movements and Violence: Participation in Underground Organizations* (Greenwich: JAI Press, 1992); Margaret Gonzales-Perez, *Women and Terrorism: Female Activity in Domestic and International Terror Groups* (Routledge: London, 2008); Kelly Oliver, *Women as Weapons for War* (New York: Columbia University Press, 2007); Jerrold M. Post, *The Mind of the Terrorist: The Psychology of Terrorism from the IRA to al-Qaeda* (New York: Palgrave MacMillan, 2007). For more on feminist organizations

see Gail Collins, *America's Women: 400 Years of Dolls, Drudges, Helpmates, and Heroines* (New York: Harper Perennial, 2003); Kimberly Springer, *Living for the Revolution: Black Feminist Organizations, 1968–1980*; Maryann Barakso, *Governing NOW: Grassroots Activism In The National Organization For Women* (Ithaca: Cornell University Press, 2004); Thompson, "Multiracial Feminism," 336–360. Becky Thompson uses the term militant women and also notes that militant women are usually not covered in the Second Wave history. See "Multiracial Feminism," 341–342.

18. Although none of these sources recognize the BPP's militant feminism, for more on the BPP, see Charles E. Jones and Judson L. Jeffries in Charles E. Jones, eds., *The Black Panther Party Reconsidered* (Baltimore: Black Classic Press, 1988); Kathleen Cleaver and George Katsiaficas, eds., *Liberation, Imagination, and the Black Panther Party: A New Look at the Panthers and their Legacy* (New York: Routledge, 2001); David Hilliard, ed., *The Black Panther Party: Service to the People Programs* (Albuquerque: University of New Mexico Press, 2008); Bobby Seale, *Seize the Time: The Story of the Black Panther Party and Huey P. Newton* (Baltimore: Black Classic Press, 1991).

19. Judson L. Jeffries, "Revising Panther History in Baltimore," in *Comrades: A Local History of the Black Panther Party*, ed. Judson L. Jeffries (Bloomington: Indiana University Press, 2007), 21.

20. *Ibid.*, 19–24.

21. Judson L. Jeffries and Malcolm Foley, "To Live and Die in LA," in *Comrades: A Local History of the Black Panther Party*, ed. Judson L. Jeffries (Bloomington: Indiana University Press, 2007), 267.

22. Judson L. Jeffries and Ryan Nissim-Sabat, "Introduction: Painting a More Complete Portrait of the Black Panther Party," in *Comrades: A Local History of the Black Panther Party*, ed. Judson L. Jeffries (Bloomington: Indiana University Press, 2007), 7.

23. For more on women's experiences in the Black Panther Party, see Elaine Brown, *A Taste of Power: A Black Woman's Story* (New York: Doubleday Books, 1992); Assata Shakur, *Assata: An Autobiography* (Chicago: Lawrence Hill Books, 1987); Angela Davis, *Angela Davis: An Autobiography* (New York: International Publishers, 1988).

24. Roxanne Dunbar-Ortiz, "Female Liberation as the Basis for Social Revolution," *No More Fun and Games: A Journal of Female Liberation*, No. 2 (February 1969), 109, 112.

25. *Ibid.*, 111.

26. For more on this theme, see Huey P. Newton, "Huey P. Newton Talks to the Movement About the Black Panther Party, Cultural Nationalism, SNCC, Liberals and White Revolutionaries," in *The Black Panthers Speak*, ed. Philip S. Foner (New York: Da Capo Press, 1995), 50–66; Bernadine Dohrn, "White Mother Country Radicals," *New Left Notes*, July 29, 1968. Roxanne Dunbar-Ortiz read feminist theory put forward by WUO founder Bernardine Dohrn (and viewed her "as a potential ally," when it came to women's liberation), but eventually was disenchanted with the direction the WUO was taking. Roxanne Dunbar-Ortiz, *Outlaw Woman: A Memoir of the War Years, 1960–1975* (San Francisco: City Lights, 2001), 126, 177, 196–197, 210–211, 397.

27. Weather, "Honky Tonk Women," National War Council Packet, December 1969; reprint, *Weatherman*, Harold Jacobs, ed. (Ramparts, 1970), 314 (page citations are to the reprint edition).

28. For more on the discussion of race, class, and gender when assessing oppression, see Patricia Hill Collins, *Black Feminist Thought: Knowledge, Consciousness, and the Politics of Empowerment* (New York: Routledge, 2000); Crenshaw, "Mapping the Margins," 1241–1299; Evelyn Higginbotham, "African-American Women's History and the Metalanguage of Race," *Signs*, Vol. 17, No. 2 (Winter 1992): 251–274; Susan Kemp and Judith Squires, eds., *Feminisms* (Oxford: Oxford University Press, 1997).

29. See Dan Berger, *Outlaws of America: The Weather Underground and the Politics of Solidarity* (Edinburgh: AK Press, 2006), 219–220, 291, 293; Jeremy Varon, *Bringing the War Home: The Weather Underground, The Red Army Faction, and Revolutionary Violence in the Sixties and Seventies* (Berkeley: University of California Press, 2004), 59–60, 149.

30. *Ibid.*

31. Alice Echols, *Daring to be Bad: Radical Feminism in America, 1967–1975* (Minneapolis: University of Minnesota Press,

1989); Bread and Roses Collective, "Weatherman Politics and the Women's Movement," *Women*, 1970; reprint, *Weatherman*, ed. Harold Jacobs (Ramparts, 1970), 327 (page citations are to the reprint edition); Doris Wright, "Angry Notes from a Black Feminist," in *Dear Sisters: Dispatches From the Women's Liberation Movement*, eds. Rosalyn Baxandall and Linda Gordon (New York: Basic Books, 2000), 37.

32. Shulamith Firestone, *The Dialectic of Sex: The Case for Feminist Revolution* (New York: Morrow, 1970).

33. For some of the position papers or pieces that exemplify this complex type of feminism for the WUO, see WUO, *Prairie Fire: The Politics of Revolutionary Anti-Imperialism* (San Francisco and New York: Prairie Fire Distribution Committee, 1974); Bernardine Dohrn, "Toward a Revolutionary Women's Movement," *New Left Notes*, Special Issue, March 8, 1969, 4; also available at SDS/WUO Document Archive, http://www.antiauthoritarian.net/sds_wuo/nln_iwd_1969/ (accessed 26 June 2016); "A Mighty Army: An Investigation of Women Workers," *Osawatomie*, Summer 1975, No. 2, 6–13. *Prairie Fire* was written collectively, with WUO members editing/revising the text together.

34. bell hooks, "Feminism: A Movement to End Sexist Oppression," in Susan Kemp and Judith Squires, eds., *Feminisms* (Oxford: Oxford University Press, 1997), 22–27. Becky Thompson also explains that the second wave was associated with a white point of view, one that marginalized the experiences and needs of women of color. See Thompson, "Multiracial Feminism: Recasting the Chronology of Second Wave Feminism," 337. This second wave feminism is coined "hegemonic feminism." See Chela Sandoval, *Methodology of the Oppressed* (Minneapolis: University of Minnesota Press, 2000), 41–42. For an alternative to hegemonic feminism, also see Benita Roth, "The Making of the Vanguard Center: Black Feminist Emergence in the 1960's and 1970's," in *Still Lifting, Still Climbing: African American Women's Contemporary Activism*, ed. Kimberly Springer (New York: New York University Press, 1999), 70–90. Roth also points out that white feminists of the era ignored poor and working women's issues. See 76.

Chapter 1

1. The Women's Brigade, "Health, Education, and Welfare: An Enemy of Women, San Francisco, March 6, 1974 Communiqué," 6 March 1974; reprint, *The Weather Eye: Communiqués from the Weather Underground*, ed. Jonah Raskin (San Francisco: Union Square Press, 1974), 100–101. For more on activism related to welfare, see Kazuyo Tsuchiya "The National Welfare Rights Organization 1966–1975," at http://www.blackpast.org/aah/national-welfare-rights-organization-1966–1975 (accessed 18 June 2018); Premilla Nadasen, *Welfare Warriors: The Welfare Rights Movement in the United States* (New York: Routledge, 2005).

2. The Women's Brigade, "Health, Education, and Welfare: An Enemy of Women, San Francisco, March 6, 1974 Communiqué," 102, 104.

3. The Weatherwomen were protesting the sterilizations of women in Alabama, specifically Minnie Lee and Mary Alice Relf. Sterilizations were increasing in the early seventies, especially among poor, minority women. For a discussion of sterilization and black women, see Angela Davis, *Women, Race, and Class* (New York: Random House, 1981); The Combahee River Collective Statement (1978) at http://www.sfu.ca/iirp/documents/Combahee%201979.pdf (accessed 27 September 2017). In 1974, the Weatherwomen were voicing outrage at the fact that poor and minority women were coerced into sterilization, often times as part of a condition of HEW support. This issue became a rallying cry for feminist groups in 1977. For more on this, see Chicago Committee to End Sterilization Abuse, "Sterilization Abuse: A Task for the Women's Movement," (January 1977) available at the CWLU Herstory Archive, https://www.uic.edu/orgs/cwluherstory/CWLUArchive/cesa.html (accessed 27 September 2017); also see the legal case Relf et al. vs. Weinberger et. al. Civil Action No. 73-1557 U.S. District Court. Washington, D.C. March 15, 1974.

4. *Ibid.* As governor, Reagan instituted welfare reform in 1971 that reduced the number of people who were eligible for welfare. See http://governors.library.ca.gov/33-reagan.html (accessed 12 September 2017).

5. For more on the Black Panther Party, see Judson L. Jeffries and Ryan Nissim-Sabat, "Introduction: Painting a More Complete Portrait of the Black Panther Party," in *Comrades: A Local History of The Black Panther Party*, ed. Judson L. Jeffries (Bloomington: Indiana University Press, 2007), 1–3.

6. This section title ("White Mother Country Radicals") is taken from Bernardine Dohrn's piece in the *New Left Notes*, July 29, 1968.

7. Terry H. Anderson, *The Movement and the 60's: Protest in America From Greensboro to Wounded Knee* (Oxford: Oxford University Press, 1995); David Gilbert, *Consumption: Domestic Imperialism. A New Left Introduction to the Political Economy of American Capitalism* (New York: Movement for a Democratic Society, circa 1968); David Gilbert and David Loud, *U.S. Imperialism* (New York: Students for a Democratic Society, 1967).

8. For a list and brief discussion of these international actions, see John Gaddis, *The Cold War: A New History* (New York: Penguin Press, 2005).

9. Judith Clavir Albert and Stewart Edward Albert, "The Mass Culture of Rebellion," in Judith Clavir Albert and Stewart Edward Albert, eds., *The Sixties Papers: Documents of a Rebellious Decade* (London: Praeger Press, 1984), 15–18.

10. For more on mobilization and nonviolence in the Civil Rights Movement, see Anderson, *The Movement and the 60's*; Barbara Ransby, *Ella Baker and the Black Freedom Movement: A Radical Democratic Vision* (Chapel Hill: University of North Carolina Press, 2003); Bruce Watson, *Freedom Summer: The Savage Season That Made Mississippi Burn and Made America a Democracy* (New York: Viking Press, 2010); Kimberly Springer, ed., *Still Lifting, Still Climbing: African American Women's Contemporary Activism* (New York: New York University Press, 1999); Belinda Robnett, *How Long? How Long? African American Women in the Struggle for Civil Rights* (New York: Oxford University Press, 1997); Constance Curry, et al., *Deep in Our Hearts: Nine White Women in the Freedom Movement* (Athens: University of Georgia Press, 2000).

11. Fannie Lou Hamer, "Interview with Fannie Lou Hamer by Neil McMillen: Winona Mississippi," April 14, 1972, Center for Oral History and Cultural Heritage, University of Southern Mississippi. Available at Digital SNCC Gateway, https://sncc digital.org/events/beatings-winona-jail/ (accessed 21 March 2019), 2.

12. Ruth Rosen, *The World Split Open: How the Modern Women's Movement Changed America* (New York: Penguin Books, 2001), 100–101.

13. Fannie Lou Hamer, "An Oral History with Fannie Lou Hamer," Interview by Dr. Neil McMillen, April 14, 1972, Center for Oral History and Cultural Heritage, University of Southern Mississippi, available at https://digitalcollections.usm.edu/uncategorized/digitalFile_60627e2c-db14-4a52-9fa6-4bd137274733/ (accessed 21 March 2019), 10.

14. In regards to Stokely Carmichael, who was advocating Black Power (a political program to organize and unite the black community as its own autonomous, self-determined entity), the FBI worriedly noted that as a "black militant nationalist" he was calling for black unity and preparation "for paramilitary training." See Federal Bureau of Investigation, *COINTELPRO Black Extremist File*, Section 3, 6.

15. See Federal Bureau of Investigation, Memorandum, Counterintelligence Program: Black Nationalist—Hate Groups Internal Security (25 August 1967), quoted and reproduced in Ward Churchill and Jim Vander Wall, *The COINTELPRO Papers: Documents from the FBI's Secret Wars Against Dissent in the United States* (Cambridge: South End Press, 1990), 92.

16. Kwame Ture (formerly known as Stokely Carmichael) and Charles V. Hamilton, *Black Power: The Politics of Liberation* (Vintage, 1992), xvii. Originally published New York, Random House, 1967.

17. Judson L. Jeffries and Ryan Nissim-Sabat, "Introduction: Painting a More Complete Portrait of the Black Panther Party," 1–2.

18. Quoted in Judson L. Jeffries and Ryan Nissim-Sabat, "Introduction: Painting a More Complete Portrait of the Black Panther Party," 3.

19. Federal Bureau of Investigation, *COINTELPRO Black Extremist File*, Section 2, 47; Federal Bureau of Investigation, Memorandum, Counterintelligence Pro-

gram: Black Nationalist—Hate Groups Racial Intelligence Black Panther Party (27 September 1968), quoted and reproduced in Churchill and Vander Wall, *The COINTELPRO Papers: Documents from the FBI's Secret Wars Against Dissent in the United States*, 124.

20. For more on the transition from black-nationalism to a Marxist-inspired international revolutionary platform of the Black Panther Party, see Kathleen Cleaver and George Katsiaficas, eds., *Liberation, Imagination, and the Black Panther Party: A New Look at the Panthers and their Legacy* (New York: Routledge, 2001); Philip S. Foner, ed., *The Black Panthers Speak* (New York: Da Capo Press, 1995); Federal Bureau of Investigation, *COINTELPRO Black Extremist File*, Section 2, 47.

21. Justin D. García, "Young Lords," *Multicultural America: A Multimedia Encyclopedia*, Carlos E. Cortés and Jane E. Sloan, eds., Vol. 4 (Sage Reference, 2014), 2216–2217.

22. Young Lords Organization, "13 Point Program and Platform of the Young Lords Organization," *Palante*, 8 May 1970, Volume 2, Number 2; reprint, *The Young Lords: A Reader*, ed. Darrel Enck-Wanzer (New York: New York University Press, 2010), 9 (page citations are to the reprint edition) and Black Panthers, "The Ten Point Program," available at the Marxist Internet Archive https://www.marxists.org/history/ usa/workers/black-panthers/1966/10/15. htm (Accessed 21 June, 2018). For more on the development of the Young Lords, see Juan Gonzalez, *Harvest of Empire: A History of Latinos in America* (New York: Penguin, 2001); Miguel "Mickey" Melendez, *We Took the Streets: Fighting for Latino Rights with the Young Lords* (New York: St. Martin's Press, 2003). The Young Lords' Thirteen Point Program is also available at Latino Education Network Service, http:// palante.org/YLPProg.html (accessed 3 January 2017).

23. Quoted in Rychetta Watkins, *Black Power, Yellow Power and the Making of Revolutionary Identities* (Jackson: University Press of Mississippi, 2012), 35.

24. *Ibid.*, 36.

25. *Ibid.*, 9.

26. For more on the history of SDS, see Cathy Wilkerson, *Flying Close to the Sun*

(New York: Seven Stories Press, 2007); Sale Kirkpatrick, *SDS* (New York: Random House, 1973). Also see the Port Huron statement itself, which alludes to these themes and stakes out a SDS's political alliance with a civil rights agenda, and with SNCC and BPP. See Port Huron Statement (1962) available at www.coursesa.matrix.msu.edu/~hst 306/documents/huron.html (Accessed 26 August, 2017). The Federal Bureau of Investigation monitored SDS; see Federal Bureau of Investigation, *COINTELPRO New Left HQ File*, part 1, 23.

27. For more on the history of SDS and its support of black determination efforts or its alignment with the BPP, see Kirkpatrick, *SDS*; Dan Berger, *Outlaws of America: The Weather Underground and the Politics of Solidarity* (Edinburgh: AK Press, 2006); Todd Gitlin, *The Sixties: Years of Hope, Days of Rage* (New York: Bantam, 1993); ERAP: Danny Pope, Alain Jehlen, Evan Metcalf and Cathy Wilkerson, "Chester, PA: A Case Study in Community Organization," (New York: Students for a Democratic Society, circa 1965), available at the SDS/WUO Document Archive at http://www.anti authoritarian.net/sds_wuo/erap_chester_ pa/ (accessed 28 June 2017). Also see Judith Clavir Albert and Stewart Edward Albert, "The Rise of the New Left," in Judith Clavir Albert and Stewart Edward Albert, eds., *The Sixties Papers: Documents of a Rebellious Decade* (London: Praeger Press, 1984), 11.

28. Berger, *Outlaws of America*, 37–39. Also see Paul Potter's speech "We Must Name the System," at the first anti-war march on Washington, April, 1965, available at the SDS/WUO Document Archive at http://www.antiauthoritarian.net/sds_ wuo/sds_documents/paul_potter.html (accessed 13 June 2017). Also on the dangers of imperialism, capitalism, military interventions (identified as corporate liberalism) see Carl Oglesby, *Ravens in the Storm: A Personal History of the 1960's Antiwar Movement* (New York: Scribner, 2008).

29. See various resolutions to this effect, all available at http://www.sds-1960s.org/ documents.htm (accessed 12 July 2017): No author, "Resolution on SNCC," June 18, 1966; Greg Calvert, "In White America: Liberal Conscience vs. Radical Consciousness," February 1967; Noel Ignatin and Ted Allen,

"White Blindspot Essays on Combating White Supremacy and White-Skin Privilege,"1967; Mike Klonsky, "Toward a Revolutionary Youth Movement," December 1968.

30. Bernardine Dohrn, "When Hope and History Rhyme," in *Sing A Battle Song: The Revolutionary Poetry, Statements, and Communiqués of the Weather Underground, 1970–1974*, eds. Bernardine Dohrn, Bill Ayers, Jeff Jones (New York: Seven Stories Press, 2006), 9.

31. For more on this trend, see Ron Jacobs, *The Way the Wind Blew: A History of the Weather Underground* (New York: Verso, 1997). One faction within SDS, known as the Jesse James Gang, was advocating violent, militant action *alongside* educational organizing. Also see Jeremy Varon, *Bringing the War Home: The Weather Underground, The Red Army Faction, and Revolutionary Violence in the Sixties and Seventies* (Berkeley: University of California Press, 2004), 47; Dohrn, "When Hope and History Rhyme," in *Sing A Battle Song: The Revolutionary Poetry, Statements, and Communiqués of the Weather Underground, 1970–1974*, eds. Bernardine Dohrn, Bill Ayers, Jeff Jones (New York: Seven Stories Press, 2006), 9–10.

32. Dohrn, "When Hope and History Rhyme," 9.

33. Max Elbaum, *Revolution in the Air: Sixties Radicals Turn to Lenin, Mao, and Che* (London: Verso, 2002), 24–25.

34. *Ibid.*, 25.

35. *Ibid.*, 25–26.

36. *Ibid.*, 26.

37. See Bill Ayers, "Revisiting the Weather Underground," in *Sing A Battle Song: The Revolutionary Poetry, Statements, and Communiqués of the Weather Underground, 1970–1974*, eds. Bernardine Dohrn, Bill Ayers, Jeff Jones (New York: Seven Stories Press, 2006), 25.

38. Bill Ayers and Jim Mellen, "Hot Town: Summer in the City or I Ain't Gonna Work On Maggie's Farm No More," *New Left Notes*, April 4, 1969; reprint, *Weatherman*, ed. Harold Jacobs (Ramparts Press, 1970), 36, 37 (page citations are to the reprint edition).

39. "Revolutionaries Must Fight Nationalism" equated the struggle for self-determination and independence with selfishness. See WSA/PL, "Revolutionaries Must Fight Nationalism," June 1969, available at

https://archive.org/stream/Revolutionaries MustFightNationalism/nationalismpl69# page/n0/mode/2up (accessed 3 January 2017).

40. For a more detailed explanation of the Progressive Labor Party (PL), see Ron Jacobs, *The Way the Wind Blew*, 5, 9–11.

41. Gilbert, *Love and Struggle*, 117.

42. SDS, "The Black Panther Party: Towards the Liberation of a Colony," *New Left Notes*, April 4, 1969. Also see Bernardine Dohrn in "White Mother Country Radicals" *New Left Notes*, July 29, 1968.

43. Dohrn, "White Mother Country Radicals."

44. Karin Ashley, Bill Ayers, Bernardine Dohrn, John Jacobs, Jeff Jones, Gerry Long, Howie Machtinger, Jim Mellen, Terry Robins, Mark Rudd and Steve Tappis, "You Don't Need a Weatherman to Know Which Way the Wind Blows," *New Left Notes*, June 18, 1969; reprint, *Weatherman*, ed. Harold Jacobs (Ramparts Press, 1970), 72–73 (page citations are to the reprint edition). Also available online at SDS/WUO Document Archive, http://www.antiauthoritarian.net/sds_wuo/weather/weatherman_document.txt (accessed 18 June 2017).

45. For more on this maneuver, see Berger, *Outlaws of America*, 82–89; Ron Jacobs, *The Way the Wind Blew*, 13–18; Varon, *Bringing the War Home*, 49.

46. Harold Jacobs, "The Emergence of Weatherman: Introduction," *Weatherman*, ed. Harold Jacobs (Ramparts Press, 1970), 1.

47. I employ the WUO label to identify the group through its many instantiations, except when referring to the initial development of the organization in this chapter. For the name change, see Gilbert, *Love and Struggle*, 166.

48. Jonah Raskin, "Introduction," May 1974; reprint, *The Weather Eye: Communiqués from the Weather Underground*, ed. Jonah Raskin (San Francisco: Union Square Press, 1974), 2.

49. Ashley, et al., "You Don't Need a Weatherman to Know Which Way the Wind Blows," 72–73.

50. Ron Jacobs, *The Way the Wind Blew*, 36.

51. Kathy Boudin, Bernardine Dohrn, and Terry Robbins, "Bringing the War Back Home: Less Talk, More National Action," *New Left Notes*, August 23, 1969; reprint,

Weatherman, ed. Harold Jacobs (Ramparts Press, 1970), 176 (page citations are to the reprint edition).

52. *FIRE!*, November 7, 1969, as quoted in Ron Jacobs, *The Way the Wind Blew*, 39.

53. Cover page, *FIRE!*, December 6, 1969.

54. For more on the openly militant position of Weather/WUO, see Eldridge Cleaver, "On Weatherman," *The Berkeley Tribe*, November 7, 1969; reprint, *Weatherman*, ed. Harold Jacobs (Ramparts Press, 1970), 293–295 (page citations are to the reprint edition); Ron Jacobs, *The Way the Wind Blew*, 22–23; Berger, *Outlaws of America*, 98, 103–104, 107–108; "Dykes and Fags Want to Know: Interview with Lesbian Political Prisoners: Queers United in Support of Political Prisoners Linda Evans, Laura Whitehorn, and Susan Rosenberg, 1991," in *Let Freedom Ring: A Collection of the Documents from the Movement to Free U.S. Political Prisoners*, ed. Matt Meyer (Oakland: PM Press, 2008), 380–381.

55. Cathy Wilkerson quoted in Ronald Frasier, *1968: A Student Generation in Revolt* (New York: Pantheon, 1988), 312.

56. Mark Rudd and Terry Robbins quoted by Ron Jacobs in *The Way the Wind Blew*, 23.

57. Wilkerson, *Flying Close to the Sun*, 281–282.

58. Susan Stern, *With the Weathermen: The Personal Journal of a Revolutionary Woman*, ed. Laura Browder (New Brunswick: Rutgers University Press, 2007), 49.

59. Laura Whitehorn, interview by author, 23 October 2014.

60. Quoted in Varon, *Bringing the War Home*, 62.

61. This title ("Living Your Conscience within the Heartland of a World-Wide Monster") is based on a sentence within the Weatherman paper, previously cited.

62. Varon, *Bringing the War Home*, 74.

63. Varon, *Bringing the War Home*, 1, 45–46, 49, 54; Gilbert, *Love and Struggle*, 77–78; Harold Jacobs, *Weatherman*, 3–8; Berger, *Outlaws of America*, 52, 171, 184, 194.

64. Karl Marx and Frederick Engels, *Economic and Philosophic Manuscripts of 1844 and the Communist Manifesto*, translated by Martin Milligan (Amherst: Prometheus Books, 1988). Also see Gerald A. Cohen, *Karl Marx's Theory of History: A Defence*, 2nd edition (Oxford, Oxford University Press,

2001); Gerald A. Cohen, *History, Labour and Freedom* (Oxford: Oxford University Press, 1988); Peter Singer, *Marx* (New York: Sterling, 1980), 57–118.

65. Karl Marx, *On Colonialism: Articles from the New York Tribune and Other Writings* (New York: International Publishers, 1972); Vladimir Lenin, *Imperialism, the Highest Stage of Capitalism* (Marxist Internet Archive, 1999 [1917]), available online at http://www.marxists.org/archive/lenin/works/1916/imp-hsc/ (accessed 9 July 2017); Frantz Fanon, *The Wretched of the Earth*, trans. Richard Philcox (New York: Grove Press, 2005 [1963]).

66. Jonah Raskin, "Introduction," May 1974, 4.

67. Harold Jacobs, "The Emergence of Weatherman: Introduction," 8. For more of the Marxist influence on the WUO, also see the FBI file on the WUO, The Federal Bureau of Investigation, *Weatherman Underground*, part 1a.

68. Ashley, et al., "You Don't Need A Weatherman," 52.

69. The Federal Bureau of Investigation, *Weatherman Underground*, part 1a, 34.

70. Herbert Marcuse, "Repressive Tolerance," in Robert Paul Wolff, Barington Moore, Jr., and Herbert Marcuse, *A Critique of Pure Tolerance* (Boston: Beacon Press, 1969).

71. Ron Jacobs, *The Way the Wind Blew*, 4, 5; Varon, *Bringing the War Home*, 42.

72. Herbert Marcuse, *One Dimensional Man* (Boston: Beacon Press, 1991[1964]).

73. Herbert Marcuse, An *Essay on Liberation* (Boston: Beacon Press, 1969), 81.

74. Ron Jacobs, *The Way the Wind Blew*, 4, 5; Bernardine Dohrn, "When Hope and History Rhyme," 7. Also, Naomi Jaffe, a member of the WUO, was a graduate student under Herbert Marcuse at Brandeis University. See Becky Thompson, *A Promise and a Way of Life: White Antiracist Activism* (Minneapolis: University of Minnesota Press, 2001), 391.

75. George Lavan, ed., *Che Guevara Speaks* (New York: Pathfinder Books, 1997), 147 and 158, respectively.

76. Ashley, et al., "You Don't Need A Weatherman," 70.

77. Varon, *Bringing the War Home*, 57.

78. Regis Debray, *Revolution in the Revolution?* (New York: Grove Press, 1967).

79. Ron Jacobs, *The Way the Wind Blew*, 17.

80. Larry Grathwohl and Frank Reagan. *Bringing Down America: An FBI Informant with the Weathermen* (New Rochelle: Arlington House Publishers, Inc., 1976); reprint, Lexington: Tina Trent, 2013, 61 (page citations are to the reprint edition).

81. The Federal Bureau of Investigation, *Weatherman Underground*, part 1a, 35, 37.

82. Ron Jacobs, *The Way the Wind Blew*, 17–18.

83. Berger, *Outlaws of America*, 54. Also see The Reminisces of David Gilbert (June 16, 17, 18, 19, 1985), 193, in the Columbia Center for Oral History (hereafter CCOHC).

84. Gilbert, *Love and Struggle*, 27.

85. Jane Lazarre, "Conversations With Kathy Boudin" (New York: Friends of Kathy Boudin, ca. 1984), 7.

86. Shin'ya Ono, "A Weatherman: You Do Need a Weatherman To Know Which Way the Wind Blows," *Leviathan*, December, 1969; reprint, *Weatherman*, ed. Harold Jacobs (Ramparts Press, 1970), 234 (page citations are to the reprint edition).

87. *The Weather Underground*, DVD, Sam Greene and Bill Siegel (Free History Project, 2002).

88. See Ron Jacobs, *The Way the Wind Blew*, 21.

89. Women's actions at the Days of Rage will be discussed in subsequent chapters. For more on the Days of Rage, see Varon, *Bringing the War Home*, 75–82; Ron Jacobs, *The Way the Wind Blew*, 28–31; Berger, *Outlaws of America*, 107–112.

90. Kathy Boudin, Bernardine Dohrn, and Terry Robbins, "Bringing the War Back Home: Less Talk, More National Action," 176.

91. *Ibid.*, 177.

92. *Ibid.*

93. *Ibid.*, 178.

94. For more on the trial, see Judy Clavir and John Spitzer, eds., *The Conspiracy Trial: The Extended Edited Transcript of the Trial of the Chicago Eight* (Indianapolis: Bobbs-Merrill Company, 1970); J. Anthony Lukas, "8 Go on Trial Today in Another Round in Chicago Convention Strife," *New York Times*, 24 September 1969, 29; Anthony Lukas, "Seale Put in Chains at Chicago 8 Trial," *New York Times*, 30 October 1969, 1.

95. Lukas, "8 Go on Trial Today in An-other Round in Chicago Convention Strife," 29; Lukas, "Seale Put in Chains at Chicago 8 Trial," 1.

96. Lukas, "Seale Put in Chains at Chicago 8 Trial," 1.

97. For more on the trial, see Judy Clavir and John Spitzer, eds., *The Conspiracy Trial: The Extended Edited Transcript of the Trial of the Chicago Eight* (Indianapolis: Bobbs-Merrill Company, 1970); Lukas, "8 Go on Trial Today in Another Round in Chicago Convention Strife," 29; Lukas, "Seale Put in Chains at Chicago 8 Trial," 1.

98. Kathy Boudin, Bernardine Dohrn, and Terry Robbins, "Bringing the War Back Home: Less Talk, More National Action," 178.

99. *Ibid.*, 178, 179.

100. *Ibid.*, 179.

101. Tom Thomas, "The Second Battle of Chicago 1969"; reprint, *Weatherman*, ed. Harold Jacobs (Ramparts Press, 1970), 209 (page citations are to the reprint edition); Shin'ya Ono, "A Weatherman: You Do Need a Weatherman To Know Which Way the Wind Blows," 271.

102. See Jacobs, *The Way the Wind Blew*, 31.

103. Jonah Raskin, "Introduction," 4–5.

104. This was actually the second Anti-War Moratorium. The first was held on Oct. 15, 1969 and had localized protests against the war, usually around college campuses. For more, see Zinn Education Project, "Nov. 15, 1969: Second Anti-War Moratorium," available at Zinn Education Project: Teaching People's History, at https://www.zinnedproject.org/news/tdih/second-antiwar-moratorium/ (accessed 12 January 2019).

105. "Washington, November 15, 1969," *Fire!* November 21, 1969; reprint, *Weatherman*, ed. Harold Jacobs (Ramparts Press, 1970), 275 (page citations are to the reprint edition).

106. "Washington, November 15, 1969," 275.

107. *Ibid.*, 276.

108. *Ibid.*, 275.

109. Christianna Silva, "Who Was Fred Hampton, the Black Panther Shot and Killed In His Bed By Chicago Police 48 Years Ago?," *Newsweek*, 4 December 2017, available at http://www.newsweek.com/fred-hampton-black-panther-shot-killed-chicago-730503

(accessed 2 June 2018). Also see Ted Gregory, "The Black Panther Raid and the Death of Fred Hampton," *Chicago Tribune*, available at http://www.chicagotribune.com/news/nationworld/politics/chi-chicagodays-pantherraid-story-story.html (accessed 23 June 2018).

110. Jonah Raskin, "Introduction," 5.

111. Meg Starr, "Laura Whitehorn," in *Enemies of the State* (Montreal: Abraham Guillen Press and Arm the Spirit, 2002), 10.

112. Wilkerson, *Flying Close to the Sun*, 313.

113. For a discussion of the War Council and their mindset about it, see Harold Jacobs, "Inside the Weather Machine: Introduction," *Weatherman*, ed. Harold Jacobs (Ramparts Press, 1970), 309–311.

114. For a list of bombings, see David Gilbert, *SDS/WUO: Students for a Democratic Society and the Weather Underground* (Montreal: Arm the Spirit Press and Abraham Guillen Press, 2002), 32–38. Also, it should be noted that if the Prairie Fire Organizing Committee (an above ground group associated with the WUO and formed by WUO members not underground) is subsumed under the WUO label, then the bombings lasted until February 1977 (one more bombing and one attempted bombing would be included in the list).

115. The Reminisces of David Gilbert, 217; Bill Ayers, *Fugitive Days* (Boston: Beacon Press, 2001), Kindle Edition, Chapter 29.

116. WUO New York Region, "Clifford Glover 103rd Precinct: New York City, May 18, 1973 Communiqué," 18 May 1973; reprint, *The Weather Eye: Communiqués from the Weather Underground*, ed. Jonah Raskin (San Francisco: Union Square Press, 1974), 66–68. Also see Gilbert, *SDS/WUO*, 35; WUO, "The Bombing of the Capitol: Washington DC, February 28, 1971 Communiqué," 28 February 1971; reprint, *The Weather Eye: Communiqués from the Weather Underground*, ed. Jonah Raskin (San Francisco: Union Square Press, 1974), 34–39. Also see Gilbert, *SDS/WUO*, 34; The Women's Brigade, "Health, Education, and Welfare: An Enemy of Women, San Francisco, March 6, 1974 Communiqué," 6 March 1974; reprint, *The Weather Eye: Communiqués from the Weather Underground*, ed. Jonah Raskin (San Francisco: Union Square Press, 1974), 100–106. Also see Gilbert, *SDS/WUO*, 36.

117. The Reminisces of David Gilbert, 217.

118. Bill Ayers, *Fugitive Days* (Boston: Beacon Press, 2001), Kindle Edition, Chapter 29.

119. For more on this term, see for example, Emma Goldman, "The Psychology of Political Violence," in *Red Emma Speaks: An Emma Goldman Reader*, ed. Alix Kates Shulman (New York: Humanity Books), 256–279; Candace Falk, ed., *Emma Goldman: A Documentary History of the American Years, Made for America, 1890–1901* (Chicago: University of Illinois Press, 2003), 9.

120. Cril Payne, *Deep Cover: An FBI Agent Infiltrates the Radical Underground* (New York: Newsweek Books, 1979), 16.

121. Ron Jacobs, *The Way the Wind Blew*, 40; Berger, *Outlaws of America*, 116.

122. Thai Jones, *A Radical Line: From the Labor Movement to the Weather Underground, One's Family Century of Conscience* (New York: Free Press, 2004), Kindle Edition, Chapter 9.

123. For a list of bombings claimed by the WUO, see: Gilbert, *SDS/WUO*, 29–38 and Jonah Raskin, "Chronology and Table of Contents," in *The Weather Eye: Communiqués From the Weather Underground*, ed. Jonah Raskin (Minton Press: San Francisco, 1974), 12–15.

124. Bill Ayers, *Fugitive Days*, Chapter 26.

125. Berger, *Outlaws of America*, 116.

126. Warren Hinckle, "Introduction," *Scanlan's Monthly* 1, no. 8 (January 1971), 12. Also see Berger, *Outlaws of America*, 116.

127. Hinckle, "Introduction," 5.

128. Grathwohl and Reagan, *Bringing Down America*, xviii.

129. *Ibid.*, xix.

130. See Gilbert, *Love and Struggle*, 162; Bill Ayers, *Fugitive Days*, Chapter 26.

131. Ayers, *Fugitive Days*, Chapter 26.

132. Warren Hinckle, "Introduction," 12.

133. Fred J. Solowey, "Berrigan Appears at Fest; Continues to Elude FBI," *The Cornell Daily Sun*, Vol. 86, No. 122, 20 April 1970, 1. The Young Lords also had a militant protest/action in New York City where they engaged with the police in summer of 1971. Berger, *Outlaws of America*, 115. For more on the Young Lords, see Melendez,

We Took the Streets: Fighting for Latino Rights With the Young Lords.

134. For more on the woman question, see Barbara Winslow, "Primary and Secondary Contradictions in Seattle, 1967–1969," in *The Feminist Memoir Project: Voices From Women's Liberation*, eds. Rachel Blau Duplessis and Ann Snitow (New Brunswick: Rugters University Press, 2007), 227.

135. Harold Jacobs, "Inside the Weather Machine: Introduction," 303–304; Gilbert, *Love and Struggle*, 186–187; Ron Jacobs, *The Way the Wind Blew*, 69; *Underground*, DVD, directed by Emile de Antonio (Turin Film, 1976), "Alternative Views: 'The de Antonio Legacy,'" Part 3.

136. Ron Jacobs, *The Way the Wind Blew*; Wilkerson, *Flying Close to the Sun*; Thomas Powers, *Diana: The Making of a Terrorist* (Boston: Houghton Mifflin, 1998); Bill Ayers, *Fugitive Days*, Chapter 25.

137. For some of the papers that explain this feminist stance, see Ashley, et al., "You Don't Need A Weatherman," 79–80; Bernardine Dohrn, "Toward a Revolutionary Women's Movement," 4, also available at SDS/WUO Document Archive, http://www.antiauthoritarian.net/sds_wuo/nln_iwd_1969/ (accessed 26 June 2017); Cathy Wilkerson, "Toward a Revolutionary Women's Militia," *New Left Notes*, July 8, 1969, 6–7; also available at SDS/WUO Document Archive, http://www.antiauthoritarian.net/sds_wuo/weather/sds_wilkerson.txt (accessed 13 June 2017); "Honky Tonk Women," 313 (page citations are to the reprint edition); WUO, "Weather Letter," *Rat*, July 15, 1970; reprint, *Weatherman*, ed., Harold Jacobs (Ramparts, 1970), 458 (page citations are to the reprint edition); A Weatherwoman, "Inside the Weather Machine," *Rat*, February 6, 1970; reprint, *Weatherman*, ed. Harold Jacobs (Ramparts, 1970), 323 (page citations are to the reprint edition); "A Mighty Army: An Investigation of Women Workers," 6–13; "The Politics of Daycare," *Osawatomie*, Summer 1975, No. 2, 14.

138. WUO, *Prairie Fire: The Politics of Revolutionary Anti-Imperialism* (San Francisco and New York: Prairie Fire Distribution Committee, 1974); "A Mighty Army: An Investigation of Women Workers," 6–13; "The Politics of Daycare," 14; Bernardine Dohrn, "Our Class Stand," *Osawatomie*, Autumn 1975, No. 3, 3–6; "The Battle of Boston: An Investigation of ROAR," *Osawatomie*, Spring 1975, No. 1, 7–12, especially 12; "Population Control," *Osawatomie*, Spring 1975, No. 1, 13–14; Celia Sojourn, "Where We Stand: The Women's Question is a Class Question," *Osawatomie*, Winter 1975-76, No. 4., 3. Celia Sojourn is a pseudonym.

139. Gilbert, *Love and Struggle*, 166; Varon, *Bringing the War Home*, 183. Also see Bernardine Dohrn, "New Morning, Changing Weather: December 6, 1970 Communiqué," 6 December 1970; reprint, *The Weather Eye: Communiqués form the Weather Underground*, ed. Jonah Raskin (San Francisco: Union Square Press, 1974), 26.

140. Grathwohl and Reagan, *Bringing Down America*, 158.

141. *Ibid.*

142. The Women's Brigade, "Health, Education, and Welfare: An Enemy of Women, San Francisco, March 6, 1974 Communiqué," 106.

Chapter 2

1. Cathy Wilkerson, *Flying Close to the Sun* (New York: Seven Stories Press, 2007), 108.

2. *Ibid.*

3. *Ibid.*, 109.

4. *Ibid.*

5. Dan Berger, *Outlaws of America: The Weather Underground and the Politics of Solidarity* (Edinburgh: AK Press, 2006), 219–220, 291, 293; Jeremy Varon, *Bringing the War Home: The Weather Underground, The Red Army Faction, and Revolutionary Violence in the Sixties and Seventies* (Berkeley: University of California Press, 2004), 59–60, 149.

6. Karin Ashley, Bill Ayers, Bernardine Dohrn, John Jacobs, Jeff Jones, Gerry Long, Howie Machtinger, Jim Mellen, Terry Robins, Mark Rudd and Steve Tappis, "You Don't Need a Weatherman to Know Which Way the Wind Blows," *New Left Notes*, June 18, 1969; reprint, *Weatherman*, ed. Harold Jacobs (Ramparts Press, 1970), 80 (page citations are to the reprint edition). Also available online at SDS/WUO Document Archive, http://www.antiauthoritarian.net/sds_wuo/weather/weatherman_document.txt (accessed 18 June 2017).

7. Thomas Powers, *Diana: The Mak-*

ing of a Terrorist (Boston: Houghton Mifflin, 1998), 20.

8. *Ibid.*, 20–22. For more on this conservatism and rigidity of gender roles for women, especially with respect to education, see Ruth Rosen, *The World Split Open: How the Modern Women's Movement Changed America* (New York: Penguin Group, 2001), 41.

9. The conservative 50s still permeated the atmosphere at the beginning of the 1960s. For more on the sense of conservatism of the 1950s, see Carolyn Lewis, *Prescription for Heterosexuality: Sexual Citizenship in the Cold War Era* (Chapel Hill: University of North Carolina Press, 2010); Terry H. Anderson, *The Movement and the 60's: Protest in America From Greensboro to Wounded Knee* (Oxford: Oxford University Press, 1995); Gail Collins, *America's Women: 400 Years of Dolls, Drudges, Helpmates, and Heroines* (New York: Harper Perennial, 2003).

10. The Reminisces of Cathy Wilkerson (February 17, 1985), 11, CCOHC.

11. Elizabeth (Betita) Martinez, "History Makes Us, We Make History," in *The Feminist Memoir Project: Voices From the Women's Liberation*, eds. Rachel Blau DuPlessis and Ann Snitow (New Brunswick: Rutgers University Press, 2007), 118.

12. Ruth Rosen coins this term in her discussion of women's lives in the shadow of the 1950s. See Chapter 1 in *The World Split Open*, especially 36. Also see Collins, *America's Women*, 422, 426, 428.

13. Sixties liberalism is used here to indicate a more free, less rigid way of life for women, as Rosen uses it in her work. See *The World Split Open*, chapter 3.

14. Rosen, *The World Split Open*, 39.

15. *Ibid.*, 63. Also see Barbara Epstein, "Ambivalence About Feminism," in *The Feminist Memoir Project: Voices From the Women's Liberation*, eds. Rachel Blau DuPlessis and Ann Snitow (New Brunswick: Rutgers University Press, 2007), 144.

16. Rosen, *The World Split Open*, 66. Also see 64–66.

17. *Ibid.*, 67.

18. Marjorie J. Spruill, *Divided We Stand: The Battle Over Women's Rights and Family Values that Polarized American Politics* (New York: Bloomsbury Publishing, 2017), 17.

19. *Ibid.*, 70–72. For more on Title VII starting out as a joke see M. E. Gold, "A tale of two amendments: The reasons Congress added sex to Title VII and their implication for the issue of comparable worth," *Duquesne Law Review*, 19 (1980), 453–477. Also see Collins, *America's Women*, 433.

20. *New York Times* editorial, August 21, 1965, 37. Also quoted in Rosen, *The World Split Open*, 72; Collins, *America's Women*, 434.

21. Dana Densmore, "A Year of Living Dangerously: 1968," in *The Feminist Memoir Project: Voices From the Women's Liberation*, eds. Rachel Blau DuPlessis and Ann Snitow (New Brunswick: Rutgers University Press, 2007), 72.

22. Casey Hayden and Mary King, "Sex and Caste: A Kind of Memo," 1965. Available at http://www.historyisaweapon.com/defcon1/sexcaste.html (accessed 4 July 2013).

23. See Cynthia Fleming, *Soon We Will Not Cry: The Liberation of Ruby Doris Smith Robinson* (Lanham: Rowman & Littlefield, 1998). For an account of women in SNCC that further complicates women's roles in the organization, see Faith S. Holsaert et al., eds., *Hands on the Freedom Plow: Personal Accounts By Women in SNCC* (Urbana: University of Illinois Press, 2010).

24. Benita Roth, *Separate Roads to Feminism: Black, Chicana, and White Feminist Movements in America's Second Wave* (Cambridge: Cambridge University Press, 2004), 85.

25. *Ibid.*, 85–86.

26. Densmore, "A Year of Living Dangerously: 1968," 73.

27. *Ibid.*

28. Winslow, "Primary and Secondary Contradictions," 227.

29. *Ibid.*

30. *Ibid.*, 232.

31. Rosalyn Fraad Baxandall, "Catching the Fire," in *The Feminist Memoir Project: Voices From the Women's Liberation*, eds. Rachel Blau DuPlessis and Ann Snitow (New Brunswick: Rutgers University Press, 2007), 210–211.

32. This title is based on a phrase ("sexist ramparts") from a quotation from Weatherman David Gilbert. See David Gilbert, *Love and Struggle: My Life in SDS, The Weather Underground, and Beyond* (Oakland: PM Press, 2012), 58.

33. Judith Clavir Albert and Stewart Edward Albert, "The Rise of a New Left," in *The Sixties Papers: Documents of a Rebellious Decade*, ed. Judith Clavir Albert (Westport: Prager, 1984), 11.

34. Gilbert, *Love and Struggle*, 56.

35. The Reminisces of Cathy Wilkerson, 19.

36. Gilbert, *Love and Struggle*, 58.

37. Gilbert, *Love and Struggle*, 58; David Gilbert, *SDS/WUO: Students for a Democratic Society and the Weather Underground* (Montreal: Arm the Spirit Press and Abraham Guillen Press, 2002), 13.

38. Gilbert, *Love and Struggle*, 58.

39. "Liberation of Women," *New Left Notes* 10 July 1967, 4. See Roxanne Dunbar-Ortiz, *Outlaw Woman: A Memoir of the War Years, 1960–1975* (San Francisco: City Lights, 2001), 173–174, who identifies Dohrn as the author of the report.

40. "Liberation of Women," *New Left Notes* 10 July 1967, 4.

41. *Ibid.*

42. *Ibid.*

43. *Ibid.*

44. *Ibid.*

45. Gilbert, *Love and Struggle*, 59. Also see The Reminisces of David Gilbert (June 16, 17, 18, 19, 1985), 184–185, CCOHC.

46. Andrew Kopkind, "The Real SDS Stands Up," (Chicago: Hard Times, June 30-July 5, 1969), available at the SDS/WUO Document Archive at http://www.sds-1960s.org/Kopkind-1969convention.pdf (accessed 5 September 2017), also available in *Weatherman*, ed. by Harold Jacobs, 15–28; The Reminisces of Jeff Jones (October 24, 1984), 42, CCOHC; Max Elbaum, *Revolution in the Air: Sixties Radicals Turn to Lenin, Mao, and Che* (New York: Verso Press, 2002), 70.

47. Sisters of WUO, "Letter from Sisters in the WUO," *The Split of the Weather Underground Organization: Struggling against White and Male Supremacy* (John Brown Book Club, 1976), 36.

48. *Ibid.*

49. For more on the base/superstructure relation, see Peter Singer, *Marx* (New York: Sterling Books, 1980), 67–77.

50. *Ibid.*

51. The Reminisces of Jeff Jones, 42.

52. *Ibid.* Gilbert, *Love and Struggle*, 59. Also see The Reminisces of David Gilbert, 184–185.

53. Ashley, et al., "You Don't Need A Weatherman," 80.

54. *Ibid.*, 79.

55. *Ibid.*, 80.

56. *Ibid.*, 70.

57. *Ibid.*

58. Bernardine Dohrn, "When Hope and History Rhyme," in *Sing A Battle Song: The Revolutionary Poetry, Statements, and Communiqués of the Weather Underground, 1970–1974*, eds. Bernardine Dohrn, Bill Ayers, Jeff Jones (New York: Seven Stories Press, 2006), 10.

59. See The Reminisces of Cathy Wilkerson, 54; Bernardine Dohrn, "The Liberation of Vietnamese Women," *New Left Notes*, October 25, 1968. For more on Vietnamese women and their involvement in the war, see Karen Gottschang Turner with Phan Thanh Hao, *Even the Women Must Fight: Memories of War From North Vietnam* (New York: John Wiley and Sons, 1998); Sandra C. Taylor, *Vietnamese Women at War: Fighting for Ho Chi Minh and the Revolution* (Lawrence: University Press of Kansas, 1999).

60. The Reminisces of Cathy Wilkerson, 54.

61. Dohrn, "The Liberation of Vietnamese Women."

62. Winslow, "Primary and Secondary Contradictions," 244.

63. Berger, *Outlaws of America*, 58.

64. Susan Stern, *With the Weathermen: The Personal Journal of a Revolutionary Woman*, ed. Laura Browder (New Brunswick: Rutgers University Press, 2007), 79.

65. Winslow, "Primary and Secondary Contradictions," 227.

66. Gilbert, *Love and Struggle*, 56.

67. Gilbert, *Love and Struggle*, 114–115. Also see The Reminisces of David Gilbert, 171–172.

68. Gilbert, *Love and Struggle*, 71.

69. *Ibid.*, 71–72.

70. Naomi Jaffe and Bernardine Dohrn, "The Look is You," *New Left Notes*, March 18, 1968, 5.

71. *Ibid.*

72. *Ibid.*

73. While Berger mentions this piece written by Jaffe and Dohnrn in his *Outlaws of America*, his treatment of it is brief—four sentences—and does not fully address the nuances and theoretical richness present in the text. See Berger, 58. Ron Jacobs also

mentions this piece, but gives it only two sentences. See Ron Jacobs, *The Way the Wind Blew: A History of the Weather Underground* (New York: Verso, 1997), 11. Varon, in *Bringing the War Home*, does not mention it at all.

74. Clara Bingham, *Witness to the Revolution: Radicals, Resisters, Vets, Hippies, and the Year America Lost Its Mind and Found Its Soul* (New York: Random House, 2016), Kindle Edition, Chapter 7.

75. David Gilbert, *Love and Struggle*, 60.

76. For more on citizenship and women, see Linda Kerber, *No Constitutional Right to be Ladies: Women and the Obligations of Citizenship* (New York: Hill and Young, 1998). As Kerber argues, women were not generally seen as being capable of soldiering, and were therefore denied that obligation, and the benefits, of full citizenship.

77. For more on Vietnamese women fighters, see Arlene Eisen Bergman, *Women of Viet Nam* (San Francisco: People's Press, 1974).

78. See Stern, *With the Weathermen*, 86.

79. Laura Whitehorn, interview by author, 23 October 2014.

80. Gilbert, *Love and Struggle*, 116.

81. Lorraine Rosal, "Who Do They Think Could Bury You?," *New Left Notes*, August 23, 1969; reprint, *Weatherman*, ed. Harold Jacobs (Ramparts Press, 1970), 147 (page citations are to the reprint edition).

82. *Ibid.*

83. *Ibid.*

84. *Ibid.*

85. *Ibid.*, 148.

86. *Ibid.*

87. *Ibid.*, 149. Rosal does not mention what the specific leadership positions were.

88. Stern, *With the Weathermen*, 95, 103.

89. *Ibid.*, 89–90. Stern was living at the time with Garrity and Indian in a house across the street from the Weather collective.

90. Stern, *With the Weathermen*, 106, 115. Stern also recalls that Jay often cooked.

91. *Ibid.*, 116.

92. Larry Grathwohl and Frank Reagan, *Bringing Down America: An FBI Informant with the Weathermen* (New Rochelle: Arlington House Publishers, Inc., 1976); reprint, Lexington: Tina Trent, 2013, 19 (page citations are to the reprint edition).

93. *Ibid.*, 89.

94. *Ibid.*, 88–89.

95. *Ibid.*, 70–71, 83, 116–117.

96. The Reminisces of David Gilbert, 244.

97. Ron Jacobs, *The Way the Wind Blew*, 46.

98. Berger, *Outlaws of America*, 293.

99. Ron Jacobs, *The Way the Wind Blew*, 46.

100. Stern, *With the Weathermen*, 248.

101. *Ibid.*

102. Gilbert, *Love and Struggle*, 54, 55.

103. Stern, *With the Weathermen*, 170, 198; Wilkerson, *Flying Close to the Sun*, 213; Jane Alpert, *Growing Up Underground* (New York: Citadel Press, 1981), 330; Mark Rudd, *Underground: My Life with SDS and the Weathermen* (New York: Harper Collins, 2009), 122.

104. Rudd, *Underground*, 122.

105. Jane Alpert, *Growing Up Underground*, 327, 330.

106. Sisters of WUO, "Letter from Sisters in the WUO," 39.

107. Bernardine Dohrn, "Tape from Bernardine Dohrn" in *The Split of the Weather Underground Organization: Struggling against White and Male Supremacy* (John Brown Book Club, 1976), 35. We can only speculate as to why she released this statement, but the evidence, as discussed below, shows it to be inaccurate.

108. Berger, *Outlaws of America*, 83, 111; Ron Jacobs, *The Way the Wind Blew*, 26, 30, 47, 51; Varon, *Bringing the War Home*, 81, 85, 98, 180, 182; Rudd, *Underground*, 151; Kopkind, "The Real SDS Stands Up," 27; Stern, *With the Weathermen*, 148, 151; Wilkerson, *Flying Close to the Sun*, 211, 214, 256, 304, 357; Bill Ayers, *Fugitive Days* (Boston: Beacon Press, 2001), Kindle Edition, Chapters 19, 20, 25, 27; Ayers, "Revisiting the Weather Underground," in *Sing A Battle Song: The Revolutionary Poetry, Statements, and Communiqués of the Weather Underground, 1970–1974*, eds. Bernardine Dohrn, Bill Ayers, Jeff Jones (New York: Seven Stories Press, 2006), 24; Thai Jones, *A Radical Line: From the Labor Movement to the Weather Underground, One's Family Century of Conscience* (New York: Free Press, 2004), Kindle Edition, Chapters 7, 8, 9; The Reminisces of Jeff Jones, 40; The Reminisces of David Gilbert, 78; The Weather

Underground, "A Declaration of a State of War: May 21, 1970 Communiqué," 21 May 1970; reprint, *The Weather Eye: Communiqués from the Weather Underground*, ed. Jonah Raskin (San Francisco: Union Square Press, 1974), 16 (page citations are to the reprint edition); Weather Underground, "New Morning, Changing Weather: December 6, 1970 Communiqué," 26; Federal Bureau of Investigation, *Weatherman Underground File*, Part 2a.

109. Ashley, et al., "You Don't Need A Weatherman"; Naomi Jaffe and Bernardine Dohrn, "The Look is You"; Bernardine Dohrn, "Toward a Revolutionary Women's Movement"; Bernardine Dohrn, "An Open Letter To The U.S. Workers," *Osawatomie*, Vol. 2, No. 1, April-May 1976, 11.

110. WUO, "Weather Letter," *Rat*, July 15, 1970; reprint, *Weatherman*, ed., Harold Jacobs (Ramparts, 1970), 460 (page citations are to the reprint edition).

111. Grathwohl and Reagan, *Bringing Down America*, 99; Federal Bureau of Investigation, *Weathermen*, part 4, 64.

112. David Gilbert, *SDS/WUO: Students for a Democratic Society and the Weather Underground* (Montreal: Arm the Spirit Press and Abraham Guillen Press, 2002), 20.

113. Wilkerson, *Flying Close to the Sun*, 275.

114. Gilbert, *SDS/WUO*, 20; Wilkerson, *Flying Close to the Sun*, 275.

115. Stern, *With the Weathermen*, 89, 206; Jones, *A Radical Line*, Chapter 9.

116. The Reminisces of David Gilbert, 320.

117. See Jonah Raskin, *Out of the Whale: Growing Up in the American Left, An Autobiography* (New York: Links Books, 1974); Jones, *A Radical Line*, Chapter 1, 7, 8, 9; Kathy Boudin, Eleanor Raskin, Brian Glick, and Gustin Reicherbach, *The Bust Book* (Legal Rap, 1969).

118. Ayers, *Fugitive Days*, Chapter 19; Federal Bureau of Investigation, *Weather Underground*, part 2, 27 and part 3, 12.

119. Jones, *A Radical Line*, Chapter 9.

120. Ayers, *Fugitive Days*, Chapter 18.

121. *Ibid.*, Chapter 20.

122. This title is based on the WUO position paper, "Honky Tonk Women." See Weather, "Honky Tonk Women," National War Council Packet, December 1969; reprint, *Weatherman*, Harold Jacobs, ed. (Ram-

parts, 1970), 320 (page citations are to the reprint edition). The sentence cited goes on to say that these revolutionary women, the Weatherwomen, do not just demand "Bread and Roses ... but bombs and rifles" to achieve women's liberation.

123. For example, the Bread and Roses collective dismissed the WUO's feminism in "Weatherman Politics and the Women's Movement"; See Bread and Roses Collective, "Weatherman Politics and the Women's Movement," *Women*, 1970; reprint, *Weatherman*, ed. Harold Jacobs (Ramparts, 1970), 327–336 (page citations are to the reprint edition).

124. James Rocha and Mona Rocha, "Love, Sex, and Social Justice: The Anarcha-Feminist Free Love Debate," *Anarchist Studies*, Vol. 27, No. 1 (2019), 63–82. For a brief look at similarities between anarcha-feminists and third wavers in terms of sex positivity, see J. H. Morris, "Free Sex Relations," *The Firebrand*, 3 May 1896; Lucy Parsons, "Objections to Variety," *The Firebrand*, 27 September 1896; A.E.K., "It Depends on the Woman," *The Firebrand*, 24 April 1897; Emma Goldman, "Marriage," *The Firebrand*, 18 July 1897; Voltairine de Cleyre, "They Who Marry Do Ill," reprinted in A.J. Brigati, ed., *The Voltairine de Cleyre Reader* (Oakland: AK Press, 2004), 13.

125. Kimberlé Crenshaw, 1991, "Mapping the Margins: Intersectionality, Identity Politics, and Violence Against Women of Color" *Stanford Law Review*, 43(6): 1241–1299; Noelle McAfee, "Feminist Philosophy," The Stanford Encyclopedia of Philosophy (Fall 2018 Edition), Edward N. Zalta (ed.), available at https://plato.stanford.edu/entries/feminist-philosophy/ (accessed 1 July 2018); Kimberly Springer, "Third Wave Black Feminism?" *Signs: Journal of Women in Culture and Society*, Vol. 27, No.4 (Summer 2002): 1059–1082. Also see Jo Freeman, The Women's Liberation Movement: It's Origins, Structures, and Ideas," 1971, available at https://dukelibraries.contentdm.oclc.org/digital/api/collection/p15957coll6/id/706/page/0/inline/p15957coll6_706_0 (accessed 1 July 2018). Freeman explains that those in the early women's movement "tend to be predominantly white, middle-class and college educated." See 2.

126. For an example of another scholar who examines how the waves structure is

disrupted, see Wini Breines, "What's Love Got to Do with It? White Women, Black Women, and Feminism in the Movement Years," *Signs: Journal of Women in Culture and Society*, Vol. 27, No. 4 (Summer 2002): 1095–1133.

127. Angie Maxwell and Todd Shields, "Introduction: Toward a New Understanding of Second-Wave Feminism," in *The Legacy of Second Wave Feminism in American Politics* (Palgrave McMillan, 2017), 4–5.

128. *Ibid.*, 10–11.

129. Audre Lorde, "The Master's Tools Will Never Dismantle the Master's House," in *Sister Outsider: Essays and Speeches by Audre Lorde* (Berkeley: Crossing Press, 2007), 110. Lorde made that criticism in 1979.

130. Meg Starr, "Laura Whitehorn," in *Enemies of the State* (Montreal: Abraham Guillen Press and Arm the Spirit, 2002), 17.

131. Freeman, "The Women's Liberation Movement: It's Origins, Structures, and Ideas," 8.

132. *Ibid.*, 2.

133. *Ibid.*, 8–9.

134. *Ibid.*, 3, 4–6. Consciousness raising (CR) can be understood as a group of women discussing a particular topic and realizing how that topic is interconnected in their lives and how it causes oppression when it is not challenged. CR can lead to political action because what one assumes to be a personal problem can be also be experienced by others and solved through collective, political activism. Consider a simple example: a husband comes home after work and trips over the children's toys, then he gets angry at the wife, but he does not once consider that he should pick up the toys himself—this scenario is something that can be discussed/shared, and women can realize that they all experience this type of issue in their everyday lives. Then, based on the discussion, sexist gender norms can be analyzed as restrictive, and connected to the patriarchy. A program for breaking free of traditional gender norms can then be planned. Various feminist groups of the second wave practiced CR, on a variety of topics. Depending on the group, men were either not allowed to participate, or were only allowed in limited roles. For more on this issue, see Kathie Sarachild, "Feminist

Consciousness Raising and 'Organizing,'" in *Voices From Women's Liberation*, ed. Leslie B. Tanner (New York: Signet Books, 1970), 154–157. Also see the section entitled "Consciousness Raising" in the same book, 231–254.

135. Sisters of WUO, "Letter from Sisters in the WUO," previously cited. This document tried to point out that the brand of feminism that the WUO had did not fit the Sister's brand of feminism. It also correctly pointed out that a concern with sexism was central to the split form SDS.

136. *Ibid.*, 36.

137. In agreement with the Sisters on this interpretation, see Berger, *Outlaws of America*, 219.

138. Celia Sojourn, "Where We Stand: The Women's Question is a Class Question," *Osawatomie*, Winter 1975-76, No. 4., 3.

139. *Ibid.*, 3, 5.

140. For more on this, see Harold Jacobs, "Inside the Weather Machine: Introduction," *Weatherman*, ed. Harold Jacobs (Ramparts Press, 1970), 303. Also see Wilkerson, *Flying Close to the Sun*, 244. Historian Alice Echols further discusses the term "politico." For more on female separatist groups and politico feminists, see Alice Echols, *Daring to be Bad: Radical Feminism in America, 1967–1975* (Minneapolis: University of Minnesota Press, 1989), 84–85.

141. The Reminisces of Cathy Wilkerson, 50, 51.

142. See Dunbar-Ortiz, *Outlaw Woman*, 150.

143. Berger, *Outlaws of America*, 219–220.

144. "Break The Chains," *Osawatomie*, Autumn 1975, No. 3, 7–13; the special section on women is on 12.

145. Ashley, et al., "You Don't Need A Weatherman," 79–80.

146. "A Mighty Army: An Investigation of Women Workers," 6–13.

147. *Ibid.*, 6.

148. *Ibid.*, 6, 9.

149. Dohrn, "Tape from Bernardine Dohrn," 34–35.

150. Gilbert, *Love and Struggle*, 60.

151. Sisters of WUO, "Letter from Sisters in the WUO," 36.

152. Clara Bingham, *Witness to the Revolution: Radicals, Resisters, Vets, Hippies, and*

the Year America Lost Its Mind and Found Its Soul (New York: Random House, 2016), Kindle Edition, Chapter 17.

153. Berger, *Outlaws of America*, 293.

154. Gilbert, *Love and Struggle*, 60.

155. Clara Bingham, *Witness to the Revolution*, Chapter 17.

156. See Rosal, "Who Do They Think Could Bury You?," 149.

157. *Ibid.*

158. *Ibid.*

159. Dohrn, "Toward a Revolutionary Women's Movement," 4.

160. Becky Thompson, *A Promise and a Way of Life: White Antiracist Activism* (Minneapolis: University of Minnesota Press, 2001), 121, 130.

161. See Elizabeth Spelman, *The Inessential Woman* (Boston: Beacon Press, 1988); Iris Young, *Justice and the Politics of Difference* (Princeton: Princeton University Press, 1990); Becky Thompson, "Multiracial Feminism: Recasting the Chronology of Second Wave Feminism," *Feminist Studies*, Vol. 28, No. 2 (Summer 2002): 336–360. Also see Marilyn Boxer, "Rethinking the Social Construction and International Career of the Concept 'Bourgeois Feminism,'" *The American Historical Review*, Vol. 112, No.1 (February 2007): 131–158. Boxer explains that socialist feminism is opposed to bourgeois feminism as a way to create a binary in feminism, but that both strands are part of the feminist movement.

162. This quotation ("Feminist to a person") comes from Dohrn, "When Hope and History Rhyme," 11.

163. Varon, *Bringing the War Home*, 293, 294. While Varon concedes that the WUO was more receptive to feminism by the late 1970s, he nevertheless concludes that the WUO attacked anything that would take away from its anti-imperialist focus. Even more strongly, Berger concludes, "Weather did not have a feminist internal culture." Berger's assessment is based on the sexist actions of men described above. Berger draws this conclusion even after pointing out that, by 1970, women made up three quarters of the members of WUO, and after noting that women challenged sexism from men in criticism, self-criticism sessions. In response, Berger says, "few men in the organization viewed the struggle against patriarchy as important, and women's initia-

tives did not change the overall culture of the WUO." See Berger, *Outlaws of America*, 291–294.

164. Ron Jacobs, *The Way the Wind Blew*, 24.

165. Berger, *Outlaws of America*, 172, 203, 219, 293.

166. For more on the different kinds of feminism, see Alison Jaggar, "Political Philosophies of Women's Liberation," in *Feminism and Philosophy*, eds. Mary Vetterling-Braggin, Frederick A. Elliston and Jane English (Totowa: Rowman & Littlefield, 1977); Alison Jaggar, *Feminist Politics and Human Nature* (Totowa: Rowman and Littlefield, 1983). Jaggar distinguishes between liberal feminism, radical feminism, and Marxist or socialist feminism. Also see Becky Thompson, "Multi Racial Feminism"; bell hooks, "Feminism: A Movement to End Sexist Oppression," in Susan Kemp and Judith Squires, eds., *Feminisms* (Oxford: Oxford University Press, 1997), 22–27; Benita Roth, *Separate Roads To Feminism: Black, Chicana, and White Feminist Movements in America's Second Wave* (Cambridge: Cambridge University Press, 2004); Benita Roth, "The Making of the Vanguard Center: Black Feminist Emergence in the 1960's and 1970's," in *Still Lifting, Still Climbing: African American Women's Contemporary Activism*, ed. Kimberly Springer (New York: New York University Press, 1999), 71. Roth argues that there were other feminisms besides the white middle class feminism usually associated with the second wave (which, she also argues, was not representative of the oppressions or needs of women of color).

167. Berger, *Outlaws of America*, 293.

168. Dohrn, "When Hope and History Rhyme," 11.

Chapter 3

1. Cathy Wilkerson, *Flying Close to the Sun* (New York: Seven Stories Press, 2007), 288.

2. Ann Standley, "The Role of Black Women in the Civil Rights Movement," in Vicky Crawford, Jacqueline Anne Rouse, and Barbara Woods, eds., *Women in the Civil Rights Movement: Trailblazers and Torchbearers, 1941–1965* (Bloomington: Indiana University Press, 1990), 187, 194.

3. For more on this topic, see Mary

King and Casey Hayden, "Sex and Caste: A Kind of Memo," 1965. Available at http://www.historyisaweapon.com/defcon1/sexcaste.html (accessed 4 July 2013). Also Cynthia Fleming, *Soon We Will Not Cry: The Liberation of Ruby Doris Smith Robinson* (Lanham: Rowman & Littlefield, 1998); Constance Curry, et al., *Deep in Our Hearths: Nine White Women in the Freedom Movement* (Athens: University of Georgia Press, 2000); Vicky Crawford, Jacqueline Anne Rouse, and Barbara Woods, eds., *Women in the Civil Rights Movement: Trailblazers and Torchbearers, 1941–1965* (Bloomington: Indiana University Press, 1990); Ruth Rosen, *The World Split Open: How the Modern Women's Movement Changed America* (New York: Penguin Group, 2001), 100–101, 106–107. This framework might be made even more complicated due to the fact that white women and black women were coming to the movement with differing experiences, namely that white women did not necessarily understand the local contexts of the South during this time period and thus were purposefully assigned less difficult work in offices (or were assigned this office work as a pragmatic move to ensure the safety of activists in the field). As Cynthia Washington reasoned, this assignment was based on the women's qualifications. Washington recalls that she herself had her own project she was directing in Mississippi, but viewed herself as having experience. See Ann Standley, "The Role of Black Women in the Civil Rights Movement," 197. Eventually though, even Washington concluded sexism existed in SNCC. See especially198.

4. See Barbara Ransby, *Ella Baker and the Black Freedom Movement: A Radical Democratic Vision* (Chapel Hill: University of North Carolina Press, 2003), 184–186.

5. Ann Standley, "The Role of Black Women in the Civil Rights Movement," 195.

6. *Ibid.*

7. See Elaine Brown, *A Taste of Power: A Black Woman's Story* (New York: Doubleday Books, 1992); Assata Shakur, *Assata: An Autobiography* (Chicago: Lawrence Hill Books, 1987); Angela Davis, *Angela Davis: An Autobiography* (New York: International Publishers, 1988).

8. To date, only 52 women have been in the Senate. See "Women in the Senate," https://www.senate.gov/artandhistory/ history/common/briefing/women_senators.htm (accessed 4 July 2018). In the House, between 1955 and 1976 there were only 39 women. See http://history.house.gov/ Exhibitions-and-publications/WIC/ Historical-Essays/Changing-Guard/ Introduction/ (accessed 8 August 2018). For the President's cabinet, see www.potus.com/ rmnixon.html (accessed 8 August 2018).

9. See Center for American Women and Politics, "Women in Elective Office 2018," http://www.cawp.rutgers.edu/current-numbers (accessed 4 July 2018). As of June 2018, the CATO Institute's Board of Directors had two women out of 19 directors. See http://www.cato.org/board-of-directors (accessed 4 June 2018). The American Enterprise Institute's Board of Trustees had no woman trustee. See http://www.aei.org/ about/board-of-trustees/ (accessed 4 July 2018).

10. Harold Jacobs, "Inside the Weather Machine: Introduction," *Weatherman*, ed. Harold Jacobs (Ramparts Press, 1970), 303–304.

11. A Weatherwoman, "Inside the Weather Machine," *Rat*, February 6, 1970; reprint, *Weatherman*, ed. Harold Jacobs (Ramparts, 1970), 320 (page citations are to the reprint edition).

12. Larry Grathwohl and Frank Reagan, *Bringing Down America: An FBI Informant with the Weathermen* (New Rochelle: Arlington House Publishers, Inc., 1976); reprint, Lexington: Tina Trent, 2013, 120, 132–133 (page citations are to the reprint edition).

13. Bill Ayers, *Fugitive Days* (Boston: Beacon Press, 2001), Kindle Edition, Chapter 23.

14. David Gilbert, *Love and Struggle: My Life in SDS, The Weather Underground, and Beyond* (Oakland: PM Press, 2012), 186–187; Thai Jones, *A Radical Line: From the Labor Movement to the Weather Underground, One's Family Century of Conscience* (New York: Free Press, 2004), Kindle Edition, Chapter 9.

15. See Alistair Horn, *A Savage War of Peace: Algeria 1954–1962* (New York: New York Review Books, 2011); Erika A. Kuhlman, *A to Z of Women in World History* (New York: Infobase Publishing, 2002); *The Battle of Algiers*, directed by Gillo Pontecorvo (1966).

16. *Ibid.*

17. Larry Grathwohl and Frank Reagan, *Bringing Down America*, 18–19 (page citations are to the reprint edition).

18. "Stormy Weather," *San Francisco Good Times*, January 8, 1970; reprint, *Weatherman*, ed. Harold Jacobs (Ramparts, 1970), 347 (page citations are to the reprint edition).

19. Gilbert, *Love and Struggle*, 125.

20. For more on the discussion of fragile masculinity in the face of women's increasing flexibility in gender roles, see Carolyn Lewis, *Prescription for Heterosexuality: Sexual Citizenship in the Cold War Era* (Chapel Hill: University of North Carolina Press, 2010), Chapter 3. For more on masculinity in twentieth century U.S., see James Gilbert, *Men in the Middle: Searching for Masculinity in the 1950's* (Chicago: University of Chicago Press, 2005); Bill Osgerby, *Playboys in Paradise: Masculinity, Youth, and Leisure Style in Modern America* (London: Bloomsbury Academic, 2001).

21. Lorraine Rosal, "Who Do They Think Could Bury You?," *New Left Notes*, August 23, 1969; reprint, *Weatherman*, ed. Harold Jacobs (Ramparts Press, 1970), 149 (page citations are to the reprint edition).

22. *Ibid.*

23. *Ibid.*, 149.

24. *Ibid.*, 150.

25. *Ibid.*

26. A Weatherwoman, "Inside the Weather Machine," 322.

27. Rosal, "Who Do They Think Could Bury You?," 149.

28. A Weatherwoman, "Inside the Weather Machine," 326.

29. WUO, "Weather Letter," *Rat*, July 15, 1970; reprint, *Weatherman*, ed., Harold Jacobs (Ramparts, 1970), 458 (page citations are to the reprint edition).

30. The Reminisces of David Gilbert (June 16, 17, 18, 19, 1985), 244, CCOHC.

31. *Ibid.*

32. Research seems to support the view that female leadership results in more cooperative approaches and female empowerment, while male leadership results in more competitive and exploitative styles of leadership, which are aimed at individual and not communal gains. See J. Brad Chapman, "Comparison of Male and Female Leadership Styles," *Academy of Management*, 18, 3 (September 1975): 645–650; Roslyn H. Chernesky and Marcia J. Bombick, "Women's

Ways and Effective Management," *Affilia*, 3, 1 (March 1988): 48–61. Female leadership also fosters an interdependent style or dynamic, see Jean Lipman-Blumen, "Connective Leadership: Female Leadership Styles in the 21st Century Workplace," *Sociological Perspectives*, 35, 1 (1992): 183–203. In terms of women's leadership in social movements, such as the civil rights movement, research indicates that women's building of personal relationships aided in building coalitions and in recruiting members to the cause. See Belinda Robnett, "African American Women in the Civil Rights Movement, 1954–1965: Gender, Leadership, and Micromobilization," *AJS*, 101, 6 (May 1996): 1661–1693; Danelle Moon, *Daily Life of Women During the Civil Rights Era* (Santa Barbara: Greenwood Press, 2011).

33. A Weatherwoman, "Inside the Weather Machine," 321.

34. *Ibid.*, 322.

35. This title is inspired by a positive characterization made by Susan Stern about Bernardine Dohrn. See Susan Stern, *With the Weathermen: The Personal Journal of a Revolutionary Woman*, ed. Laura Browder (New Brunswick: Rutgers University Press, 2007), 150. Using similar language, the FBI's infiltrator Grathwohl compares Dohrn to "a high priestess" due to her oratorical skills. Grathwohl and Reagan, *Bringing Down America*, 101.

36. Gilbert, *Love and Struggle*, 118; Berger, *Outlaws of America*, 84.

37. Andrew Kopkind, "The Real SDS Stands Up," (Chicago: Hard Times, June 30–July 5, 1969), available at the SDS/WUO Document Archive at http://www.sds-1960s.org/Kopkind-1969convention.pdf (accessed 5 September 2013), also available in *Weatherman*, ed. Harold Jacobs, 26, 27.

38. *Ibid.*

39. Federal Bureau of Investigation, *Weather Underground*, part 2, 1, 2, 59, 68. Dohrn organized trips to Cuba first for SDS, then for Weather. Note that after the split, Weather considered itself the real SDS, and slowly took on the name Weather and abandoned the SDS moniker.

40. Several other Weatherwomen were involved in the trip, such as Diana Oughton, Dionne Donghi, and Elenor Raskin. See Federal Bureau of Investigation, *Weather Underground*, part 3; Ron Jacobs, *The Way*

the Wind Blew: A History of the Weather Underground (New York: Verso, 1997), 26; Ayers, Fugitive Days, Chapter 19; Jones, A Radical Line, Chapter 7.

41. Federal Bureau of Investigation, Weather Underground, part 2, 59.

42. Dohrn though was careful to maintain a balance in the struggle, so that outright violence would not take over the organization. Eventually, she even expelled the most influential proponent of violence, John Jacobs, from within the organization. This will be discussed shortly. See Ayers, Fugitive Days, Chapter 19; Jones, A Radical Line, Chapter 7.

43. See Federal Bureau of Investigation, Weather Underground, part 2, 68; Federal Bureau of Investigation, Weather Underground, part 3, 11.

44. Federal Bureau of Investigation, Weather Underground, part 3, 6; Federal Bureau of Investigation, Weather Underground, part 4, 13.

45. See Ron Jacobs, The Way the Wind Blew, 29–30; Berger, Outlaws of America, 108; Jeremy Varon, Bringing the War Home: The Weather Underground, The Red Army Faction, and Revolutionary Violence in the Sixties and Seventies (Berkeley: University of California Press, 2004), 77; Jones, A Radical Line, Chapter 8; Gilbert, Love and Struggle, 131.

46. Ayers, Fugitive Days, Chapter 20. For more on "La Pasionaria" see Dolores Ibarruri, They Shall Not Pass: The Autobiography of La Pasionaria (New York, 1976).

47. Larry Grathwohl continues his description of Dohrn, noting that also "She was sexually appealing in long dark boots, a short miniskirt, and a see-through blouse with no bra." See Grathwohl and Reagan, Bringing Down America, 101–102.

48. Grathwohl and Reagan, Bringing Down America, 101–102.

49. Stern, With the Weathermen, 141; Varon, Bringing the War Home,, 80; Jones, A Radical Line, Chapter 8.

50. Stern, With the Weathermen, 147.

51. Wilkerson, Flying Close to the Sun, 304.

52. Varon, Bringing the War Home, 81.

53. Ayers, Fugitive Days, Chapter 20.

54. Stern, With the Weathermen, 151.

55. Clara Bingham, Witness to the Revolution: Radicals, Resisters, Vets, Hippies, and the Year America Lost Its Mind and Found Its Soul (New York: Random House, 2016), Kindle Edition, Chapter 7.

56. Ibid.

57. Shin'ya Ono, "You Do Need A Weatherman To Know Which Way the Wind Blows," Leviathon, December 1969; reprint, Weatherman, ed. Harold Jacobs (Ramparts Press, 1970), 273 (page citations are to the reprint edition).

58. Stern, With the Weathermen, 149.

59. Ibid., 151. By Larry Grathwohl's account, Weatherwoman Naomi Jaffe also inspired those jailed, as he remembers her discussing the jailing as follows: "The pigs couldn't break us.... We all stuck together. We sang songs. We even got the others, the supposed criminals to join in with us. The pigs didn't know what to do." See Grathwohl and Reagan, Bringing Down America, 63.

60. Ayers, Fugitive Days, Chapter 19; Jones, A Radical Line, Chapter 7.

61. See Jones, A Radical Line, Chapter 9.

62. Wilkerson, Flying Close to the Sun, 324–326; Jonah Raskin, "Introduction," in The Weather Eye: Communiques from the Weather Underground, ed. Jonah Raskin (San Francisco: Union Square Press, 1974), 5; Ron Jacobs, The Way the Wind Blew, 47.

63. Wilkerson, Flying Close to the Sun, 336. Ron Jacobs lists both Weathermen as "purported" supporters of this plan. See Jacobs, The Way the Wind Blew, 47.

64. See Berger, Outlaws of America, 129; Gilbert, Love and Struggle, 150; Wilkerson, Flying Close to the Sun, 337.

65. Wilkerson, Flying Close to the Sun, 351.

66. Thai Jones, A Radical Line: From the Labor Movement to the Weather Underground, One's Family Century of Conscience (New York: Free Press, 2004), Kindle Edition, Chapter 9.

67. Ibid.

68. Note that this approach could be argued to be both feminist and strategic. The approach is arguably feminist in that it is creating a low pressure, low affective environment where WUO members could reflect and shed the strains imposed on them by living on the run or underground; it was an environment that focuses on healing, collaboration and relationships. At the same time, this approach could also have afforded time for Dohrn to make her point privately

to individual members so that she could be more effective in her group presentation. In any case, this interval allowed members to make decisions in a calmer environment.

69. Jones, *A Radical Line*, Chapter 9.

70. *Ibid.* Also see Wilkerson, *Flying Close to the Sun*, 351.

71. Jones, *A Radical Line*, Chapter 9.

72. Ayers, *Fugitive Days*, Chapter 24.

73. *Ibid.*

74. Jones, *A Radical Line*, Chapter 9.

75. Gilbert, *Love and Struggle*, 152.

76. The Weather Underground, "A Declaration of a State of War: May 21, 1970, Communiqué," 21 May 1970; reprint, in *The Weather Eye: Communiqués from the Weather Underground*, ed. Jonah Raskin (San Francisco: Union Square Press, 1974), 16 (page citations are to the reprint edition). An audio file of the communiqué was made available to radio stations. It is also available here: http://www.youtube.com/watch?v=jbpTvkpZluk (accessed 12 July 2017). For more on the communiqué, see Federal Bureau of Investigation, *Weather Underground File*, part 3, 45–47; Ron Jacobs, *The Way the Wind Blew*, 51; Berger, *Outlaws of America*, 136. Cril Payne, an FBI agent who infiltrated the WUO, stated that Dohrn's communiqué outraged J. Edgar Hoover, as it indicated that "the situation was rapidly progressing to the point where the group was becoming an embarrassment to the Bureau." See Cril Payne, *Deep Cover: An FBI Agent Infiltrates the Radical Underground* (New York: Newsweek Books, 1979), 16.

77. Jones, *A Radical Line*, Chapter 9.

78. Bernardine Dohrn, "New Morning, Changing Weather Communiqué: December 6, 1970," in *The Weather Eye: Communiques from the Weather Underground*, ed. Jonah Raskin (San Francisco: Union Square Press, 1974), 26–35.

79. *Ibid.*

80. *Ibid.*, 29.

81. Dohrn, "New Morning, Changing Weather Communiqué: December 6, 1970," 31–35. Also see The Reminisces of David Gilbert, 217.

82. See *The Weather Eye: Communiqués from the Weather Underground*, ed. Jonah Raskin (San Francisco: Union Square Press, 1974).

83. Johan Raskin, "Introduction," in *The Weather Eye: Communiqués from the*

Weather Underground, ed. Jonah Raskin (San Francisco: Union Square Press, 1974), 6.

84. Emile de Antonio, *Underground*, DVD.

85. *Ibid.*

86. Bernardine Dohrn, "Toward a Revolutionary Women's Movement," *New Left Notes*, Special Issue, March 8, 1969, 4; also available at SDS/WUO Document Archive, http://www.antiauthoritarian.net/sds_wuo/nln_iwd_1969/ (accessed 26 June 2017).

87. *Ibid.*

88. This title is inspired by Diana Oughton's words in a letter to her parents. See Thomas Powers, *Diana: The Making of a Terrorist* (Boston: Houghton Mifflin, 1998), 100.

89. Federal Bureau of Investigation, *Diana Oughton*, part 1. "Memories of Diana," *Time*, 30 March 1970; reprint, in *Weatherman*, ed. Harold Jacobs (Ramparts Press, 1970), 486 (page citations are to the reprint edition).

90. Powers, *Diana*, 10, 22, 24, 30; Lucinda Franks and Thomas Powers, "Story of Diana: The Making of a Terrorist, Part 1," United Press International, 1970, http://100years.upi.com/sta_1970-09-14-p1.html (accessed 26 June 2017).

91. Powers, *Diana*, 30–35; Lucinda Franks and Thomas Powers, "Story of Diana: The Making of a Terrorist, Part 2," United Press International, 1970, http://100years.upi.com/sta_1970-09-16-p2.html (accessed 1 July 2017); Federal Bureau of Investigation, *Diana Oughton*, part 1.

92. Powers, *Diana*, 39, 43; Ayers, *Fugitive Days*, Chapter 12.

93. Powers, *Diana*, 32–45. Also see, Nicholas Cullather, *Secret History: The CIA's classified account of its operations in Guatemala, 1952–1954* (Palo Alto: Stanford University Press, 1999). This work is a book written by the CIA historian, meant to tell the story for CIA eyes only.

94. Ayers, *Fugitive Days*, Chapter 14.

95. See Powers, *Diana*, 60; Ayers, *Fugitive Days*, Chapter 12; Lucinda Franks and Thomas Powers, "Story of Diana: The Making of a Terrorist, Part 3," United Press International, 1970, http://100years.upi.com/sta_1970-09-16-p3.html (accessed 14 July 2017); Federal Bureau of Investigation, *Diana Oughton*, part 1.

96. See Ron Jacobs, *The Way the Wind Blew*, 6, 48; Powers, *Diana*, 87; Federal Bu-

reau of Investigation, *Weather Underground*, part 5, 32.

97. See Powers, *Diana*, 88–89, 90, 104.
98. *Ibid.*, 92–3.
99. Mike Klonsky, "Toward a Revolutionary Youth Movement," December 1968.
100. Powers, *Diana*, 101; Lucinda Franks and Thomas Powers, "Story of Diana: The Making of a Terrorist, Part 3."
101. Lucinda Franks and Thomas Powers, "Story of Diana: The Making of a Terrorist, Part 3."
102. Federal Bureau of Investigation, *Diana Oughton*, part 1.
103. Federal Bureau of Investigation, *Diana Oughton*, part 1 and part 2. See Federal Bureau of Investigation, *Diana Oughton*, part 2, part 3 and part 4. Also see Federal Bureau of Investigation, *Weather Underground*, part 3, 15.
104. "Memories of Diana," *Time*, 30 March 1970; reprint, in *Weatherman*, ed. Harold Jacobs (Ramparts Press, 1970), 486 (page citations are to the reprint edition). Lucinda Franks and Thomas Powers, "Story of Diana: The Making of a Terrorist, Part 3"; Lucinda Franks and Thomas Powers, "Story of Diana: The Making of a Terrorist, Part 4," United Press International, 1970, http://100years.upi.com/sta_1970-09-18-p4.html (accessed 18 July 2017); Ayers, *Fugitive Days*, Chapter 14, 15; Federal Bureau of Investigation, *Diana Oughton*, part 1 and part 2. The FBI file notes that an informant overheard Diana state that at the Days of Rage, protesters would "confront the police," "bait the pigs," and "resist arrest." See Federal Bureau of Investigation, *Diana Oughton*, part 2, part 3 and part 4. Also see Federal Bureau of Investigation, *Weather Underground*, part 3, 15.
105. Powers, *Diana*, 94.
106. Powers, *Diana*, 72, 94; Ayers, *Fugitive Days*, Chapter 13.
107. Ayers, *Fugitive Days*, Chapter 13.
108. *Ibid.*
109. *Ibid.*, Chapter 14.
110. *Ibid.*
111. *Ibid.*
112. Ayers, *Fugitive Days*, Chapter 13; Powers, *Diana*, 97, 158.
113. Ayers, *Fugitive Days*, Chapter 15.
114. *Ibid.* Larry Grathwohl, who infiltrated the WUO for the FBI, noted that he found Oughton to be concerned with the

indiscriminate use of violence, particularly against people. As Grathwohl put it, "She had great concerns for people, and the thought of destroying them was bothering her." See Grathwohl and Reagan, *Bringing Down America*, 156–7.
115. *Ibid.*, Chapter 25, 30. Note this is a supposition; there's no way to concretely know Oughton's motivations.
116. Wilkerson, *Flying Close to the Sun*, 404.
117. *Ibid.*, 343; Powers, *Diana*, 3–6.
118. Wilkerson, *Flying Close to the Sun*, 343–344; Jacobs, *The Way the Wind Blew*, 47.
119. See Lucinda Franks and Thomas Powers, "Story of Diana: The Making of a Terrorist, Part 4."
120. This section title is inspired by Stern's memoir title, *With the Weathermen: The Personal Journey of a Revolutionary Woman.*
121. Stern, *With the Weathermen*, 11, 12, 13.
122. Stern, *With the Weathermen*, 12.
123. *Ibid.*, 15.
124. *Ibid.*, 16–17.
125. *Ibid.*, 19.
126. *Ibid.*, 21–22.
127. *Ibid.*, 33.
128. *Ibid.*, 36. Thursday, August 22, 1968 is most likely the night to which she is referring.
129. Stern was also involved in the Columbia protest. See Stern, *With the Weathermen*, 48–51, 57–58. As part of her work, Stern also met Kathy Boudin, Bernardine Dohrn, and Mark Rudd. Both women inspired and intimidated Stern, who stated that she wanted to achieve their strength and self-possession one day. See Stern, *With the Weathermen*, 46–47, 59–60.
130. *Ibid.*, 71.
131. *Ibid.*, 102.
132. *Ibid.*, 102, 108.
133. *Ibid.*, 109.
134. *Ibid.*, 114–117.
135. This action was a collaboration between the women in Stern's Weather collective and the SDS women. *Ibid.*, 128.
136. *Ibid.*, 129. For more on the action also see Mike Calovinch, "Female Protestors Stage Raid on Air Force ROTC," *University of Washington Daily*, 1 October 1969.

137. Stern, *With The Weathermen*, 130–131.

138. Stern, *With the Weathermen,* 131–132; Martin Works, "Young Animals Attack ROTC," *Seattle PI*, 3 October 1969.

139. Stern, *With the Weathermen*, 72.

140. Gilbert, *Love and Struggle*, 128.

141. Gerald Dworkin, *The Theory and Practice of Autonomy* (New York: Cambridge University Press, 1988), 6, 29. For more on autonomy, see Marilyn Friedman, *Autonomy, Gender, Politics* (Oxford: Oxford University Press, 2003); Robert Noggle, "Autonomy and the Paradox of Self-Creation," in *Personal Autonomy*, ed. James Stacey Taylor (New York: Cambridge University Press, 2005); Michael McKenna, "The Relationship between Autonomous and Morally Responsible Agency," in *Personal Autonomy*, ed. James Stacey Taylor (New York: Cambridge University Press, 2005); and Alfred Mele, *Autonomous Agents* (New York: Oxford University Press). It is the standard position that personal autonomy ought not to have substantial requirements, which implies that immoral acts can be autonomous. For support for this standard position, see: Isaiah Berlin, *Liberty* (Oxford: Oxford University Press, 1969), 179–200; Paul Benson, "Feminist Intuitions and the Normative Substance of Autonomy," in *Personal Autonomy*, ed. James Stacey Taylor (New York: Cambridge University Press, 2005); John Christman, "Procedural Autonomy and Liberal Legitimacy," in *Personal Autonomy*, ed. James Stacey Taylor (New York: Cambridge University Press, 2005), 281–285, 292–294; and James Stacey Taylor, "Introduction," in *Personal Autonomy*, ed. James Stacey Taylor (New York: Cambridge University Press, 2005), 22–23. For one position that there is something troubling about counting the immoral as autonomous, see Susan Wolf, "Freedom within Reason," in *Personal Autonomy*, ed. James Stacey Taylor (New York: Cambridge University Press, 2005), 265–267.

142. Rosal, "Who Do They Think Could Bury You?," 149.

143. Weather, "Honky Tonk Women," National War Council Packet, December 1969; reprint, *Weatherman*, Harold Jacobs, ed. (Ramparts, 1970), 314 (page citations are to the reprint edition).

144. Motor City SDS, "Break on Through to the Other Side," *New Left Notes*, August 23, 1969; reprint, *Weatherman*, Harold Jacobs, ed. (Ramparts, 1970), 154 (page citations are to the reprint edition).

145. "Motor City 9," *New Left Notes*, August 23, 1969; reprint, *Weatherman*, Harold Jacobs, ed. (Ramparts, 1970), 161 (page citations are to the reprint edition).

146. Motor City SDS, 154.

147. Laura Whitehorn, interview by author, 23 October 2014; Motor City SDS, 158.

148. Motor City SDS, 155.

149. *Ibid.*

150. Interestingly though, these Weatherwomen's agency or feminism is rarely the focus in the literature, where generally speaking, this action is represented in a manner that undermines these Weatherwomen's processes, contributions, and overall agency. For example, Berger characterizes the action as follows: "Weatherwomen invaded a classroom at McComb Community College, lectured the students on war and racism, and—using karate moves—blocked those who tried to escape. The Motor City Nine were arrested and charged with disorderly conduct and assault and battery" (Berger, *Outlaws of America*, 101). While this representation is generally accurate, it makes no mention of the women's message on sexism, nor does it discuss the fact that the women employed karate chops to respond to arrogant males who did not want to listen to a feminist message. Neither is there a discussion of female leadership in that description. Indeed, the way the women organized and led the action is a testament to their agency and to their active involvement within the WUO. It is a crucial aspect of female leadership within the WUO that should not be overlooked.

Ron Jacobs does much of the same thing when he describes this action. He reports that nine women entered the classroom and spoke to the students, stating that "some male students pushed the Weatherwomen out of the way in an attempt to leave. A fight ensued. The women failed to escape before the police arrived" (Ron Jacobs, *The Way the Wind Blew*, 23). His words, while generally accurate, nevertheless impart a sense of failure for the women, in that they emerge from the text as weak, being pushed around, and unable to escape. Again, there is no

mention of their feminist message nor is
there a discussion of their leadership. Hence,
the feminist message of the Weatherwomen
is expunged, as is their commanding presence.

151. "Women's Militia," *New Left Notes*,
September 12, 1969; reprint, *Weatherman*,
Harold Jacobs, ed. (Ramparts, 1970), 163–
4 (page citations are to the reprint edition).

152. *Ibid.*

153. "School Peace Riot Poses A Big
'Why?,'" *The Pittsburgh Press*, 5 September,
1969, 1 and 12; Roger Stuart, "Kids Dug Us,"
The Pittsburgh Press, 6 September, 1969, 2;
Associated Press, "Some Schools Have Be-
come Arenas of Racial Tension," *Herald
Journal*, 25 September, 1969, 2; Reuters,
"Girls' 'Bare' Display Produces 25 Arrests,"
The Montreal Gazette, 5 September 1969,
14; United Press International, "War Pro-
testors Cause Disorder at High School," *The
News Dispatch*, 5 September 1969, 1.

154. "School Peace Riot Poses A Big
'Why?'"; "Girls' 'Bare' Display Produces 25
Arrests."

155. Laura Whitehorn, interview by author, 23 October 2014.

156. Gilbert, *Love and Struggle*, 128.

157. Moreover, while Ron Jacobs describes the high school action in his treatment of the WUO, and speaks positively
about it, he does not discuss the whole event,
leaving out the protests of the night before
occurring around Pittsburgh. See Jacobs,
The Way the Wind Blew, 26.

158. "Women's Militia," 165.

159. Grathwohl and Reagan, *Bringing
Down America*, 5.

160. *Ibid.*, 84.

161. *Ibid.*, 147.

162. Grathwohl and Reagan, *Bringing
Down America*, 155.

163. *Ibid.*, 156.

164. Bill Ayers, *Fugitive Days*, Chapter
29.

165. *Ibid.*

166. *Ibid.*

167. *Ibid.*

168. *Ibid.*

169. Tom Thomas, "The Second Battle
of Chicago 1969"; reprint, *Weatherman*, ed.
Harold Jacobs (Ramparts Press, 1970), 197
(page citations are to the reprint edition).

170. Stern, *With The Weathermen*, 147.

171. *Ibid.*

172. Thomas, "The Second Battle of Chicago," 205.

173. See Varon, *Bringing the War Home*,
80; Thomas, "The Second Battle of Chicago," 205.

174. *Ibid.*

175. Stern, *With the Weathermen*, 149.

176. *Ibid.*, 148–149.

177. Gilbert, *Love and Struggle*, 133.

178. Shin'ya Ono, "You Do Need A
Weatherman To Know Which Way the Wind
Blows," *Leviathon*, December 1969; reprint,
Weatherman, ed. Harold Jacobs (Ramparts
Press, 1970), 270 (page citations are to the
reprint edition).

179. "Dykes and Fags Want to Know: Interview with Lesbian Political Prisoners:
Queers United in Support of Political Prisoners Linda Evans, Laura Whitehorn, and
Susan Rosenberg, 1991," in *Let Freedom
Ring: A Collection of the Documents from
the Movement to Free U.S. Political Prisoners*, ed. Matt Meyer (Oakland: PM Press,
2008), 380–381.

180. Bernardine Dohrn, "The Liberation
of Vietnamese Women," *New Left Notes*,
October 25, 1968.

181. Arlene Eisen Bergman, *Women of
Viet Nam* (San Francisco: People's Press,
1974), 113, 119–120, 157, 168–209.

182. Federal Bureau of Investigation,
Weather Underground, part 4, 23; *The
Weather Underground: Report of the Subcommittee to Investigate the Administration
of the Internal Security Act and Other Internal Security Laws of the Committee on
the Judiciary*, United States Senate, Ninety-
fourth Congress, First Session (1975). *The
Weather Underground*. Washington, D.C.:
U.S. Government Printing Office, 75.

183. See Grathwohl and Reagan, *Bringing Down America*, 108.

184. Rosal, "Who Do They Think Could
Bury You?," 149.

Chapter 4

1. Anonymous Weatherwomen, "Introduction," in *Sing a Battle Song* (Red Dragon
Print, 1975).

2. *Ibid.*

3. For example, Berger dismisses the
WUO's feminism at *Outlaws of America*,
172–174. See Dan Berger, *Outlaws of America: The Weather Underground and the Pol-

itics of Solidarity (Edinburgh: AK Press, 2006).

4. Women of the Weather Underground, "A Collective Letter to the Women's Movement," July 24, 1973, in *The Weather Eye: Communiqués from the Weather Underground*, ed. Jonah Raskin (San Francisco: Union Square Press, 1974), 68.

5. For more on the aims of the second wave, see Rachel Blau DuPlessis and Ann Snitow, "A Feminist Memoir Project," in *The Feminist Memoir Project: Voices From the Women's Liberation*, eds. Rachel Blau DuPlessis and Ann Snitow (New Brunswick: Rutgers University Press, 2007), 3–24; Rosalyn Baxandall and Linda Gordon "Introduction," in *Dear Sisters: Dispatches From the Women's Liberation Movement*, eds. Rosalyn Baxandall and Linda Gordon (New York: Basic Books, 2000), 11–13, 16; Robin Morgan, ed., *Sisterhood is Powerful: An Anthology of Writings From the Women's Liberation Movement* (New York: Random House, 1970); "Introduction," *Feminisms*, eds. Sandra Kemp and Judith Squires (Oxford: Oxford University Press, 1997), 3. Also see National Organization for Women, "The National Organization for Women's 1966 Statement of Purpose" at http://www.now.org/history/purpos66.html (accessed 9 September 2017). Ruth Rosen also discusses the aims of the second wave in *The World Split Open*. See Ruth Rosen, *The World Split Open: How the Modern Women's Movement Changed America* (New York: Penguin Group, 2001), 63–294.

6. Robin Morgan, "Goodbye to All That," *The Rat*, February 9–23, 1970, 6–7; reprint, *The Sixties Papers: Documents of a Rebellious Decade*, ed. Judith Clavir Albert (Westport: Prager, 1984), 510 (page citations are to the reprint edition).

7. *Ibid.*, 510, 514. Morgan identified the New Left movement, the ecological movement, as well as other groups as male led and as imbued with male privilege; society, for Morgan, was marred by male gender norms.

8. A Weatherwoman, "Inside the Weather Machine," *Rat*, February 6, 1970; reprint, *Weatherman*, ed. Harold Jacobs (Ramparts, 1970), 323 (page citations are to the reprint edition); Harold Jacobs, "Inside the Weather Machine: Introduction," *Weatherman*, ed. Harold Jacobs (Ramparts Press, 1970), 303.

9. Anonymous Weatherwomen, "Mountain Moving Day," 1973, 3.

10. Anonymous Weatherwomen, "Mountain Moving Day," 1973, 1.

11. Anonymous Weatherwomen, "Introduction," *Sing a Battle Song*.

12. This title is based on a phrase, "chained to a family structure that allows us no freedom," which comes from the WUO packet "Honky Tonk Women" that was passed out at the December 1969 national WUO (War Council) meeting. See Weather, "Honky Tonk Women," National War Council Packet, December 1969; reprint, *Weatherman*, Harold Jacobs, ed. (Ramparts, 1970), 316 (page citations are to the reprint edition).

13. See Betty Friedan, *The Feminine Mystique* (New York: Norton and Company, 2013 [1963]), Kindle Edition, 1, 303, 77 respectively. Many feminists of the second wave era took up Friedan's critical framework that linked patriarchy to the propagation of gender roles that resulted in oppression in women's lives. For some examples, see the SCUM Manifesto, which linked domesticity and motherhood to the patriarchy and saw them as destructive to women's self-development. See Valerie Solanas, "SCUM Manifesto"; reprint, *Radical Feminism: A Documentary Reader*, ed. Barbara A. Crow (New York: New York University Press, 2000), 201–222, especially 206 (page citations are to the reprint edition). For more on the critique of domesticity, see Pat Mainardi, "Politics of Housework"; reprint, *Radical Feminism: A Documentary Reader*, ed. Barbara A. Crow (New York: New York University Press, 2000), 525–529; Betsy Warrior, "Housework: Slavery or Labor of Love"; reprint, *Radical Feminism: A Documentary Reader*, ed. Barbara A. Crow (New York: New York University Press, 2000), 530–533.

14. See Cathy Wilkerson, "Toward a Revolutionary Women's Militia," *New Left Notes*, July 8, 1969, 6–7; also available at SDS/WUO Document Archive, http://www.antiauthoritarian.net/sds_wuo/weather/sds_wilkerson.txt (accessed 13 June 2017).

15. Anonymous Weatherwomen, "Riding the Subways," *Sing a Battle Song*, 13–14.

16. For more on the second shift, see Arlie Russel Hocschild and Anne Machung, *The Second Shift* (New York: Penguin Books, 1989).

17. For just a few examples of second wave critiques of housework and the second shift or the double day, see Rachel Blau DuPlessis and Ann Snitow, "A Feminist Memoir Project," in *The Feminist Memoir Project: Voices From Women's Liberation*, eds. Rachel Blau DuPlessis and Ann Snitow (New Brunswick: Rutgers University Press, 2007), 11; Rosalyn Baxandall and Linda Gordon, "Work," in *Dear Sisters: Dispatches From the Women's Liberation Movement*, eds. Rosalyn Baxandall and Linda Gordon (New York: Basic Books, 2000), 254; "Wages for Housework"; reprint, *Dear Sisters: Dispatches From the Women's Liberation Movement*, eds. Rosalyn Baxandall and Linda Gordon (New York: Basic Books, 2000), 258; Pat Mainardi, "The Politics of Housework," cited previously.

18. For more on the second shift, see Russel Hocschild and Machung, *The Second Shift*, cited above.

19. From the files of Naomi Jaffe; in author's files.

20. Anonymous Weatherwomen, "Six Sisters: Summer Study in Struggle for Health, Education and Welfare," Summer 1973, 1–2.

21. *Ibid.*, 7.

22. WUO, *Prairie Fire: The Politics of Revolutionary Anti-Imperialism* (San Francisco: Communications Co., 1974), 126–127. As mentioned in the Introduction, footnote 2, both men and women often wrote position papers. *Prairie Fire* was a collaborative effort, where ideas were presented, discussed, written, then rewritten and edited together, with all WUO collectives revising/editing. Some of the contributing members are known for their contributions, as they have claimed involvement with the creation of *Prairie Fire* (for example, Bill Ayers, Jeff Jones, Bernardine Dohrn) while the majority prefer to stay anonymous. The Weatherwomen were primarily in charge of the chapter on women and feminism. For more on the development of *Prairie Fire*, see Bernardine Dohrn, "When Hope and History Rhyme," in *Sing A Battle Song: The Revolutionary Poetry, Statements, and Communiqués of the Weather Underground, 1970–1974*, eds. Bernardine Dohrn, Bill Ayers, Jeff Jones (New York: Seven Stories Press, 2006), 6, 11; David Gilbert, *Love and Struggle: My Life in SDS, The Weather Underground, and Beyond* (Oakland: PM Press, 2012), 199.

23. WUO, *Prairie Fire*, 126.

24. See WUO, "A Mighty Army: An Investigation of Women Workers," *Osawatomie*, Summer 1975, No. 2, 6.

25. Celia Sojourn, "Where We Stand: The Women's Question is a Class Question," *Osawatomie*, Winter 1975-76, No. 4., 4. *Osawatomie* was a WUO publication, put together by men and women in the WUO. Thusly, I use "WUO" when referring to articles written in it. Celia Sojourn was an alias/pseudonym representing multiple authors (and, also exhibiting the example the WUO members set for themselves with such revolutionary women as Sojourner Truth). See the *Prairie Fire* section in *Sing a Battle Song: The Revolutionary Poetry, Statements, and Communiqués of the Weather Underground, 1970- 1974*, eds. Bernardine Dohrn, Bill Ayers, Jeff Jones (New York: Seven Stories Press, 2006), 234; Berger, *Outlaws of America*, 186.

26. Wilkerson, "Toward a Revolutionary Women's Militia," 6–7.

27. This WUO view echoed second wave critiques along the same lines. For a few examples of similar positions held by second wave groups, see Margaret Benston, "The Political Economy of Women's Liberation," Radical Education Project, 1969; "Wages for Housework"; reprint, *Dear Sisters: Dispatches From the Women's Liberation Movement*, eds. Rosalyn Baxandall and Linda Gordon (New York: Basic Books, 2000), 258. For the quote from the Redstockings, see Redstockings, "Redstockings Manifesto," in *Sisterhood is Powerful: An Anthology of Writings From the Women's Liberation Movement*, ed. Robin Morgan (New York: Random House, 1970), 533.

28. Robin Morgan, "Introduction," in *Sisterhood Is Powerful: An Anthology of Writings From the Women's Liberation Movement*, ed. Robin Morgan (New York: Random House, 1970), xxxii.

29. Sojourn, "The Women's Question is a Class Question," 3.

30. *Ibid.*

31. WUO, *Prairie Fire*, 126.

32. *Ibid.* This analysis of domesticity as enforced by family structure was also present in second wave writings. For a few examples of second wave discussions of women

and domesticity/child rearing within a marriage, see Alix Kates Shulman, "A Marriage Agreement," 1970; reprint, *Dear Sisters: Dispatches From the Women's Liberation Movement*, eds. Rosalyn Baxandall and Linda Gordon (New York: Basic Books, 2000), 218–219; Beverly Jones, "The Dynamics of Marriage and Motherhood," in *Sisterhood Is Powerful: An Anthology of Writings From the Women's Liberation Movement*, ed. Robin Morgan (New York: Random House, 1970), 46–61.

33. Wilkerson, "Toward a Revolutionary Women's Militia," 7.

34. Cathy Wilkerson, *Flying Close to the Sun* (New York: Seven Stories Press, 2007), 260.

35. *Ibid.* Wilkerson doesn't know herself as she went traveling before she saw it printed and did not notice the change.

36. Wilkerson, "Toward a Revolutionary Women's Militia," 7.

37. National Organization for Women, "The National Organization for Women's 1966 Statement of Purpose" at http://www.now.org/history/purpos66.html (accessed 9 September 2017). For examples of second wave groups discussing the wage gap, also see Rosen, *The World Split Open*, 65–69; "59 cents, A Woman's Dollar"; reprint, *Dear Sisters: Dispatches From the Women's Liberation Movement*, eds. Rosalyn Baxandall and Linda Gordon (New York: Basic Books, 2000), 272; Miriam Gilbert, "Women in Medicine," in *Sisterhood Is Powerful: An Anthology of Writings From the Women's Liberation Movement*, ed. Robin Morgan (New York: Random House, 1970), 62–66; Laura Furman, "A House is Not a Home: Women in Publishing," in *Sisterhood Is Powerful: An Anthology of Writings From the Women's Liberation Movement*, ed. Robin Morgan (New York: Random House, 1970), 66–70; Judith Ann, "The Secretarial Proletariat," in *Sisterhood Is Powerful: An Anthology of Writings From the Women's Liberation Movement*, ed. Robin Morgan (New York: Random House, 1970), 86–100.

38. Weather, "Honky Tonk Women," 316.

39. Robin Morgan, "Introduction," xxxiii, also see xv, xxxii.

40. See Alice Echols, *Daring to be Bad: Radical Feminism in America, 1967–1975* (Minneapolis: University of Minnesota Press, 1989), 387.

41. See Bread and Roses Collective, "Weatherman Politics and the Women's Movement," *Women*, 1970; reprint, *Weatherman*, ed. Harold Jacobs (Ramparts, 1970), 327–336 (page citations are to the reprint edition).

42. See Bread and Roses Collective, "Declaration of Women's Independence," 1970; reprint, *Dear Sisters: Dispatches From the Women's Liberation Movement*, eds. Rosalyn Baxandall and Linda Gordon (New York: Basic Books, 2000), 45–46.

43. Sojourn, "The Women's Question is a Class Question," 3.

44. See Kathy McAfee and Myrna Wood, "Bread and Roses," *Feminism in Our Time: The Essential Writings, WWII to the Present*, ed. Miriam Schneir (New York: Vintage Books, 1994), 135. The essay's title is not related to the Bread and Roses collective, but the essay defends a similar position.

45. WUO, *Prairie Fire*, 127.

46. *Ibid.*

47. See WUO, "A Mighty Army: An Investigation of Women Workers," *Osawatomie*, Summer 1975, No. 2, 6–9.

48. WUO, *Prairie Fire*, 127.

49. The second wave was also interested in the idea of organizing female workers so as to gain better working conditions and pay. For just an example, see Renee Blakkan, "Women Unionize Office Jobs," 1974; reprint, *Dear Sisters: Dispatches From the Women's Liberation Movement*, eds. Rosalyn Baxandall and Linda Gordon (New York: Basic Books, 2000), 270. Morgan was fired for trying to unionize her workplace. See Robin Morgan, "Introduction," xiv. For more on women's efforts to gain equal wages to those of men, including support for collective bargaining rights, see Dorothy Sue Cobble, *The Other Women: Workplace Justice and Social Rights in Modern America* (Princeton: Princeton University Press, 2004); Eileen Boris, *Home to Work: Motherhood and the Politics of Industrial Homework in the United States* (Cambridge: Cambridge University Press, 1994); Alice Kessler Harris, *Out to Work: The History of Wage Earning Women* (Oxford: Oxford University Press, 2003); Priscilla Murolo, A. B. Chitty, and Joe Sacco, *From the Folks Who Brought You the Weekend: A Short, Illustrated History of Labor in the United States* (New York: The New York Press, 2001); Alice

Kessler Harris, *In Pursuit of Equity: Women, Men, and the Quest for Economic Citizenship in 20th Century America* (Oxford: Oxford University Press, 2001); Nan Enstad, *Ladies of Labor, Girls of Adventure: Working Women, Popular Culture and Labor Politics at the Turn of the Twentieth Century* (New York: Columbia University Press, 1999).

50. This title, "We Can't Get No Satisfaction," comes from a subheading used in the "Honky Tonk Women" WUO (War Council) meeting packet from December, 1969. See Weather, "Honky Tonk Women," 317.

51. For examples of second wavers' critique of gender norms, see Rachel Blau DuPlessis and Ann Snitow, "A Feminist Memoir Project," 12; Meredith Tax, "There Was a Young Woman Who Swallowed a Lie...," 1969; reprint, *Dear Sisters: Dispatches From the Women's Liberation Movement*, eds. Rosalyn Baxandall and Linda Gordon (New York: Basic Books, 2000), 293; Jean Tepperman, "Witch," 1969; reprint, *Dear Sisters: Dispatches From the Women's Liberation Movement*, eds. Rosalyn Baxandall and Linda Gordon (New York: Basic Books, 2000), 296.

52. See Kathy McAfee and Myrna Wood, "Bread and Roses," 134.

53. See Echols, *Daring to Be Bad*, 388.

54. See Redstockings, "Redstockings Manifesto," 1970; reprint, *Radical Feminism: A Documentary Reader*, ed. Barbara A. Crow (New York: New York University Press, 2000), 224.

55. Morgan, "Introduction," xix.

56. Wilkerson, "Toward a Revolutionary Women's Militia," 6–7.

57. *Ibid.*

58. Weather, "Honky Tonk Women," 316–317.

59. See WUO, *Prairie Fire*, 128.

60. Anonymous Weatherwomen, "Mountain Moving Day," 1973, 1.

61. *Ibid.*

62. WUO, *Prairie Fire*, 128.

63. For just a few examples, see Linda Phelps, "Death is the Spectacle," 1971; reprint, *Dear Sisters: Dispatches From the Women's Liberation Movement*, eds. Rosalyn Baxandall and Linda Gordon (New York: Basic Books, 2000), 175–179; Bev Grant, "A Pretty Girl Is Like a Commodity," 1968; reprint, *Dear Sisters: Dispatches From the Women's*

Liberation Movement, eds. Rosalyn Baxandall and Linda Gordon (New York: Basic Books, 2000), 180; Bev Grant, "Ain't She Sweet," 1968; reprint, *Dear Sisters: Dispatches From the Women's Liberation Movement*, eds. Rosalyn Baxandall and Linda Gordon (New York: Basic Books, 2000), 180. Also see Rosen, *The World Split Open*, 159, 160–161.

64. Weather, "Honky Tonk Women," 316–317.

65. *Ibid.*, 317.

66. WUO, *Prairie Fire*, 128.

67. Weather, "Honky Tonk Women," 317. Feminist groups of the time period, such as the New York Radical Women fought against beauty ideals in protests. See Rosen, *World Split Open*, 159–161; Echols, *Daring to be Bad*, 92–95, 388.

68. A similar position was held by the New York Radical Women. See New York Radical Women, "No More Miss America," 1968; reprint, *Dear Sisters: Dispatches From the Women's Liberation Movement*, eds. Rosalyn Baxandall and Linda Gordon (New York: Basic Books, 2000), 184.

69. Echols, *Daring to be Bad*, 93.

70. New York Radical Women, "No More Miss America."

71. Weather, "Honky Tonk Women," 317.

72. *Ibid.* As previously mentioned, second wavers were also involved in the fight against beauty standards. For just a few examples, see New York Radical Women, "No More Miss America," 184; Judy Freespirit and Aldebaran, "Fat Liberation Manifesto," 1973; reprint *Dear Sisters: Dispatches From the Women's Liberation Movement*, eds. Rosalyn Baxandall and Linda Gordon (New York: Basic Books, 2000), 191. Also see Redstockings, "The Miss America Protest," http://www.redstockings.org/index.php? option=com_content&view=article&id= 59&Itemid=103 (accessed 10 November 2017). Also see Rosen, *The World Split Open*, 159–162; Echols, *Daring to be Bad*, 92–95.

73. Second wave feminists were deeply involved in the fight for reproductive freedom. For just a few examples, see JANE, "Women Learn to Perform Abortions," 1973; reprint, *Dear Sisters: Dispatches From the Women's Liberation Movement*, eds. Rosalyn Baxandall and Linda Gordon (New York: Basic Books, 2000), 145–47 (JANE was a collective within the Chicago Women's Lib-

eration Union, a group that delivered abortion access and in which some collective members performed the abortions themselves); Irene Peslikis, "Women Must Control the Means of Reproduction," 1967 (drawing); reprint, *Dear Sisters: Dispatches From the Women's Liberation Movement*, eds. Rosalyn Baxandall and Linda Gordon (New York: Basic Books, 2000), 134; Rosen, *The World Split Open*, 157–159, 176, 177. Also see sections from Heather Boots and Vivian Rothstein on abortion in Clara Bingham, *Witness to the Revolution: Radicals, Resisters, Vets, Hippies, and the Year America Lost Its Mind and Found Its Soul* (New York: Random House, 2016), Kindle Edition, Chapter 17.

74. See *The Weather Underground: Report of the Subcommittee to Investigate the Administration of the Internal Security Act and Other Internal Security Laws of the Committee on the Judiciary*, United States Senate, Ninety-fourth Congress, First Session (1975). *The Weather Underground*, 13; Federal Bureau of Investigation, *Weatherman Underground*, part 1, part 3, 12–27. Also see Venceremos Brigade at www.venceremosbrigade.net/ (accessed 3 September 2017).

FBI informant Larry Grathwohl remembers that Weatherwoman Karen Bittner was discussing the Venceremos Brigade as an opportunity for members to learn/observe gender equality, as he noted that Bittner said that the Brigade was "fantastic opportunity, especially for the women: 'Women aren't second class citizens in Cuba.'" Larry Grathwohl and Frank Reagan. *Bringing Down America: An FBI Informant with the Weathermen* (New Rochelle: Arlington House Publishers, Inc., 1976); reprint, Lexington: Tina Trent, 2013, 117–118 (page citations are to the reprint edition).

75. The Venceremos Brigade, *Venceremos Brigade: Young Americans Sharing the Life and Work of Revolutionary Cuba—Diaries, Letters, Interviews, Tapes, Essays, Poetry by the Venceremos Brigade*, eds. Carol Brightman and Sandra Lawson (New York: Simon & Schuster, 1971), 258. Material from the book comes from the first two brigades (February-April, 1970) and therefore includes former SDS members, who at the time were WUO. Also see Federal Bureau of Investigation, *Weatherman Underground*,

part 1, 26–29; Federal Bureau of Investigation, *Weatherman Underground*, part 3, 12–27.

76. For more on Roe v. Wade and the fight to legalize abortion, see Leslie J. Reagan, *When Abortion Was a Crime* (Berkeley: University of California Press, 1997); Rosen, *The World Split Open*, 157–159.

77. Wilkerson, *Flying Close to the Sun*, 78–80.

78. Anonymous Weatherwomen, "Six Sisters," 10. They also cautioned that abortion centers might serve young women, but health centers that focus on the needs of "older, or poor people" must also be developed.

79. WUO, *Prairie Fire*, 88.

80. *Ibid.*, 128.

81. As previously noted, position papers on these issues, sometimes satirical in nature so as to illustrate that women were held to a pro-natal norm to their own detriment, were also crafted. For just a few examples, see Lucinda Cisler, "On Abortion and Abortion Law," 1969; reprint, *Dear Sisters: Dispatches From the Women's Liberation Movement*, eds. Rosalyn Baxandall and Linda Gordon (New York: Basic Books, 2000), 140–143; Sarah Wernick Lockeretz, "Hernia: A Satire on Abortion Law Repeal"; reprint, *Dear Sisters: Dispatches From the Women's Liberation Movement*, eds. Rosalyn Baxandall and Linda Gordon (New York: Basic Books, 2000), 144–145. Also consider the Redstockings' actions (a New York feminist group) in trying to repeal abortion laws by interrupting legislative hearings in New York. See Echols, *Daring to Be Bad*, 140–142. Also see Rosen, *The World Split Open*, 157–159,176, 177, 209. Also see Morgan, "Introduction," xix; National Organization for Women, "The Right of a Woman to Determine Her Own Reproductive Process," 1967; reprint, *Feminist Chronicles*, eds. Toni Carabillo, Judy Meuli, and June Bundy Csida (Los Angeles: Women's Graphics, 1993), 191–193.

82. WUO, *Prairie Fire*, 88.

83. *Ibid.*, 128.

84. *Ibid.*

85. See Susan Brownmiller, "The Mass Psychology of Rape," 1975; reprint, *Dear Sisters: Dispatches From the Women's Liberation Movement*, eds. Rosalyn Baxandall and Linda Gordon (New York: Basic Books, 2000), 197.

86. See Susan Brownmiller, "The Mass Psychology of Rape," 196–197. For just a few other examples of second wave discourse regarding rape, see Karen Lindsey, Holly Newman, and Fran Taylor, "Rape: The All American Crime," 1975; reprint, *Dear Sisters: Dispatches From the Women's Liberation Movement*, eds. Rosalyn Baxandall and Linda Gordon (New York: Basic Books, 2000), 195–196; Rosen, *The World Split Open*, 181–185.

87. Benita Roth, *Separate Roads To Feminism: Black, Chicana, and White Feminist Movements in America's Second Wave* (Cambridge: Cambridge University Press, 2004), 201. Roth defines ethos as a "value judgment/directive about how to do radical action."

88. Morgan, "Goodbye to All That," 510.

89. Bread and Roses Collective, "Weatherman Politics and the Women's Movement," 334.

90. These two pieces (Morgan's and "Inside a Weather Machine") were actually published at the same time, as if Morgan and the anonymous Weatherwoman were engaged with each other in a public conversation across the pages of *Rat*. See Harold Jacobs, "Inside the Weather Machine: Introduction," 305.

91. A Weatherwoman, "Inside the Weather Machine," 321, 322.

92. Susan Stern, *With the Weathermen: The Personal Journal of a Revolutionary Woman*, ed. Laura Browder (New Brunswick: Rutgers University Press, 2007), 94.

93. See Emile de Antonio, *Underground*, DVD.

94. WUO, *Prairie Fire*, 132.

95. *Ibid.*

96. A Weatherwoman, "Inside the Weather Machine," 322.

97. WUO, *Prairie Fire*, 132.

98. Bill Ayers, *Fugitive Days* (Boston: Beacon Press, 2001), Kindle Edition, Chapter 18; Thai Jones, *A Radical Line: From the Labor Movement to the Weather Underground, One's Family Century of Conscience* (New York: Free Press, 2004), Kindle Edition, Chapter 8; Wilkerson, *Flying Close to the Sun*, 268, 270.

99. See the introduction to the karate section in *Dear Sisters: Dispatches from the Women's Liberation Movement*, eds. Rosalyn Baxandall and Linda Gordon (New York: Basic Books, 2000), 206. Also see Susan Pacale, Rachel Moon, and Leslie Tanner,

"Karate As Self-Defense for Women," 1970; reprint, *Dear Sisters: Dispatches from the Women's Liberation Movement: Broadsides, Manifestos and Other Documents From the Twentieth Century's Most Influential Movement*, eds. Rosalyn Baxandall and Linda Gordon (New York: Basic Books, 2000), 208.

100. Morgan, "Introduction," xiv.

101. See New York Radical Women, "Principles," in *Sisterhood Is Powerful: An Anthology of Writings From the Women's Liberation Movement*, ed. Robin Morgan (New York: Random House, 1970), 520. The Redstockings also called for female unity as a source of power. See Redstockings, "Redstockings Manifesto," 533–536.

102. Redstockings, "Redstockings Manifesto," 533–536.

103. See Echols, *Daring to Be Bad*, 158–159, 387. Also see Roxanne Dunbar-Ortiz, "Outlaw Woman: Chapters from a Feminist Memoir in Progress," in *The Feminist Memoir Project: Voices from Women's Liberation*, eds. Rachel Blau DuPlessis and Ann Snitow (New Brunswick: Rutgers University Press, 2007), 90–114.

104. Female collectives/groups were seen as nurturing and empowering to women by feminist groups of the era and by the WUO. For just a few examples of second wavers on the importance of female collectives, see Priscilla Long, "We Called Ourselves Sisters," in *The Feminist Memoir Project: Voices From Women's Liberation*, eds. Rachel Blau DuPlessis and Ann Snitow (New Brunswick: Rutgers University Press, 2007), 324–337; Kathie Sarachild, "Consciousness-Raising: A Radical Weapon," in *Feminist Revolution* (New York: Random House, circa 1978), 144–150, also available at http://library.duke.edu/rubenstein/scriptorium/wlm/fem/sarachild.html (accessed 8 November 2017); The Women's Caucus, Political Science Department, University of Chicago, "The Halls of Academe," in *Sisterhood Is Powerful: An Anthology of Writings From the Women's Liberation Movement*, ed. Robin Morgan (New York: Random House, 1970), 101.

105. Instances of female leadership within WUO were previously discussed in Chapter 3. In "Goodbye to All That," Morgan condemns female leadership within WUO, instead demanding that women form their own movement. Morgan, "Goodbye to All That," 515.

106. Rosal, 149. Rosal also notes that the women's caucus in the Columbus collective was seen by the women "as a place for women to have organizing experiences and to develop an analysis of male chauvinism and supremacy as tools of the ruling class, an analysis of the relationship between white-working class women and the international proletariat, an analysis of the economic ramifications of the oppression of women, particularly young women, caused by a crisis in imperialism."

107. Anonymous Weatherwomen, "Six Sisters."

108. See Anonymous Weatherwomen, "Six Sisters," 4–16.

109. Anonymous Weatherwomen, "For L.," *Sing a Battle Song*, 26.

110. Anonymous Weatherwomen, "Sisterhood Is Not Magic" *Sing a Battle Song*, 2.

111. A Weatherwoman, "Inside the Weather Machine," 323.

112. *Ibid.*

113. See Morgan, "Goodbye to All That," 515. The collective letter noted here can be taken as a response to Morgan's critique of working alongside men.

114. Women of the Weather Underground, "A Collective Letter to the Women's Movement," 78.

115. Anonymous Weatherwomen, "Straight Talk" *Sing a Battle Song*, 23–24.

116. Anonymous Weatherwomen, "For a Troubled Sister," *Sing a Battle Song*, 14–15.

117. Bread and Roses, "A Declaration of Women's Independence," in *Dear Sisters: Dispatches form the Women's Liberation* Movement, eds. Rosalyn Baxandall and Linda Gordon (New York: Basic Books, 2000), 45.

118. Roxanne Dunbar-Ortiz, "Female Liberation as the Basis for Social Revolution," in *Sisterhood Is Powerful: An Anthology of Writings From the Women's Liberation Movement*, ed. Robin Morgan (New York: Random House, 1970), 477–492, especially 492.

119. Wilkerson, "Toward a Revolutionary Women's Militia," 7.

120. *Ibid.*

121. As previously noted, this label was what the sessions were called by WUO members. See Stern, *With the Weathermen*, 102. Berger notes that sexism and male privilege were part of the criticism, self-criticism ses-

sions frequently, yet nevertheless concludes that these sessions were unhelpful. He states, "Male supremacy was a frequent criticism—which isn't to say that men learned from or listened to the criticism, or even that all the criticisms were useful." See Berger, *Outlaws of America*, 105. This stance seems to ignore the important feminist work that women were undertaking in these sessions. Having the conversations in the first place illustrates that there was an awareness of the importance of smashing sexism. Whether or not the work was hard or unrewarding should not take away from the efforts of the people who were involved in it.

122. Gilbert, *Love and Struggle*, 124.

123. The FBI's infiltrator Larry Grathwohl somewhat worriedly noted that Weatherwomen were demanding equality in his collective and throughout the WUO, as well. According to Grathwohl, women wanted to be "completely independent" from men; men needed to accept women's liberation and equality in all matters, even when it came to sex or not viewing women as "sex objects." See Grathwohl and Reagan, *Bringing Down America*, 158.

124. Wilkerson, "Toward a Revolutionary Women's Militia," 7.

125. "National War Council," *FIRE!*, December 6, 1969, 9.

126. A Weatherwoman, "Inside the Weather Machine," 325.

127. WUO, "Who We Are," *Osawatomie*, Summer 1975, No. 2, 2; Berger, *Outlaws of America*, 207.

Chapter 5

1. Women of the Weather Underground, "A Collective Letter to the Women's Movement," July 24, 1973, in *The Weather Eye: Communiqués from the Weather Underground*, ed. Jonah Raskin (San Francisco: Union Square Press, 1974), 78–79.

2. Women of the Weather Underground, "A Collective Letter to the Women's Movement," 72. To the WUO, "Third World" referred to poor, usually non-industrialized nations, often times with colonial pasts, which were fighting for independence and national liberation.

3. See Anonymous Weatherwomen, "Six Sisters: Summer Study of Women in

Struggle for Health, Education, and Welfare," Summer 1973, 1, 6, 7.

4. The third wave aims to incorporate all identity types in its feminist practice, including race, class, and sexual identity. Thus, the third wave is interested in respecting/integrating all points of view, all kinds of backgrounds, all kinds of sexualities or gender identities. See Naomi Zack, *Inclusive Feminism: A Third Wave Theory of Women's Commonality* (Oxford: Rowman & Littlefield, 2005); Stacy Gillis, Gillian Howie, and Rebecca Munford, *Third Wave Feminism: A Critical Exploration* (New York: Palgrave Macmillan, 2007); Claire Snyder, "What Is Third Wave Feminism? A New Directions Essay," *Signs*, Vol. 34, No. 1 (Autumn 2008): 175–196; Leslie Heywood and Jennifer Drake, eds., *Third Wave Agenda: Being Feminist, Doing Feminism* (Minneapolis: University of Minnesota Press, 1997). As noted earlier, my use of the wave motif in this chapter is meant to be conceptual in that it will establish that the WUO's brand of feminism fits in what is already recognized as feminist in the historical third wave classification even though they are not part of the historical third wave.

5. The Women's Brigade, "Health, Education, and Welfare: An Enemy of Women, San Francisco, March 6, 1974 Communiqué," 6 March 1974; reprint, *The Weather Eye: Communiqués from the Weather Underground*, ed. Jonah Raskin (San Francisco: Union Square Press, 1974), 105.

6. The third wave is usually associated with an embrace of various types of sexuality, and with a refusal to prejudge sexual activity. See Claire Snyder, "What Is Third-Wave Feminism? A New Directions Essay," 175–6. Snyder also states that "third wavers feel entitled to ... claim sexual pleasure as they desire it." See page 179. She also notes that the third wavers' sex positivity is an amplified outgrowth of the second wavers' views toward sex, even though second wavers are usually associated with anti-sex views (for an alternative view regarding second wavers being anti-sex, see Jane Gerhard, *Desiring Revolution: Second Wave Feminism and The Rewriting of American Sexual Thought, 1920–1982* [New York: Columbia University Press, 2001]). For more on the third wave, also see Leslie Heywood, ed., *The Women's Movement Today: An En-*

cyclopedia of Third-Wave Feminism, vol. 1, A–Z (Westport: Greenwood, 2006), 260; Leslie Heywood and Jennifer Drake, eds., *Third Wave Agenda: Being Feminist, Doing Feminism*, 4. For more on sex positivity and third wave feminism, see Merri Lisa Johnson, *Jane Sexes It Up: True Confessions of Feminist Desire* (New York: Four Walls Eight Windows, 2002); Jaclyn Friedman and Jessica Valenti, eds., *Yes Means Yes: Visions of Female Sexual Power and a World Without Rape* (Berkeley: Seal Press, 2008); Nadine Strossen, "A Feminist Critique of the Feminist Critique of Pornography," *Virginia Law Review*, Vol. 79, No. 5 (Aug., 1993): 1099–1190; Ruth Rosen, *The World Split Open: How the Modern Women's Movement Changed America* (New York: Penguin Group, 2001), 353–357. For the origins of the "sex positive" label usually associated with third wave feminism, see Ellen Willis, "Lust Horizons: Is the Women's Movement Pro-sex?," *Village Voice*, June 17–23, 1981.

7. WUO, *Prairie Fire: The Politics of Revolutionary Anti-Imperialism* (San Francisco: Communications Co., 1974), 129.

8. bell hooks, "Feminism: A Movement to End Sexist Oppression," in Susan Kemp and Judith Squires, eds., *Feminisms* (Oxford: Oxford University Press, 1997), 23, 25, 27.

9. *Ibid.*, 25.

10. Leslie Heywood and Jennifer Drake, eds., *Third Wave Agenda: Being Feminist, Doing Feminism*, 7; Claire Snyder, "What Is Third-Wave Feminism? A New Directions Essay," 176.

11. *Ibid.*

12. Anonymous Weatherwomen, "Mountain Moving Day," 1973, 2.

13. *Ibid.*

14. *Ibid.*

15. WUO, *Prairie Fire*, 130–131.

16. *Ibid.*, 131–132. Also see Women of the Weather Underground, "A Collective Letter to the Women's Movement," 72; Anonymous Weatherwomen, "Mountain Moving Day," 2.

17. Bernardine Dohrn, "Toward a Revolutionary Women's Movement," *New Left Notes*, Special Issue, March 8, 1969, 4; also available at SDS/WUO Document Archive, http://www.antiauthoritarian.net/sds_wuo/nln_iwd_1969/ (accessed 26 June 2017).

18. *Ibid.*

19. For hooks' concern, see hook, "Feminism: A Movement to End Sexist Oppression," page 23. The quote is from Cathy Wilkerson. See Wilkerson, "Toward a Revolutionary Women's Militia," *New Left Notes*, July 8, 1969, 7; also available at SDS/WUO Document Archive, http://www.anti authori tarian.net/sds_wuo/weather/sds_wilkerson. txt (accessed 13 June 2017).

20. Celia Sojourn, "Where We Stand: The Women's Question is a Class Question," *Osawatomie*, Winter 1975–76, No. 4, 5.

21. The WUO was deeply anti-racist. For more on its anti-racist positions and its solidarity with minority groups, especially African Americans, see WUO, "The Battle Of Boston: An Investigation of ROAR," *Osawatomie*, Spring 1975, No. 1, 7–12; Anonymous Weatherwomen, "Venom II," *Sing a Battle Song* (Red Dragon Print, 1975), 43. Weatherwoman Laura Whitehorn spent several days in Boston, guarding African American families from attack from their white neighbors during the busing/school integration crisis in the seventies. Previously, she had worked in support of the Black Panther Party. See "Former Political Prisoner Laura Whitehorn," at http://www. kersplebedeb.com/mystuff/profiles/white horn.html (accessed 12 December 2017); Laura Whitehorn, "Introduction to the *War Before*," at http://www.feministpress.org/ sites/default/files/content/War_Before_ Intro.pdf (accessed 12 December 2017).

22. Sojourn, "Where We Stand: The Women's Question is a Class Question," 4.

23. Women were also experimented on in Haiti, Massachusetts, and New York. See Linda Gordon, *The Moral Property of Women: A History of Birth Control Politics in America* (Champaign: University of Illinois Press, 2007), 287–288; Elaine Tyler May, *America and the Pill: A History of Promise, Peril, and Liberation* (New York: Perseus Books, 2010).

24. Dohrn, "Toward a Revolutionary Women's Movement," 4.

25. *Ibid.*

26. The article was part of the winter 1975–1976 issue of *Osawatomie*.

27. Sojourn, "Where We Stand: The Women's Question is a Class Question," 3.

28. *Ibid.*

29. Anonymous Weatherwomen, *Sing a Battle Song*.

30. *Ibid.*

31. *Ibid.*, 9–10. The poem dates from November 1974. The poetry collection was released in 1975.

32. Anonymous Weatherwomen, "Women's Lament," *Sing a Battle Song*, 27–28.

33. *Ibid.*

34. *Ibid.*, 27.

35. Anonymous Weatherwomen, "Women's Lament," *Sing a Battle Song*, 28.

36. See Assata Shakur, *Assata: An Autobiography* (Chicago: Lawrence Hill Books, 1987), 3–17.

37. Anonymous Weatherwomen, "For Assata Shakur," *Sing a Battle Song*, 4.

38. Anonymous Weatherwomen, "Food Lines in Oakland," *Sing a Battle Song*, 36. This poem dates from February 1974.

39. J. Ann Tickner, "You Just Don't Understand: Troubled Estrangements Between Feminists and IR Theorists," *International Studies Quarterly* 41 (1997): 611–632.

40. Cynthia Enloe, *Bananas, Beaches and Bases: Making Feminist Sense of International Politics* (Berkeley: University of California Press, 2000).

41. For more on how women are affected by imperialism, see United Nations, *Human Development Report* (Oxford: Oxford University Press, 1995).

42. WUO, *Prairie Fire*, 87.

43. *Ibid.*, 90.

44. See Anonymous Weatherwomen, "Six Sisters," 7, 8.

45. WUO, *Prairie Fire*, 87.

46. *Ibid.*

47. *Ibid.*

48. Cynthia Enloe, *Maneuvers: The International Politics of Militarizing Women's Lives* (Berkeley: University of California Press, 2000), 108–111, 151.

49. *Ibid.*, 151–152.

50. WUO, *Prairie Fire*, 88.

51. *Ibid.*, 87. The Rockefellers and the Ford Foundation were listed as encouraging sterilizations.

52. See *Prairie Fire*, 88.

53. WUO, "Population Control," *Osawatomie*, Spring 1975, No. 1, 13.

54. WUO, *Prairie Fire*, 87.

55. Celia Sojourn, "Puerto Rico Is The Test Of Fire Of Anti-Imperialism," *Osawatomie*, Vol. 2, No. 1, April–May 1976, 8.

56. *Ibid.*

57. Bernardine Dohrn, "An Open Letter

To The U.S. Workers," *Osawatomie*, Vol. 2, No. 1, April-May 1976, 11. In a previous issue of *Osawatomie*, the WUO published "The Women's Question is a Class Question," where they noted that 34 percent of Puerto Rican women had been sterilized. See Celia Sojourn, "Where We Stand: The Women's Question is a Class Question," 5.

58. Anonymous Weatherwomen, "Malthusian Mythologies," *Sing a Battle Song*, 19–20.

59. Sojourn, "Where We Stand: The Women's Question is a Class Question," 5.

60. Anonymous Weatherwomen, "Six Sisters," 1, 6.

61. WUO, *Prairie Fire*, 133.

62. Among pieces that identify these positions in support of Native Americans, see the WUO's Health, Education and Welfare Communiqué, previously cited; WUO, "Weather Underground Organization Bombs Kennecott Corporation: Salt Lake City, Utah, September 4, 1975 Communiqué," 4 September 1975; reprint, *Sing A Battle Song: The Revolutionary Poetry, Statements, and Communiqués of the Weather Underground, 1970–1974*, eds. Bernardine Dohrn, Bill Ayers, Jeff Jones (New York: Seven Stories Press, 2006), 224; WUO, *Prairie Fire*, 12, 20, 40, 50, 104, 110, 123, 127; Bernardine Dohrn, "When Hope and History Rhyme," in *Sing A Battle Song: The Revolutionary Poetry, Statements, and Communiqués of the Weather Underground, 1970–1974*, eds. Bernardine Dohrn, Bill Ayers, Jeff Jones (New York: Seven Stories Press, 2006), 13.

63. Weather, "Honky Tonk Women," National War Council Packet, December 1969; reprint, *Weatherman*, Harold Jacobs, ed. (Ramparts, 1970), 313 (page citations are to the reprint edition.

64. The poem dates from 1972. See Anonymous Weatherwomen, "People's War," *Sing a Battle Song*, 5, 7. Ho Chi Minh was the leader of North Vietnam.

65. Anonymous Weatherwomen, "Mountain Moving Day," 2–3.

66. *Ibid.*

67. Women of the Weather Underground, "A Collective Letter to the Women's Movement," 76.

68. Meg Starr, "Laura Whitehorn," in *Enemies of the State* (Montreal: Abraham Guillen Press and Arm the Spirit, 2002), 14–15. The advice was derived from a story where "the French were decisively driven out of one village after another" due to collaboration between peasants and cadres of the party.

69. *Ibid.*, 20.

70. A Weatherwoman, "Inside the Weather Machine," *Rat*, February 6, 1970; reprint, *Weatherman*, ed. Harold Jacobs (Ramparts, 1970), 326 (page citations are to the reprint edition).

71. Weather, "Honky Tonk Women," 314.

72. *Ibid.*, 313.

73. *Ibid.*, 314.

74. *Ibid.*

75. See Bread and Roses Collective, "Weatherman Politics and the Women's Movement," *Women*, 1970; reprint, *Weatherman*, ed. Harold Jacobs (Ramparts, 1970), 328 (page citations are to the reprint edition).

76. See Anonymous Weatherwomen, "Mountain Moving Day," 2, 3.

77. Harold Jacobs, "Inside the Weather Machine: Introduction," in *Weatherman*, ed. Harold Jacobs (Ramparts, 1970), 303.

78. *Ibid.*

79. Mimi Marinucci, *Feminism is Queer: The Intimate Connection between Queer and Feminist Theory* (London: Zed Books, 2012), Kindle Edition, Chapter 8. Marinucci points out that this solidarity has not been found throughout the history of feminism, which included a great deal of "bias against lesbian women, gay men, bisexual people, and transgender people." This point fits with the contention that while many feminists of the time period were homophobic, the WUO's attempt to be sensitive of LGBTQ rights was more representative of third wave feminism. Also see Annamarie Jagose, "Feminism's Queer Theory," *Feminism & Psychology* 19, No. 2 (2009): 157–174.

80. Jane Alpert, *Growing Up Underground* (New York: Citadel Press, 1981), 330. In this same conversation, Dohrn explained that being in the WUO does not mean that one has to hide his or her beliefs or way of being. Dohrn stated, "We respect anyone who can survive underground, and we'll never ask you to compromise your beliefs, feminist or otherwise." See Alpert, *Growing Up Underground*, 329.

81. Anonymous Weatherwomen, "For Two Sisters," *Sing a Battle Song*, 25. This poem dates from Summer 1973.

82. Larry Grathwohl and Frank Reagan. *Bringing Down America: An FBI Informant with the Weathermen* (New Rochelle: Arlington House Publishers, Inc., 1976); reprint, Lexington: Tina Trent, 2013, 158 (page citations are to the reprint edition).
83. *Ibid.*
84. *Ibid.*
85. Women of the Weather Underground, "A Collective Letter to the Women's Movement," 78.
86. Starr, "Laura Whitehorn," 20.
87. David Gilbert, *Love and Struggle: My Life in SDS, The Weather Underground, and Beyond* (Oakland: PM Press, 2012), 140.
88. Dan Berger, *Outlaws of America: The Weather Underground and the Politics of Solidarity* (Edinburgh: AK Press, 2006), 105.
89. David Gilbert, *Love and Struggle*, 193. Gilbert does not state the city for this collective.
90. Weather, "Honky Tonk Women," 318.
91. Gilbert, *Love and Struggle*, 140.
92. WUO, *Prairie Fire*, 129.
93. Linda LeMoncheck, *Loose Women, Lecherous Men: A Feminist Philosophy of Sex* (Oxford: Oxford University Press, 1997), 70.
94. *Ibid.*
95. *Ibid.*
96. Neeru Tandon, *Feminism: A Paradigm Shift* (New Delhi: Atlantic Publishers and Distributors, 2008), 67.
97. Wilkerson, "Toward a Revolutionary Women's Militia," 7.
98. Harold Jacobs, "Inside the Weather Machine: Introduction," 301.
99. See Gilbert, *Love and Struggle*, 98.
100. Harold Jacobs, "Inside the Weather Machine: Introduction," 301.
101. Gilbert, *Love and Struggle*, 140–141, 193.
102. Starr, "Laura Whitehorn," 20.
103. A Weatherwoman, "Inside the Weather Machine," 325.
104. Weather, "Honky Tonk Women," 319.
105. A Weatherwoman, "Inside the Weather Machine," 322.
106. *Ibid.*
107. *Ibid.*
108. *Ibid.*, 325.
109. Susan Stern, *With the Weathermen: The Personal Journal of a Revolutionary Woman*, ed. Laura Browder (New Brunswick: Rutgers University Press, 2007), 110–111.
110. Ron Jacobs, *The Way the Wind Blew: A History of the Weather Underground* (New York: Verso, 1997), 24.
111. Stern, *With the Weathermen*, 121–122.
112. See Gilbert, *Love and Struggle*, 125.
113. WUO, "Weather Letter," *Rat*, July 15, 1970; reprint, *Weatherman*, ed., Harold Jacobs (Ramparts, 1970), 460 (page citations are to the reprint edition).
114. See Women of the Weather Underground, "A Collective Letter to the Women's Movement," 75.
115. Heather Corinna, "An Immodest Proposal," in *Yes Means Yes: Visions of Female Sexual Power & A World Without Rape*, eds. Jaclyn Friedman and Jessica Valenti (Berkeley: Seal Press, 2008), 191.
116. Stern, *With the Weathermen*, 122. David Gilbert adds orgies to the list of sexually experimental acts but notes that he only attended one. In evaluating such encounters, he states: "I suspect that while some may have found orgies new and exciting, most just went through the motions to maintain the image of being liberated." See Gilbert, *Love and Struggle*, 141. Weatherman Mark Rudd sums up smash monogamy as follows: "It was a moment of extreme sexual experimentation. Group sex, homosexuality, casual sex hook-ups were all tried as we attempted to break out of the repression of the past into the revolutionary future." See Mark Rudd, *Underground: My Life with SDS and the Weathermen* (New York: Harper Collins, 2009), 164. When assessing sexual liberation within the WUO, Bernardine Dohrn adds that the WUO "experimented famously with strategies for sexual liberation and lesbian rights." See Bernardine Dohrn, "When Hope and History Rhyme," 12. If the FBI's infiltrator Larry Grathwohl is to be believed on these matters, he was involved in a sexual relationship with Weatherwoman Naomi Jaffe. He noted that she was very open about her sexual desires and very matter of fact about sexual intercourse; she viewed traditional courting/mating practices as outdated. She was also a proponent of smash monogamy. See Grathwohl and Reagan, *Bringing Down America*, 75, 95–96.
117. Gilbert, *Love and Struggle*, 140.

118. A Weatherwoman, "Inside the Weather Machine," 325.

119. Carole Vance, "Pleasure and Danger: Towards a Politics of Sexuality," in *Feminisms*, eds. Sandra Kemp and Judith Squires (Oxford: Oxford University Press, 1997), 334.

120. For an opposing viewpoint, namely that some women felt that men used them during the sexual revolution, see Paula Kamen, *Young Women Remake the Sexual Revolution* (New York: NYU Press, 2000). Kamen cites a 1976 survey where women taking the Pill felt pressured to have sex. See page 99. Also see Rosen, *World Split Open*, 151–152. For a stance against this viewpoint, see Jane Gerhard, *Desiring Revolution*. There must have been room on this continuum—between these two endpoints—where some women's circumstances, sexual autonomy and subjectivity allowed for pleasure and empowerment. For example, consider Susan Stern who gloried in her sexuality and unabashedly admitted that she was "caught up in a sexual frenzy." Stern, *With the Weathermen*, 41.

121. This title ("A Vibrant Part of the Women's Movement") is taken from one of Dohrn's claims describing the WUO's part in the women's liberation movement. See Bernardine Dohrn, "When Hope and History Rhyme," 11.

122. Mark Rudd used women in this way, interpreting smash monogamy as an opportunity for him to sleep around with as many women as possible. He writes of the experience, "my fantasies were being fulfilled: I could have almost any of these beautiful, strong revolutionary women I desired." See Mark Rudd, *Underground*, 164. Stern indicts Rudd's behavior. See Stern, *With the Weathermen*, 176.

123. Bill Ayers, "Revisiting the Weather Underground," in *Sing A Battle Song: The Revolutionary Poetry, Statements, and Communiqués of the Weather Underground, 1970–1974*, eds. Bernardine Dohrn, Bill Ayers, Jeff Jones (New York: Seven Stories Press, 2006), 34.

Conclusion

1. Cathy Wilkerson, *Flying Close to the Sun* (New York: Seven Stories Press, 2007), 345.

2. *Ibid.*, 346.

3. *Ibid.*, 346–347. Also see "Timeline," "Revisiting the Weather Underground," in *Sing A Battle Song: The Revolutionary Poetry, Statements, and Communiqués of the Weather Underground, 1970–1974*, eds. Bernardine Dohrn, Bill Ayers, Jeff Jones (New York: Seven Stories Press, 2006), 61.

4. For example, Thomas Powers dismisses the WUO at 169–170, see Thomas Powers, *Diana: The Making of a Terrorist* (Boston: Houghton Mifflin, 1998); he also dismisses Diana as a hysterical female at 186. Also see Dan Berger who discusses this dismissal at *Outlaws of America*, 263, see Dan Berger, *Outlaws of America: The Weather Underground and the Politics of Solidarity* (Edinburgh: AK Press, 2006).

5. Lucinda Franks and Thomas Powers, "Story of Diana: The Making of a Terrorist, Part 4," United Press International, 1970, http://100years.upi.com/sta_1970-09-18-p4.html (accessed 18 July 2017).

6. Bill Ayers, "Revisiting the Weather Underground," in *Sing A Battle Song: The Revolutionary Poetry, Statements, and Communiqués of the Weather Underground, 1970–1974*, eds. Bernardine Dohrn, Bill Ayers, Jeff Jones (New York: Seven Stories Press, 2006), 26.

7. WUO, *Prairie Fire: The Politics of Revolutionary Anti-Imperialism* (San Francisco: Communications Co., 1974), 87.

8. See Berger, *Outlaws of America*, 334; Mark Rudd, *Underground: My Life with SDS and the Weathermen* (New York: Harper Collins, 2009), 299.

9. Rudd, *Underground*, 299.

10. Kaitlin Menza, "How Women Can Strike Fear into the Patriarchy," *Marie Claire*, 7 March 2017.

11. Jeremy Varon, *Bringing the War Home: The Weather Underground, The Red Army Faction, and Revolutionary Violence in the Sixties and Seventies* (Berkeley: University of California Press, 2004), 292; Ron Jacobs, *The Way the Wind Blew: A History of the Weather Underground* (New York: Verso, 1997), 83.

12. Diana Block, *Arm the Spirit: A Woman's Journey Underground and Back* (Oakland: AK Press, 2009), 106.

13. Block, *Arm the Spirit*, 102.

14. Ron Jacobs, *The Way the Wind Blew*, 84.

15. Berger, *Outlaws of America*, 234.

16. Jeremy Varon, *Bringing the War Home*, 298.

17. Block, *Arm the Spirit*, 106.

18. Ron Jacobs, *The Way the Wind Blew*, 88.

19. Berger, *Outlaws of America*, 239.

20. Ron Jacobs, *The Way the Wind Blew*, 88–89. Also see Rudd, *Underground*, 305–306.

21. Ron Jacobs, *The Way the Wind Blew*, 89; Berger, *Outlaws of America*, 240; Varon, *Bringing the War Home*, 299.

22. Ron Jacobs, *The Way the Wind Blew*, 86–87; Block, *Arm the Spirit*, 124–125; Thai Jones, *A Radical Line: From the Labor Movement to the Weather Underground, One's Family Century of Conscience* (New York: Free Press, 2004), Kindle Edition, Chapter 10.

23. Berger, *Outlaws of America*, 240.

24. See *Sing A Battle Song: The Revolutionary Poetry, Statements, and Communiqués of the Weather Underground, 1970–1974*, eds. Bernardine Dohrn, Bill Ayers, Jeff Jones (New York: Seven Stories Press, 2006), 389.

25. *Ibid.*

26. Ayers, "Revisiting the Weather Underground," 38, 39–40, 4; Bernardine Dohrn, "When Hope and History Rhyme," in *Sing A Battle Song: The Revolutionary Poetry, Statements, and Communiqués of the Weather Underground, 1970–1974*, eds. Bernardine Dohrn, Bill Ayers, Jeff Jones (New York: Seven Stories Press, 2006), 12, 13, 18. Bernardine Dohrn is also critical of the U.S. interventions in Iraq and Afghanistan in terms of what they mean for women's rights. Also see Menza, "How Women Can Strike Fear into the Patriarchy."

27. See State of New York Division of Parole, "Minutes of Parole Board Hearing: Kathy Boudin," August 2003, 9, 10.

28. Meg Starr, "Laura Whitehorn," in *Enemies of the State* (Montreal: Abraham Guillen Press and Arm the Spirit, 2002), 8.

29. *Ibid.*, 8, 24.

30. Laura Whitehorn, interview by author, 23 October 2014.

31. Menza, "How Women Can Strike Fear into the Patriarchy."

32. *Ibid.*

33. Becky Thompson, *A Promise and a Way of Life: White Antiracist Activism* (Minneapolis: University of Minnesota Press, 2001), 391.

34. Mike Klonsky, "Mike Klonsky Blog," http://klonsky.blogspot.com (accessed 13 January 2017).

35. See *Sing A Battle Song: The Revolutionary Poetry, Statements, and Communiqués of the Weather Underground, 1970–1974*, eds. Bernardine Dohrn, Bill Ayers, Jeff Jones (New York: Seven Stories Press, 2006), 390.

36. Larry McShane, "One Time Radical Judith Clarke Released From Prison After 38 Years," *New York Daily News*, 10 May 2019; Tom Robbins, "Judith Clark's Radical Transformation," *The New York Times Magazine*, 12 January, 2012.

37. Meg Starr, "David Gilbert," in *Enemies of the State* (Montreal: Abraham Guillen Press and Arm the Spirit, 2002), 38.

38. *Ibid.*, 45.

39. Ayers, "Revisiting the Weather Underground," 21.

40. The Reminisces of Jeff Jones (October 24, 1984), 89, CCOHC.

41. Anonymous Weatherwomen, "Mountain Moving Day," 1973, 1.

42. Dohrn, "When Hope and History Rhyme," 2.

43. *Ibid.*, 12.

44. The Proud Eagle Tribe, "Letter," *The Harvard Crimson*, 15 October 1970, also available at http://www.thecrimson.com/article/1970/10/15/letter-ptonight-the-proud-eagle-tribe/ (accessed 2 January 2017). This letter was left by the Proud Eagle Tribe—made up of Weatherwomen—for *The Harvard Crimson*, Harvard's newspaper. The action was planned and led by women in solidarity with Assata Shakur and in solidarity with the peoples of Vietnam, as Harvard's Center for International Affairs had initiated the "strategic hamlet program for the Viet war." This action is yet another example of how the Weatherwomen blended anti-imperialist, political aims with feminist aims.

Bibliography

A.E.K. "It Depends on the Woman," *The Firebrand*, 24 April 1897.

Albert, Judith Clavir, and Stewart Edward Albert, eds. *The Sixties Papers: Documents of a Rebellious Decade.* Westport: Praeger, 1984.

Ali, Tariq, and Susan Watkins. *1968: Marching in the Streets.* New York: Free Press. 1998.

Alpert, Jane. *Growing Up Underground.* New York: Citadel, 1990.

Alpert, Jane. "Mother Right." *Ms.*, August 1975.

Anderson, Terry. *The Movement and the Sixties.* Oxford: Oxford University Press, 1996.

Ann, Judith. "The Secretarial Proletariat." In *Sisterhood Is Powerful: An Anthology of Writings from the Women's Liberation Movement,* ed. Robin Morgan, 86–100. New York: Random House, 1970.

Anonymous Weatherwomen. "For a Troubled Sister." In *Sing a Battle Song,* 14–15. Red Dragon Print, 1975.

Anonymous Weatherwomen. "For Assatta Shakur." In *Sing a Battle Song,* 3–4. Red Dragon Print, 1975.

Anonymous Weatherwomen. "For L." In *Sing a Battle Song,* 26. Red Dragon Print, 1975.

Anonymous Weatherwomen. "Introduction." In *Sing a Battle Song.* Red Dragon Print, 1975.

Anonymous Weatherwomen. "Malthusian Mythologies." In *Sing a Battle Song,* 19–20. Red Dragon Print, 1975.

Anonymous Weatherwomen. "Mountain Moving Day." 1973.

Anonymous Weatherwomen. "People's War." In *Sing a Battle Song,* 5–7. Red Dragon Print, 1975.

Anonymous Weatherwomen. "Riding the Subways." In *Sing a Battle Song,* 13–14. Red Dragon Print, 1975.

Anonymous Weatherwomen. *Sing a Battle Song.* Red Dragon Print, 1975.

Anonymous Weatherwomen. "Six Sisters." Summer 1973.

Anonymous Weatherwomen. "Straight Talk." In *Sing a Battle Song,* 23–24. Red Dragon Print, 1975.

Anonymous Weatherwomen. "Venom II." In *Sing a Battle Song,* 43. Red Dragon Print, 1975.

Anonymous Weatherwomen. "Women's Lament." In *Sing a Battle Song,* 27–28. Red Dragon Print, 1975.

Anthony, Earl. *Picking Up the Gun.* New York: Dial Press, 1970.

Ashley, Karin, Bill Ayers, Bernardine Dohrn, John Jacobs, Jeff Jones, Gerry Long, Howie Machtinger, Jim Mellen, Terry Robins, Mark Rudd, and Steve Tappis. "You Don't Need a Weatherman to Know Which Way the Wind Blows." *New Left Notes,* 18 June 1969. Reprint, *Weatherman,* ed. Harold Jacobs, 51–90. Ramparts Press, 1970.

Associated Press. "Some Schools Have Become Arenas of Racial Tension." *Herald Journal,* 25 September 1969.

Ayers, Bill. *Fugitive Days: A Memoir.* Kindle Edition. Boston: Beacon, 2001.

Ayers, Bill. "Revisiting the Weather Underground." In *Sing a Battle Song: The Revolutionary Poetry, Statements, and Com-*

muniqués of the Weather Underground, 1970–1974, eds. Bernardine Dohrn, Bill Ayers, Jeff Jones, 21–42. Kindle Edition. New York: Seven Stories Press, 2006.

Ayers, Bill, and Jim Mellen. "Hot Town: Summer in the City or I Ain't Gonna Work on Maggie's Farm No More." New Left Notes, 4 April 1969. Reprint, Weatherman, ed. Harold Jacobs, 29–38. Ramparts Press, 1970.

Barakso, Maryann. Governing NOW: Grassroots Activism in the National Organization for Women. Ithaca: Cornell University Press, 2004.

Barnes, Jack. Malcolm X, Black Liberation & the Road to Worker's Power. New York: Pathfinder, 2009.

Bartky, Sandra. Femininity and Domination: Studies in the Phenomenology of Oppression. New York: Routledge, 1990.

Bartky, Sandra. "Two Lectures" in Colin Gordon (ed.), Power/Knowledge: Selected Interviews and Other Writings, 1972–1977. New York: Pantheon, 1980.

Bates, Laura. Everyday Sexism. London: Simon & Schuster, 2014.

Bates, Tom. Rads: The 1970 Bombing of the Army Math Research Center at the University of Wisconsin and Its Aftermath. New York: HarperCollins, 1992.

The Battle of Algiers. DVD. Directed by Gillo Pontecorvo. 1966.

"The Battle of Boston: An Investigation of ROAR." Osawatomie, Spring 1975, No. 1, 7–12.

Baxandall, Rosalyn, and Linda Gordon. "Introduction." In Dear Sisters: Dispatches from the Women's Liberation Movement, eds. Rosalyn Baxandall and Linda Gordon, 1–18. New York: Basic Books, 2000.

Baxandall, Rosalyn, and Linda Gordon. "Work." In Dear Sisters: Dispatches from the Women's Liberation Movement, eds. Rosalyn Baxandall and Linda Gordon, 254. New York: Basic Books, 2000.

Baxandall, Rosalyn, and Linda Gordon, eds. Dear Sisters: Dispatches from the Women's Liberation Movement. New York, NY: Basic Books, 2000.

Baxandall, Rosalyn Fraad. "Catching the Fire." In The Feminist Memoir Project: Voices from the Women's Liberation, eds. Rachel Blau DuPlessis and Ann Snitow, 208–224. New Brunswick: Rutgers University Press, 2007.

Benson, Paul. "Feminist Intuitions and the Normative Substance of Autonomy." In Personal Autonomy, ed. James Stacey Taylor, 124–142. New York: Cambridge University Press, 2005.

Benston, Margaret. "The Political Economy of Women's Liberation." Radical Education Project, 1969.

Berger, Dan. Outlaws of America: The Weather Underground and the Politics of Solidarity. Edinburgh: AK Press, 2006.

Berlin, Isaiah. Liberty. Oxford: Oxford University Press, 1969.

Berrigan, Dan. The Trial of the Cattonsville Nine. Boston: Beacon Press, 1970.

Bingham, Clara. Witness to the Revolution: Radicals, Resisters, Vets, Hippies, and the Year America Lost Its Mind and Found Its Soul. New York: Random House, 2016.

The Black Panther Party. "The Black Panther Party: Platform and Program." Reprinted in The Sixties Papers: Documents of a Rebellious Decade, eds. Judith Clavir Albert and Stewart Edward Albert, 159–164. London: Praeger Press, 1984.

Blakkan, Renee. "Women Unionize Office Jobs." 1974. Reprint, Dear Sisters: Dispatches from the Women's Liberation Movement, eds. Rosalyn Baxandall and Linda Gordon, 270–272. New York: Basic Books, 2000.

Blau DuPlessis, Rachel, and Ann Snitow. "A Feminist Memoir Project." In The Feminist Memoir Project: Voices from the Women's Liberation, eds. Rachel Blau DuPlessis and Ann Snitow, 3–24. New Brunswick: Rutgers University Press, 2007.

Blau Duplessis, Rachel, and Ann Snitow, eds. The Feminist Memoir Project: Voices from Women's Liberation. New Brunswick: Rutgers University Press, 2007.

Block, Diana. Arm the Spirit: A Woman's Journey Underground and Back. Oakland: AK Press, 2009.

"Board of Directors." http://www.cato.org/board-of-directors (accessed 4 June 2018).

"Board of Trustees." http://www.aei.org/about/board-of-trustees/ (accessed 4 July 2018).

Bordo, Susan. Unbearable Weight. Berkeley: University of California Press, 2004.

Boris, Eileen. Home to Work: Motherhood and the Politics of Industrial Homework in the United States. Cambridge: Cambridge University Press, 1994.

Boudin, Kathy, Bernardine Dohrn, and Terry Robbins. "Bringing the War Back Home: Less Talk, More National Action." *New Left Notes*, 23 August 1969. Reprint, *Weatherman*, ed. Harold Jacobs, 175–182. Ramparts Press, 1970.

Boudin, Kathy, Eleanor Raskin, Brian Glick, and Gustin Reichbach. *The Bust Book: What to Do Till the Lawyer Comes.* Legal Rap, 1969.

Boxer, Marilyn. "Rethinking the Social Construction and International Career of the Concept 'Bourgeois Feminism.'" *The American Historical Review*, 112, No. 1 (2007): 131–158.

Bread and Roses Collective. "Declaration of Women's Independence." 1970. Reprint, *Dear Sisters: Dispatches from the Women's Liberation Movement*, eds. Rosalyn Baxandall and Linda Gordon, 45–47. New York: Basic Books, 2000.

Bread and Roses Collective. "Weatherman Politics and the Women's Movement." *Women*, 1970. Reprint, ed. Harold Jacobs, 327–336. *Weatherman*. Ramparts, 1970.

"Break the Chains." *Osawatomie*. Autumn 1975, No. 3, 7–13.

Breines, Paul, ed. *Critical Interruptions: New Left Perspectives on Herbert Marcuse.* New York: Herder & Herder, 1970.

Breines, Wini. "What's Love Got to Do with It? White Women, Black Women, and Feminism in the Movement Years." *Signs: Journal of Women in Culture and Society*, 27(4): 1095–1133.

Brown, Elaine. *A Taste of Power: A Black Woman's Story.* New York: Doubleday Books, 1992.

Brownmiller, Susan. "The Mass Psychology of Rape." 1975. Reprint, *Dear Sisters: Dispatches from the Women's Liberation Movement*, eds. Rosalyn Baxandall and Linda Gordon, 196. New York: Basic Books, 2000.

Bugliosi, Vincent, and Curt Gentry. *Helter Skelter: The True Story of the Manson Murders.* New York: Bantam Books, 1975.

Calovinch, Mike. "Female Protestors Stage Raid on Air Force ROTC." *University of Washington Daily*, 1 October 1969.

Calvert, Greg. "In White America: Liberal Conscience Vs. Radical Consciousness." Archived at http://www.sds-1960s.org/documents.htm. February 1967.

Castelluci, John. *The Big Dance: The Untold Story of Weatherman Kathy Boudin and the Terrorist Family That Committed the Brink Robbery Murder.* New York: Dodd, Mead & Company, 1986.

Center for American Women and Politics. "Women in the U.S. Congress 2015." http://www.cawp.rutgers.edu/fast_facts/levels_of_office/documents/cong.pdf (accessed 4 July 2018).

"A Changing of the Guard: Traditionalists, Feminists, and the New Face of Women in Congress, 1955–1976." http://history.house.gov/Exhibitions-and-publications/WIC/Historical- Essays/Changing-Guard/Introduction/ (accessed 8 August 2013).

Chapman, Brad J. "Comparison of Male and Female Leadership Styles." *Academy of Management*, Vol. 18, No. 3 (September 1975): 645–650.

Chepesiuk, Ron. *Sixties Radicals: Then and Now.* Jefferson, North Carolina: McFarland, 1995.

Chernesky, Roslyn H., and Marcia J. Bombick. "Women's Ways and Effective Management." *Affilia*, Vol. 3, No. 1 (March 1988): 48–61.

Chicago Committee to End Sterilization Abuse. "Sterilization Abuse: A Task for the Women's Movement." Archived at CWLU Herstory Archive https://www.uic.edu/orgs/cwluherstory/CWLU Archive/cesa.html. January 1977.

Choate, Laura H. *Girls' and Women's Wellness: Contemporary Counseling Issues and Interventions.* Alexandria: American Counseling Association, 2008.

Chomsky, Noam. *Hegemony or Survival: America's Quest for Global Dominance.* New York: Owl Books, 2004.

Christian, Barbara. "The Race for Theory." In *Gender and Theory*, Linda Kaufman, ed., 225–236. Oxford: Blackwell, 1989.

Christman, John. "Procedural Autonomy and Liberal Legitimacy." In *Personal Autonomy*, ed. James Stacey Taylor, 277–298. New York: Cambridge University Press, 2005.

Churchill, Ward. *Acts of Rebellion: The Ward Churchill Reader.* New York: Routledge, 2003.

Churchill, Ward. *Agents of Repression: The FBI'S Secret War Against the Black Panther Party and the American Indian Movement.* Cambridge: South End Press, 1988.

Churchill, Ward. *The COINTELPRO Papers: Documents from the FBI'S Secret Wars Against Dissent in the United States.* Boston: South End Press, 1990.

Cisler, Lucinda. "On Abortion and Abortion Law." 1969. Reprint, *Dear Sisters: Dispatches from the Women's Liberation Movement,* eds. Rosalyn Baxandall and Linda Gordon, 140–143. New York: Basic Books, 2000.

Clavir, Judy, and John Spitzer, eds. *The Conspiracy Trial: The Extended Edited Transcript of the Trial of the Chicago Eight.* Indianapolis: Bobbs-Merrill Company, 1970.

Clavir Albert, Judith, and Stewart Edward Albert. "The Mass Culture of Rebellion." In *The Sixties Papers: Documents of a Rebellious Decade,* eds. Judith Clavir Albert and Stewart Edward Albert, eds., 15–27. London: Praeger Press, 1984.

Clavir Albert, Judith, and Stewart Edward Albert. "The Rise of the New Left." In *The Sixties Papers: Documents of a Rebellious Decade,* eds. Judith Clavir Albert and Stewart Edward Albert, 10–14. London: Praeger Press, 1984.

Cleaver, Eldridge. "On Weatherman." *The Berkeley Tribe,* 7 November 1969. Reprint, *Weatherman,* ed. Harold Jacobs, 293–300. Ramparts Press, 1970.

Cleaver, Kathleen, and George Katsiaficas, eds. *Liberation, Imagination, and the Black Panther Party.* New York: Routledge, 2001.

Cobble, Dorothy Sue. *The Other Women: Workplace Justice and Social Rights in Modern America.* Princeton: Princeton University Press, 2004.

Cochrane, Kira. *All the Rebel Women: The Rise of the Fourth Wave of Feminism.* London: Guardian Books, 2013.

Cochrane, Kira. "The Fourth Wave of Feminism: Meet the Rebel Women." *The Guardian,* 10 December 2013.

Cohen, Gerald A. *History, Labour and Freedom.* Oxford: Oxford University Press, 1988.

Cohen, Gerald A. *Karl Marx's Theory of History: A Defence,* 2nd edition. Oxford, Oxford University Press, 2001.

Collier, Peter, and David Horowitz. *Destructive Generation: Second Thoughts About the 60's.* New York: Summit Books, 1990.

Collier-Thomas, Bettye. *Sisters in the Struggle: African American Women in the Civil Rights-Black Power Movement.* New York: New York University Press, 2001.

Collins, Gail. *America's Women: 400 Years of Dolls, Drudges, Helpmates, and Heroines.* New York: Harper Perennial, 2003.

Combahee River Collective. "The Combahee River Collective Statement." 1978.

Corinna, Heather. "An Immodest Proposal." In *Yes Means Yes: Visions of Female Sexual Power & a World Without Rape,* eds. Jaclyn Friedman and Jessica Valenti, 179–192. Berkeley: Seal Press, 2008.

Crawford, Vicky, Jacqueline Anne Rouse, and Barbara Woods, eds. *Women in the Civil Rights Movement: Trailblazers and Torchbearers, 1941–1965.* Bloomington: Indiana University Press, 1990.

Crenshaw, Kimberle. "Mapping the Margins, Intersectionality, Identity Politics, and Violence Against Women of Color." *Stanford Law Review* Vol. 43, No. 6 (1991): 1241–1299.

Crenshaw, Martha, ed. *Terrorism in Context.* University Park: Pennsylvania State University Press, 1995.

Cullather, Nicholas. *Secret History: The CIA'S Classified Account of Its Operations in Guatemala, 1952–1954.* Palo Alto: Stanford University Press, 1999.

Curry, Constance, Joan C. Browning, Dorothy Dawson Burlage, Penny Patch, Theresa Del Pozzo, Sue Thrasher, Elaine Delott Baker, Emmie Schrader Adams, and Casey Hayden. *Deep in Our Hearths: Nine White Women in the Freedom Movement.* Athens: University of Georgia Press, 2000.

Davis, Angela. *Angela Davis: An Autobiography.* New York: International Publishers, 1988.

Davis, Angela. *If They Come in the Morning: Voices of Resistance.* New York: Signet, 1971.

Davis, Angela. *Women, Race, and Class.* New York: Vintage Books, 1983.

Debray, Regis. *Revolution in the Revolution?* New York: Grove Press, 1967.

de Cleyre, Voltairine. "They Who Marry Do Ill." In *The Voltairine De Cleyre Reader,* ed. A.J. Brigati, 11–20. Oakland: AK Press, 2004.

Della Porta, Donatella. *Social Movements and Violence: Participation in Underground Organizations.* Greenwich: JAI Press, 1992.

Densmore, Dana. "A Year of Living Dangerously: 1968." In *The Feminist Memoir Project: Voices from the Women's Liberation*, eds. Rachel Blau DuPlessis and Ann Snitow, 71–89. New Brunswick: Rutgers University Press, 2007.

Dohrn, Bernardine. "The Liberation of Vietnamese Women." *New Left Notes*, 25 October 1968.

Dohrn, Bernardine. "New Morning, Changing Weather: December 6, 1970 Communiqué." 6 December 1970. Reprint, *The Weather Eye: Communiqués from the Weather Underground*, ed. Jonah Raskin, 26–34. San Francisco: Union Square Press, 1974.

Dohrn, Bernardine. "An Open Letter to the US Workers." *Osawatomie*, April-May 1976, Vol. 2, No. 1, 11.

Dohrn, Bernardine. "Our Class Stand." *Osawatomie*, Autumn 1975, No. 3, 3–6.

Dohrn, Bernardine. "Tape from Bernardine Dohrn." In *The Split of the Weather Underground Organization: Struggling Against White and Male Supremacy*, 33–35. John Brown Book Club, 1976.

Dohrn, Bernardine. "Toward a Revolutionary Women's Movement." *New Left Notes*, Special Issue, 8 March 1969.

Dohrn, Bernardine. "When Hope and History Rhyme." In *Sing a Battle Song: The Revolutionary Poetry, Statements, and Communiqués of the Weather Underground, 1970–1974*, eds. Bernardine Dohrn, Bill Ayers, Jeff Jones, 1–20. Kindle Edition. New York: Seven Stories Press, 2006.

Dohrn, Bernardine. "White Mother Country Radicals." *New Left Notes*, 29 July 1968.

Dohrn, Bernardine, Bill Ayers, and Jeff Jones, eds. *Sing a Battle Song: The Revolutionary Poetry, Statements, and Communiqués of the Weather Underground, 1970–1974*. Kindle Edition. New York: Seven Stories Press, 2006.

Dotson, Rader, ed. "Weatherman: The Long and Winding Road to the Underground." In *Defiance #2: A Radical Review*. New York: Paperback Library, 1970.

Dunbar-Ortiz, Roxanne. "Female Liberation as the Basis for Social Revolution." *No More Fun and Games: A Journal of Female Liberation* No. 2 (February 1969): 103–115.

Dunbar-Ortiz, Roxanne. "Female Liberation as the Basis for Social Revolution." In *Sisterhood Is Powerful: An Anthology of Writings from the Women's Liberation Movement*, ed. Robin Morgan, 477–492. New York: Random House, 1970.

Dunbar-Ortiz, Roxanne. "Outlaw Woman: Chapters from a Feminist Memoir in Progress." In *The Feminist Memoir Project: Voices from Women's Liberation*, eds. Rachel Blau DuPlessis and Ann Snitow, 90–114. New Brunswick: Rutgers University Press, 2007.

Dunbar-Ortiz, Roxanne. *Outlaw Woman: A Memoir of the War Years, 1960–1975*. San Francisco: City Lights, 2001.

DuPlessis, Rachel Blau, and Ann Snitow, eds. *The Feminist Memoir Project: Voices from Women's Liberation*. New York: Three Rivers Press, 1998.

Dworkin, Gerald. *The Theory and Practice of Autonomy*. New York: Cambridge University Press, 1988.

"Dykes and Fags Want to Know: Interview with Lesbian Political Prisoners: Queers United in Support of Political Prisoners Linda Evans, Laura Whitehorn, and Susan Rosenberg, 1991." In *Let Freedom Ring: A Collection of the Documents from the Movement to Free US Political Prisoners*, ed. Matt Meyer, 372–384. Oakland: PM Press, 2008.

Dylan, Bob. *Lyrics, 1962–1985*. New York: Knopf, 1985.

Echols, Alice. *Daring to Be Bad: Radical Feminism in America, 1967–1975*. Minneapolis: University of Minnesota Press, 1989.

Einstein, Zillah. *Against Empire: Feminisms, Racism and the West*. London: Zed, 2004.

Elbaum, Max. *Revolution in the Air: Sixties Radicals Turn to Lenin, Che, and Mao*. London: Verso, 2002.

Enck-Wanzer, Darrel, ed. *The Young Lords: A Reader*. New York: New York University Press, 2010.

Enloe, Cynthia. *Bananas, Beaches and Bases: Making Feminist Sense of International Politics*. Berkeley: University of California Press, 2000.

Enloe, Cynthia. *Maneuvers: The International Politics of Militarizing Women's Lives*. Berkeley: University of California Press, 2000.

Enstad, Nan. *Ladies of Labor, Girls of Adventure: Working Women, Popular Culture and Labor Politics at the Turn of the*

Twentieth Century. New York: Columbia University Press, 1999.

Epstein, Barbara. "Ambivalence About Feminism." In The Feminist Memoir Project: Voices from the Women's Liberation, eds. Rachel Blau DuPlessis and Ann Snitow, 124–148. New Brunswick: Rutgers University Press, 2007.

Estrin, Marc, ed. Recreation: Some Notes on What's What and What You Might Be Able to Do About What's What. New York: Dell Publishing, 1971.

Evans, Sarah. Personal Politics: The Roots of the Women's Liberation in the Civil Rights Movement and the New Left. New York: Vintage Books, 1980.

Evans M., Sara. "Re-Viewing the Second Wave," Feminist Studies 28.3 (Summer 2002): 258–267.

Falk, Candace, ed. "Forging Her Place: An Introduction." In Emma Goldman: A Documentary History of the American Years, Made for America, 1890–1901, 1–84. Chicago: University of Illinois Press, 2003.

Fanon, Franz. The Wretched of the Earth. Translated by Richard Philcox. New York: Grove Press, 2005.

Federal Bureau of Investigation. Black Panther Party. FOIA release. No date available.

Federal Bureau of Investigation. COINTELPRO Black Extremist. FOIA release. No date available.

Federal Bureau of Investigation. COINTELPRO New Left. FOIA release. No date available.

Federal Bureau of Investigation. Diana Oughton. FOIA release. No date available.

Federal Bureau of Investigation. Weather Underground. FOIA release. No date available.

Federal Bureau of Investigation. Weatherman Underground. FOIA release. 20 August 1976.

"59 Cents, a Woman's Dollar." Reprint, Dear Sisters: Dispatches from the Women's Liberation Movement, eds. Rosalyn Baxandall and Linda Gordon, 272. New York: Basic Books, 2000.

FIRE! 6 December 1969.

Firestone, Shulamith. The Dialectic of Sex: The Case for Feminist Revolution. New York: Morrow, 1970.

Fleming, Cynthia. Soon We Will Not Cry: The Liberation of Ruby Doris Smith Robinson. Lanham: Rowman & Littlefield, 1998.

Foner, Philip S. The Black Panthers Speak. New York: Da Capo Press, 1995.

"Former Political Prisoner Laura Whitehorn." http://www.kersplebedeb.com/my stuff/profiles/whitehorn.html (accessed 12 December 2017).

Frankfort, Ellen. Kathy Boudin and the Dance of Death. New York: Stein and Day, 1984.

Franks, Lucinda, and Thomas Powers. "Story of Diana: The Making of a Terrorist." Archived at http://100years.upi.com/sta_1970-09-14-p1.html. United Press International, 1970.

Franz, Fanon. Wretched of the Earth. Grove Press, 2005.

Frasier, Ronald, ed. 1968: A Student Generation in Revolt. New York: Pantheon Books, 1988.

Freeman, Jo. The Women's Liberation Movement: It's Origins, Structures and Ideas. 1971. Archived at https://dukelibraries.contentdm.oclc.org/digital/api/collection/p15957coll6/id/706/page/0/inline/p15957coll6_706_0. (Accessed 1 July 2018).

Freespirit, Judy, and Aldebaran. "Fat Liberation Manifesto." 1973. Reprint, Dear Sisters: Dispatches from the Women's Liberation Movement, eds. Rosalyn Baxandall and Linda Gordon, 191. New York: Basic Books, 2000.

Freire, Paulo. Pedagogy of the Oppressed. New York: Continuum, 1993.

Friedan, Betty. The Feminine Mystique. Kindle Edition. New York: Norton and Company, 2013 [1963].

Friedman, Jaclyn, and Jessica Valenti, eds. Yes Means Yes: Visions of Female Sexual Power and a World Without Rape. Berkeley: Seal Press, 2008.

Friedman, Marilyn. Autonomy, Gender, Politics. Oxford: Oxford University Press, 2003.

Furman, Laura. "A House Is Not a Home: Women in Publishing." In Sisterhood Is Powerful: An Anthology of Writings from the Women's Liberation Movement, ed. Robin Morgan, 66–70. New York: Random House, 1970.

Gaddis, John. The Cold War: A New History. New York: Penguin Press, 2005.

García, Justin D. "Young Lords." In Multicultural America: A Multimedia Encyclopedia, eds. Carlos E. Cortés and Jane E. Sloan, Vol. 4: 2216–2217. Sage Reference, 2014.

Gerhard, Jane. *Desiring Revolution: Second Wave Feminism and the Rewriting of American Sexual Thought, 1920–1982.* New York: Columbia University Press, 2001.

Gilbert, David. *Consumption: Domestic Imperialism. a New Left Introduction to the Political Economy of American Capitalism.* New York: Movement for a Democratic Society, circa 1968.

Gilbert, David. *Love and Struggle: My Life in the SDS, the Weather Underground, and Beyond.* Oakland: PM Press, 2012.

Gilbert, David. *No Surrender: Writings from an Anti-Imperialist Political Prisoner.* Montreal: Abraham Guillen Press and Arm the Spirit, 2004.

Gilbert, David. *SDS/WUO.* Montreal: Abraham Guillen Press & Arm the Spirit, 2002.

Gilbert, David, and David Loud. *U.S. Imperialism.* New York: Students for a Democratic Society, 1967.

Gilbert, David. Letter to author. 15 May 2013, 1 September 2013, 19 December 2013.

Gilbert, James. *Men in the Middle: Searching for Masculinity in the 1950's.* Chicago: University of Chicago Press, 2005.

Gilbert, Miriam. "Women in Medicine." In *Sisterhood Is Powerful: An Anthology of Writings from the Women's Liberation Movement,* ed. Robin Morgan, 62–66. New York: Random House, 1970.

Gillian, Carol. *In a Different Voice.* Cambridge: Harvard University Press, 1982.

Gillis, Stacy, Gillian Howie, and Rebecca Munford, *Third Wave Feminism: A Critical Exploration.* New York: Palgrave Macmillan, 2007.

Gitlin, Todd. *The Sixties: Years of Hope, Days of Rage.* New York: Bantam Books, 1993.

Gitlin, Todd. *The Whole World Is Watching: Mass Media in the Making and Unmaking of the New Left.* Berkeley: University of California Press, 1980.

Gold, M. E. "A tale of two amendments: The reasons Congress added sex to Title VII and their implication for the issue of comparable worth." *Duquesne Law Review, 19* (1980): 453–477.

Goldman, Emma. "Marriage." *The Firebrand,* 18 July 1897.

Goldman, Emma. "The Psychology of Political Violence." In *Red Emma Speaks: An Emma Goldman Reader,* ed. Alix Kates Shulman, 256–279. New York: Humanity Books, 1996.

Gonzales-Perez, Margaret. *Women and Terrorism: Female Activity in Domestic and International Terror Groups.* London: Routledge, 2008.

Gonzalez, Juan. *Harvest of Empire: A History of Latinos in America.* New York: Penguin, 2001.

Gordon, Linda. *The Moral Property of Women: A History of Birth Control Politics in America.* Champaign: University of Illinois Press, 2007.

Gottschang Turner, Karen, and Phan Thanh Hao. *Even the Women Must Fight: Memories of War from North Vietnam.* New York: John Wiley and Sons, 1998.

Grant, Bev. "Ain't She Sweet." 1968. Reprint, *Dear Sisters: Dispatches from the Women's Liberation Movement,* eds. Rosalyn Baxandall and Linda Gordon, 180. New York: Basic Books, 2000.

Grant, Bev. "A Pretty Girl Is Like a Commodity." 1968. Reprint, *Dear Sisters: Dispatches from the Women's Liberation Movement,* eds. Rosalyn Baxandall and Linda Gordon, 180. New York: Basic Books, 2000.

Grathwohl, Larry, and Frank Reagan. *Bringing Down America: An FBI Informer with the Weathermen.* New Rochelle, NY: Arlington House, 1976.

Gregory, Ted. "The Black Panther Raid and the Death of Fred Hampton," *Chicago Tribune.* No date available.

Hamer, Fannie Lou. "Interview with Fannie Lou Hamer: Winona Mississippi." Interview by Neil McMillen," April 14, 1972. Center for Oral History and Cultural Heritage, University of Southern Mississippi. Archived at Digital SNCC Gateway, https://snccdigital.org/events/beatings-winona-jail/.

Hamer, Fannie Lou. "An Oral History with Fannie Lou Hamer." Interview by Dr. Neil McMillen, April 14, 1972. Center for Oral History and Cultural Heritage, University of Southern Mississippi.

Hayden, Casey, and Mary King. "Sex and Caste: A Kind of Memo." Archived at http://www.historyisaweapon.com/defcon1/sexcaste.html. 1965.

Hayden, Tom. *Reunion: A Memoir.* New York: Random House, 1988.

Heywood, Leslie, and Jennifer Drake, eds. *Third Wave Agenda: Being Feminist, Doing Feminism.* Minneapolis: University of Minnesota Press, 1997.

Heywood, Leslie, ed. *The Women's Movement Today: An Encyclopedia of Third Wave Feminism, A–Z,* vol. 1. Westport: Greenwood, 2006.

Higginbotham, Evelyn. "African-American Women's History and the Metalanguage of Race." *Signs,* Vol. 17, No. 2 (Winter 1992): 251–274.

Hill Collins, Patricia. *Black Feminist Thought: Knowledge, Consciousness, and the Politics of Empowerment.* New York: Routledge, 2000.

Hilliard, David, and Lewis Cole. *This Side of Glory: The Autobiography of David Hilliard and the Story of the Black Panther Party.* Boston: Little Brown, 1993.

Hilliard, David, ed. *The Black Panther Party: Service to the People.* Albuquerque: University of New Mexico Press, 2008.

Hinckle, Warren. "Introduction." *Scanlan's Monthly,* January 1971, 4–12.

Holsaert Faith S. et al. eds. *Hands on the Freedom Plow: Personal Accounts by Women in SNCC* (Urbana: University of Illinois Press, 2010).

hooks, bell. "Feminism: A Movement to End Sexist Oppression." In *Feminisms,* eds. Susan Kemp and Judith Squires, 22–27. Oxford: Oxford University Press, 1997.

Horn, Alistair. *A Savage War of Peace: Algeria 1954–1962.* New York: New York Review Books, 2011.

Howe, Irving, ed. *Beyond the New Left.* New York: McCall Publishing, 1970.

Ibarruri, Dolores. *They Shall Not Pass: The Autobiography of La Pasionaria.* New York, 1976.

Ignatin, Noel, and Ted Allen. "White Blindspot Essays on Combating White Supremacy and White-Skin Privilege." Archived at http://www.sds-1960s.org/documents.htm. 1967.

Jacobs, Harold. "The Emergence of Weatherman: Introduction." In *Weatherman,* ed. Harold Jacobs, 1–13. Ramparts Press, 1970.

Jacobs, Harold. "Inside the Weather Machine: Introduction." In *Weatherman,* ed. Harold Jacobs, 301–311. Ramparts Press, 1970.

Jacobs, Harold, ed. *Weatherman.* Ramparts Press, 1970.

Jacobs, Ron. *The Way the Wind Blew: A History of the Weather Underground.* New York: Verso, 1997.

Jaffe, Naomi, and Bernardine Dohrn. "The Look Is You." *New Left Notes,* 18 March 1968, 5.

Jaggar, Alison. "Political Philosophies of Women's Liberation." In *Feminism and Philosophy,* eds. Mary Vetterling-Braggin, Frederick A. Elliston and Jane English. Totowa: Rowman & Littlefield, 1977.

Jagose, Annamarie. "Feminism's Queer Theory." *Feminism & Psychology* 19, No. 2 (2009): 157–174.

James, Joy. *The Angela Davis Reader.* Oxford: Blackwell, 1998.

JANE. "Women Learn to Perform Abortions." 1973. Reprint, *Dear Sisters: Dispatches from the Women's Liberation Movement,* eds. Rosalyn Baxandall and Linda Gordon, 145–147. New York: Basic Books, 2000.

Jeffries, Judson L. "Revising Panther History in Baltimore." In *Comrades: A Local History of the Black Panther Party,* ed. Judson L. Jeffries, 13–46. Bloomington: Indiana University Press, 2007.

Jeffries, Judson L., and Malcolm Foley. "To Live and Die in LA." In *Comrades: A Local History of the Black Panther Party,* ed. Judson L. Jeffries, 255–290. Bloomington: Indiana University Press, 2007.

Jeffries, Judson L., and Ryan Nissim-Sabat. "Introduction: Painting a More Complete Portrait of the Black Panther Party." In *Comrades: A Local History of the Black Panther Party,* ed. Judson L. Jeffries, 1–12. Bloomington: Indiana University Press, 2007.

Jeffries, Judson L., ed. *Comrades.* Bloomington: Indiana University Press, 2007.

John Brown Book Club, ed. *The Split of the Weather Underground Organization: Struggling Against White and Male Supremacy.* Seattle: John Brown Book Club, 1977.

Johnson, Merri Lisa. *Jane Sexes It Up: True Confessions of Feminist Desire.* New York: Four Walls Eight Windows, 2002.

Jones, Beverly. "The Dynamics of Marriage and Motherhood." In *Sisterhood Is Powerful: An Anthology of Writings from the Women's Liberation Movement,* ed. Robin Morgan, 46–61. New York: Random House, 1970.

Jones, Charles. *The Black Panther Party Reconsidered.* Baltimore: Black Classic Press, 1998.

Jones, Thai. *A Radical Line: From the Labor Movement to the Weather Underground, One Family's Century of Conscience.* Kindle Edition. New York: Free Press, 2004.

Kamen, Paula. *Young Women Remake the Sexual Revolution.* New York: NYU Press, 2000.

Kant, Immanuel. *Practical Philosophy.* Edited and translated by Mary J. Gregor. Cambridge: Cambridge University Press, 1996.

Katsiaficas, George. *The Imagination of the New Left: A Global Analysis of 1968.* Boston: South End Press, 1988.

Kemp, Susan, and Judith Squires. "Introduction." In *Feminisms,* eds. Susan Kemp and Judith Squires, 3–12. Oxford: Oxford University Press, 1997.

Kemp, Susan, and Judith Squires, eds. *Feminisms.* Oxford: Oxford University Press, 1997.

Kerber, Linda. *No Constitutional Right to Be Ladies: Women and the Obligations of Citizenship.* New York: Hill and Young, 1998.

Kessler Harris, Alice. *In Pursuit of Equity: Women, Men, and the Quest for Economic Citizenship in 20th Century America.* Oxford: Oxford University Press, 2001.

Kessler Harris, Alice. *Out to Work: The History of Wage Earning Women.* Oxford: Oxford University Press, 2003.

Kirkpatrick, Sale. *SDS.* New York: Vintage, 1974.

Klonsky, Mike. "Mike Klonsky Blog." http://klonsky.blogspot.com.

Klonsky, Mike. "Toward a Revolutionary Youth Movement." Archived at http://www.sds-1960s.org/documents.htm. December 1968.

Kopkind, Andrew. "The Real SDS Stands Up." Chicago: Hard Times, 30 June–5 July 1969. Reprint in *Weatherman,* ed. Harold Jacobs, 15–28. Ramparts Press, 1970. Also archived at the SDS/WUO Document Archive http://www.sds-1960s.org/Kopkind-1969convention.pdf. 30 June–5 July 1969.

Kuhlman, Erika A. *A to Z of Women in World History.* New York: Infobase Publishing, 2002.

Lavan, George, ed. *Che Guevara Speaks.* New York: Pathfinder Books, 1997.

Lazarre, Jane. "Conversations with Kathy Boudin." New York: Friends of Kathy Boudin, circa 1984.

LeMoncheck, Linda. *Loose Women, Lecherous Men: A Feminist Philosophy of Sex.* Oxford: Oxford University Press, 1997.

Lenin, Vladimir. *Imperialism, the Highest Stage of Capitalism.* Archived at Marxist Internet Archive http://www.marxists.org/archive/lenin/works/1916/imp-hsc/. 1917.

Lewis, Carolyn. *Prescription for Heterosexuality: Sexual Citizenship in the Cold War Era.* Chapel Hill: University of North Carolina Press, 2010.

"Liberation of Women." *New Left Notes,* 10 July 1967, 4.

Lindsey, Karen, Holly Newman, and Fran Taylor. "Rape: The All American Crime." 1973. Reprint, *Dear Sisters: Dispatches Rom the Women's Liberation Movement,* eds. Rosalyn Baxandall and Linda Gordon, 195–196. New York: Basic Books, 2000.

Ling, Peter J., and Sharon Monteith. *Gender and the Civil Rights Movement.* New Brunswick: Rutgers University Press, 2004.

Lipman-Blumen, Jean. "Connective Leadership: Female Leadership Styles in the 21st Century Workplace." *Sociological Perspectives,* Vol. 35, No. 1 (1992): 183–203.

Lockeretz Wernick, Sarah. "Hernia: A Satire on Abortion Law Repeal." Reprint, *Dear Sisters: Dispatches from the Women's Liberation Movement,* eds. Rosalyn Baxandall and Linda Gordon, 144–145. New York: Basic Books, 2000.

Long, Priscilla. "We Called Ourselves Sisters." In *The Feminist Memoir Project: Voices from Women's Liberation,* eds. Rachel Blau DuPlessis and Ann Snitow, 324–337. New Brunswick: Rutgers University Press, 2007.

Longevall, Frederick. *Choosing War: The Lost Chance for Peace and the Escalation of War in Vietnam.* Berkeley: University of California Press, 1999.

Lorde, Audre. "The Master's Tools Will Never Dismantle the Master's House." In *Sister Outsider: Essays and Speeches by Audre Lorde,* 110–113. Berkeley: Crossing Press, 2007.

Lukas, J. Anthony. "8 Go on Trial Today in Another Round in Chicago Convention Strife," *New York Times*, 24 September 1969, 29.

Lukas, J. Anthony. "Seale Put in Chains at Chicago 8 Trial," *New York Times*, 30 October 1969, 1.

MacLean, Nancy. *The American Women's Movement: 1945–2000.* Boston: Bedford Press, 2009.

Mainardi, Pat. "Politics of Housework." Reprint, *Radical Feminism: A Documentary Reader*, ed. Barbara A. Crow, 525–529. New York: New York University Press, 2000.

Marcuse, Herbert. *An Essay on Liberation.* Boston: Beacon Press, 1969.

Marcuse, Herbert. *One Dimensional Man.* Boston: Beacon Press, 1964.

Marcuse, Herbert. "Repressive Tolerance." In Robert Paul Wolff, Barington Moore, Jr., and Herbert Marcuse, *A Critique of Pure Tolerance.* Boston: Beacon Press, 1969.

Marighella, Carlos. *Minimanual of the Urban Guerrilla.* Berkeley: Long Time Comin' Press, 1969.

Marinucci, Mimi. *Feminism Is Queer: The Intimate Connection Between Queer and Feminist Theory.* Kindle Edition. London: Zed Books, 2012.

Martinez, Elizabeth (Betita). "History Makes Us, We Make History." In *The Feminist Memoir Project: Voices from the Women's Liberation*, eds. Rachel Blau DuPlessis and Ann Snitow, 115–123. New Brunswick: Rutgers University Press, 2007.

Marx, Karl. *On Colonialism: Articles from the New York Tribune and Other Writings.* New York: International Publishers, 1972.

Marx, Karl, and Frederick Engels. *Economic and Philosophic Manuscripts of 1844 and the Communist Manifesto.* Translated by Martin Milligan. Amherst: Prometheus Books, 1988.

Maxwell, Angie, and Todd Shields. "Introduction: Toward a New Understanding of Second-Wave Feminism." In *The Legacy of Second Wave Feminism in American Politics*, eds. Angie Maxwell and Todd Shields, 1–18. Palgrave McMillan, 2017.

McAfee, and Myrna Wood. "Bread and Roses." In *Feminism in Our Time: The Essential Writings, WWII to the Present*, ed.

Miriam Schneir, 130–147. New York: Vintage Books, 1994.

McAfee, Noelle. "Feminist Philosophy." *The Stanford Encyclopedia of Philosophy* (Fall 2018 Edition), ed. Edward N. Zalta.

McKenna, Michael. "The Relationship Between Autonomous and Morally Responsible Agency." In *Personal Autonomy*, ed. James Stacey Taylor, 205–234. New York: Cambridge University Press, 2005.

McShane, Larry. "One Time Radical Judith Clarke Released from Prison After 38 Years." *New York Daily News*, 10 May 2019.

Mele, Alfred. *Autonomous Agents.* New York: Oxford University Press, 1995.

Melendez, Miguel "Mickey." *We Took the Streets: Fighting for Latino Rights with the Young Lords.* New York: St. Martin's Press, 2003.

"Memories of Diana," *Time*, 30 March 1970; reprint, in *Weatherman*, ed. Harold Jacobs (Ramparts Press, 1970), 486 (page citations are to the reprint edition).

Menza, Kaitlin. "How Women Can Strike Fear in the Patriarchy: Lessons from a 1960's Radicalist." *Marie Claire.* March 7 2017.

"A Mighty Army: An Investigation of Women Workers. " *Osawatomie*, Summer 1975, No. 2, 6–13.

Miller, James. *"Democracy Is in the Streets": From Port Huron to the Siege of Chicago.* Cambridge: Harvard University Press, 1994.

Mohanty, Chandra Talpade. *Feminism Without Borders: Decolonizing Theory, Practicing Solidarity.* Durham, North Carolina: Duke University Press, 2003.

Moon, Danelle. *Daily Life of Women During the Civil Rights Era.* Santa Barbara: Greenwood Press, 2011.

Moraga, Cherrie, and Gloria Anzaldua, eds. *This Bridge Called My Back.* Third Woman Press, 2002.

Morgan, Edward. *The Sixties Experience: Hard Lessons About Modern America.* Philadelphia: Temple University Press, 1991.

Morgan, Robin. *Going Too Far: The Personal Chronicle of a Feminist.* New York: Vintage Books, 1978.

Morgan, Robin. "Goodbye to All That." *The Rat*, 9–23 February 1970, 6–7. Reprint, *The Sixties Papers: Documents of a Rebellious Decade*, eds. Judith Albert Clavir and Stewart Edward Albert, 509–516. Westport: Praeger, 1984.

Morgan, Robin. "Introduction." In *Sisterhood Is Powerful: An Anthology of Writings from the Women's Liberation Movement*, ed. Robin Morgan, xiii-xli. New York: Random House, 1970.

Morgan, Robin, ed. *Sisterhood Is Powerful: An Anthology of Writing from the Women's Liberation Movement*. New York: Random House, 1970.

Morris, J.H. "Free Sex Relations." *The Firebrand*, 3 May 1896.

"Motor City 9." *New Left Notes*, 23 August 1969. Reprint, *Weatherman*, ed. Harold Jacobs, 161–162. Ramparts, 1970.

Motor City SDS. "Break on Through the Other Side." *New Left Notes*, 23 August 1969. Reprint, *Weatherman*, ed. Harold Jacobs, 152–160. Ramparts, 1970.

Murolo, Priscilla, A. B. Chitty, and Joe Sacco. *From the Folks Who Brought You the Weekend: A Short, Illustrated History of Labor in the United States*. New York: The New York Press, 2001.

Nadasen, Premilla. *Welfare Warriors: The Welfare Rights Movement in the United States*. New York: Routledge, 2005.

National Council of Students for a Democratic Society. "Resolution on SNCC." Archived at http://www.sds-1960s.org/documents.htm. 18 June 1966.

National Organization for Women. "The National Organization for Women's 1966 Statement of Purpose." Archived at http://www.now.org/history/purpos66.html. 1966.

National Organization for Women. "The Right of a Woman to Determine Her Own Reproductive Process." 1967. Reprint, *Feminist Chronicles*, eds. Toni Carabillo, Judy Meuli, and June Bundy Csida, 191–193. Los Angeles: Women's Graphics, 1993.

"National War Council." Neromi, Hilary. *The Violent Woman: Femininity, Narrative, and Violence in Contemporary American Cinema*. Albany: State University of New York Press, 2005.

New York Radical Women. "No More Miss America." 1968. Reprint, *Dear Sisters: Dispatches from the Women's Liberation Movement*, eds. Rosalyn Baxandall and Linda Gordon, 184–815. New York: Basic Books, 2000.

New York Radical Women. "Principles." In *Sisterhood Is Powerful: An Anthology of Writings from the Women's Liberation Movement*, ed. Robin Morgan, 520. New York: Random House, 1970.

New York Times. Editorial. 21 August 1965, 37.

Newton, Huey P. "Huey Newton Talks to the *Movement*." *The Movement*, August 1968. Printed by Students for a Democratic Society, August 1968. Archived at https://archive.lib.msu.edu/DMC/AmRad/hueynewtontalks.pdf.

Newton, Huey P. *War Against the Panthers: A Study of Repression in America*. New York: Harlem River Press, 1980.

Nicholson, Linda, ed. *The Second Wave: A Reader in Feminist Theory*. New York: Routledge, 1997.

Noggle, Robert. "Autonomy and the Paradox of Self-Creation." In *Personal Autonomy*, ed. James Stacey Taylor, 87–108. New York: Cambridge University Press, 2005.

Oglesby, Carl. *Ravens in the Storm: A Personal History of the 1960's Antiwar Movement*. New York: Scribner's, 2008.

Oliver, Kelly. *Women as Weapons of War*. New York: Columbia University Press, 2007.

Olson, Lynne. Freedom's Daughters: *The Unsung Heroines of the Civil Rights Movement from 1830 to 1970*. New York: Touchstone, 2001.

Ono, Shin'ya. "You Do Need a Weatherman to Know Which Way the Wind Blows." *Leviathon*, December 1969. Reprint, *Weatherman*, ed. Harold Jacobs, 227–274. Ramparts Press, 1970.

Osgerby, Bill. *Playboys in Paradise: Masculinity, Youth, and Leisure Style in Modern America*. London: Bloomsbury Academic, 2001.

Pacale, Susan, Rachel Moon, and Leslie Tanner. "Karate as Self-Defense for Women." 1970. Reprint, *Dear Sisters: Dispatches from the Women's Liberation Movement*, eds. Rosalyn Baxandall and Linda Gordon, 207–208. New York: Basic Books, 2000.

Pardun, Robert. *Prairie Radical: A Journey Through the Sixties*. Los Gatos, California: Shire, 2001.

Parsons, Lucy. "Objections to Variety," *The Firebrand*, 27 September 1896.

Payne, Cril. *Deep Cover: An FBI Agent In-*

filtrates the Radical Underground. New York: Newsweek Books, 1979.

Peslikis, Irene. "Women Must Control the Means of Reproduction." 1967. Reprint, Dear Sisters: Dispatches from the Women's Liberation Movement, eds. Rosalyn Baxandall and Linda Gordon, 134. New York: Basic Books, 2000.

Phelps, Linda. "Death Is the Spectacle." 1971. Reprint, Dear Sisters: Dispatches from the Women's Liberation Movement, eds. Rosalyn Baxandall and Linda Gordon, 175–179. New York: Basic Books, 2000.

"The Politics of Daycare." Osawatomie, Summer 1975, No. 2, 14.

Pope, Dany, Alain Jehlen, Evan Metcalf, and Cathy Wilkerson. "Chester, PA: A Case Study in Community Organization." New York: Students for a Democratic Society. Archived at SDS/WUO Document Archive http://www.antiauthoritarian.net/sds_wuo/erap_chester_pa/. Circa 1965.

"Population Control." Osawatomie, Spring 1975, No. 1, 13–14.

Post, Jerrold M. The Mind of the Terrorist: The Psychology of Terrorism from the IRA to Al-Qaeda. New York: Palgrave MacMillan, 2007.

Potter, Paul. "We Must Name the System." April 1965.

Powers, Thomas. Diana: The Making of Terrorist. Boston: Houghton Mifflin, 1998.

"The President's Cabinet." http://www.potus.com/rmnixon.html (accessed 4 July 2018).

The Proud Eagle Tribe. "Letter." The Harvard Crimson. Also archived at http://www.thecrimson.com/article/1970/10/15/letter-ptonight-the-proud-eagle-tribe/. 15 October 1970.

Radical Education Project, ed. Debate Within SDS: RYM II Vs. Weatherman. Detroit: Radical Education Project, 1969.

Ransby, Barbara. Ella Baker and the Black Freedom Movement: A Radical Democratic Vision. Chapel Hill: The University of North Carolina Press, 2003.

Ransby, Barbara, ed. Deep in Our Hearts: Nine White Women in the Freedom Movement. Athens: University of Georgia Press, 2000.

Raskin, Johan. Out of the Whale: Growing Up in the American Left. New York: Links Books, 1974.

Raskin, Jonah. "Chronology and Table of Contents." In The Weather Eye: Commu-

niqués from the Weather Underground, ed. Jonah Raskin, 12–15. San Francisco, Union Square Press, 1974.

Raskin, Jonah, ed. The Weather Eye: Communiqués from the Weather Underground. San Francisco: Union Square Press, 1974.

Reagan, Leslie. When Abortion Was a Crime: Women, Medicine and Law in the United States, 1867–1973. Berkeley: University of California Press, 1997.

Redstockings. "The Miss America Protest." Archived at http://www.redstockings.org/index.php?option=com_content&view=article&id=59&Itemid=103. 1968.

Redstockings. "Redstockings Manifesto." In Sisterhood Is Powerful: An Anthology of Writings from the Women's Liberation Movement, ed. Robin Morgan, 533–537. New York: Random House, 1970. Also reprint, Radical Feminism: A Documentary Reader, ed. Barbara A. Crow, 223–225. New York: New York University Press, 2000.

Relf et al. vs. Weinberger et. al. Civil Action No. 73-1557 U.S. District Court. Washington, D.C. March 15, 1974.

The Reminisces of Cathy Wilkerson. 17 February 1985. Columbia Center for Oral History.

The Reminisces of David Gilbert. 16–19 June 1985. Columbia Center for Oral History.

The Reminisces of Jeff Jones. 24 October 1984. Columbia Center for Oral History.

Reuters. "Girls' 'Bare' Display Produces 25 Arrests." The Montreal Gazette, 5 September 1969.

Revolutionary Youth Movement. Call for National Action, 1969.

Robbins, Tom. "Judith Clark's Radical Transformation" The New York Times Magazine, 12 January, 2012.

Robnett, Belinda. "African American Women in the Civil Rights Movement, 1954–1965: Gender, Leadership, and Micromobilization." AJS, Vol. 101, No. 6 (May 1996): 1661–1693.

Robnett, Belinda. How Long? How Long? African American Women in the Struggle for Civil Rights. New York: Oxford University Press, 1997.

Rocha, James, and Mona Rocha. "Love, Sex, and Social Justice: The Anarcha-Feminist Free Love Debate." Anarchist Studies, Vol. 27, No. 1 (2019): 63–82.

Rosal, Lorraine. "Who Do They Think Could Bury You?" *New Left Notes,* 23 August 1969. Reprint, *Weatherman,* ed. Harold Jacobs, 147–151. Ramparts Press, 1970.

Rosen, Ruth. *The World Split Open: How the Modern Women's Movement Changed America.* New York: Penguin, 2000.

Rosenberg, Susan. *An American Radical: Political Prisoner in My Own Country.* New York: Citadel Press, 2011.

Roth, Benita. "The Making of the Vanguard Center: Black Feminist Emergence in the 1960's and 1970's." In *Still Lifting, Still Climbing: African American Women's Contemporary Activism,* ed. Kimberly Springer, 70–90. New York: New York University Press, 1999.

Roth, Benita. *Separate Roads to Feminism: Black, Chicana, and White Feminist Movements in America's Second Wave.* Cambridge: Cambridge University Press, 2004.

Rubin, Jerry. *We Are Everywhere.* New York: Harper and Row, 1971.

Rudd, Mark. *My Life with SDS and the Weathermen.* New York: William Morrow, 2009.

Russel Hocschild, Arlie, and Anne Machung. *The Second Shift.* New York: Penguin Books, 1989.

Sandoval, Chela. *Methodology of the Oppressed.* Minneapolis: University of Minnesota Press, 2000.

Sarachild, Kathie. "Consciousness-Raising: A Radical Weapon." In *Feminist Revolution,* 144–150. New York: Random House, circa 1978. Archived at http://library.duke.edu/rubenstein/scriptorium/wlm/fem/sarachild.html. Circa 1978.

Sarachild, Kathie. "Feminist Consciousness Raising and 'Organizing.'" In *Voices from Women's Liberation,* ed. Leslie B. Tanner, 153–156. New York: Signet Books, 1970.

"School Peace Riot Poses a Big 'Why?'" *The Pittsburgh Press,* 5 September 1969.

Schulman, Bruce. *The Seventies: The Great Shift in American Culture, Society, and Politics.* Cambridge: Da Capo Press, 2001.

Seale, Bobby. *Seize the Time.* Baltimore: Black Classics Press, 1991.

Seale, Bobby. "The Women of the Original Black Panther Party." *Facebook,* 24 May 2019 at 10:53 p.m.

Shakur, Assata. *Assata an Autobiography.* Chicago: Lawrence Hill Books, 1987.

Shulman, Alix Kates. "A Marriage Agreement." 1970. Reprint *Dear Sisters: Dispatches from the Women's Liberation Movement,* eds. Rosalyn Baxandall and Linda Gordon, 218–220. New York: Basic Books, 2000.

Silva, Christianna. "Who Was Fred Hampton, the Black Panther Shot and Killed in His Bed by Chicago Police 48 Years Ago?," *Newsweek,* 4 December 2017.

Singer, Peter. *Marx.* New York: Sterling, 1980.

Sisters of WUO. "Letter from Sisters in the WUO." In *The Split of the Weather Underground Organization: Struggling Against White and Male Supremacy,* 36–39. John Brown Book Club, 1976.

Sjoberg, Laura, and Caron Gentry, eds. *Women, Gender, and Terrorism.* Athens: University of Georgia Press, 2011.

Snyder, Claire. "What Is Third-Wave Feminism? A New Directions Essay." *Signs,* Vol. 34, No. 1 (Autumn 2008): 175–196.

Sojourn, Celia. "Where We Stand: The Women's Question Is a Class Question." *Osawatomie,* Winter 1975-76, No. 4., 3–5.

Solanas, Valerie. "SCUM Manifesto." Reprint, *Radical Feminism: A Documentary Reader,* ed. Barbara A. Crow, 201–222. New York: New York University Press, 2000.

Solowey, Fred J. "Berrigan Appears at Fest; Continues to Elude FBI." *The Cornell Daily Sun,* Vol. 86, No. 122, 20 April 1970, 1.

Spelman, Elizabeth. *The Inessential Woman.* Boston: Beacon Press, 1988.

Springer, Kimberly. *Living for the Revolution: Black Feminist Organizations, 1968–1980.* Durham: Duke University Press, 2005.

Springer, Kimberly. *Still Lifting, Still Climbing: African American Women's Contemporary Activism.* New York: New York University Press, 1999.

Springer, Kimberly. "Third Wave Black Feminism?" *Signs: Journal of Women in Culture and Society,* 27(4): 1060–1082.

Starr, Meg. "David Gilbert." In *Enemies of the State,* 31–47. Montreal: Abraham Guillen Press and Arm the Spirit, 2002.

Starr, Meg. "Laura Whitehorn." In *Enemies of the State,* 7–27. Montreal: Abraham Guillen Press and Arm the Spirit, 2002.

Starr, Meg. "Marylin Buck." In *Enemies of the State,* 51–67. Montreal: Abraham Guillen Press and Arm the Spirit, 2002.

State of New York Division of Parole. "Minutes of Parole Board Hearing: Kathy Boudin." August 2003.

Stern, Susan. *With the Weathermen: The Personal Journey of a Revolutionary Woman.* New Brunswick: Rutgers University Press, 1975.

"Stormy Weather." *San Francisco Good Times,* 8 January 1970. Reprint, *Weatherman,* ed. Harold Jacobs, 341–350. Ramparts, 1970.

Strossen, Nadine. "A Feminist Critique of the Feminist Critique of Pornography." *Virginia Law Review,* Vol. 79, No. 5 (Aug., 1993): 1099–1190.

Stuart, Roger. "Kids Dug Us." *The Pittsburgh Press,* 6 September 1969.

Students for a Democratic Society. "The Black Panther Party: Towards the Liberation of a Colony." *New Left Notes,* 4 April 1969.

Students for a Democratic Society. "Port Huron Statement." Archived at www.coursesa.matrix.msu.edu/~hst306/documents/huron.html. 1962.

Tandon, Neeru. *Feminism: A Paradigm Shift.* New Delhi: Atlantic Publishers and Distributors, 2008.

Tanner, Leslie B., ed. *Voices from Women's Liberation.* New York: Signet, 1970.

Tax, Meredith. "There Was a Young Woman Who Swallowed a Lie..." 1969. Reprint, *Dear Sisters: Dispatches from the Women's Liberation Movement,* eds. Rosalyn Baxandall and Linda Gordon, 293. New York: Basic Books, 2000.

Taylor, James Stacey. "Introduction." In *Personal Autonomy,* ed. James Stacey Taylor, 1–29. New York: Cambridge University Press, 2005.

Taylor, Sandra C. *Vietnamese Women at War: Fighting for Ho Chi Minh and the Revolution.* Lawrence: University Press of Kansas, 1999.

Tepperman, Jean. "Witch." 1960. Reprint, *Dear Sisters: Dispatches from the Women's Liberation Movement,* eds. Rosalyn Baxandall and Linda Gordon, 296. New York: Basic Books, 2000.

Thomas, Tom. "The Second Battle of Chicago 1969." Reprint, *Weatherman,* ed. Harold Jacobs, 196–225. Ramparts Press, 1970.

Thompson, Becky. "Multiracial Feminism: Recasting the Chronology of Second Wave Feminism." *Feminist Studies,* Vol. 24, No. 2 (Summer 2002): 337–360.

Thompson, Becky. *A Promise and a Way of Life: White Antiracist Activism.* Minneapolis: University of Minnesota, 2001.

Tickner, J. Ann. "You Just Don't Understand: Troubled Estrangements Between Feminists and IR Theorists." *International Studies Quarterly* 41 (1997): 611–632.

"Timeline." In *Sing a Battle Song: The Revolutionary Poetry, Statements, and Communiqués of the Weather Underground, 1970–1974,* eds. Bernardine Dohrn, Bill Ayers, Jeff Jones, 51–65. New York: Seven Stories Press, 2006.

Tsuchiya, Kazuyo. "The National Welfare Rights Organization 1966–1975." Archived at http://www.blackpast.org/aah/national-welfare-rights-organization-1966-1975.

Ture, Kwame, and Charles V. Hamilton. *Black Power: The Politics of Black Liberation.* New York: Vintage Books, 1992.

Tyler May, Elaine. *America and the Pill: A History of Promise, Peril, and Liberation.* New York: Perseus Books, 2010.

Underground. DVD. Directed by Emile de Antonio. Turin Film, 1976.

United Nations. *Human Development Report.* Oxford: Oxford University Press, 1995.

United Press International. "War Protestors Cause Disorder at High School." *The News Dispatch,* 5 September 1969.

United States. Kerner Commission. The Kerner Report: *The 1968 Report of the National Advisory Commission on Civil Disorder.* New York: Pantheon Books, 1988.

United States Senate. Committee on the Judiciary. Subcommmittee to Investigate the Administration of the Internal Security Act and Other Internal Security Laws. *Terroristic Activity: Hearings Before the Subcommittee to Investigate the Administration of the Internal Security Act and Other Internal Security Laws.* United States Senate, Ninety-third Congress, Second Sessions. [94th Cong., 2d sess.]. Washington, D.C.: GPO, 1974 [1975].

United States Senate. *The Weather Underground: Report of the Subcommittee to Investigate the Administration of the Internal Security Act and Other Internal Security Laws of the Committee on the Judiciary.* United States Senate, Ninety-fourth Congress, First Session. Washington, D.C.: GPO, 1975.

Vance, Carole. "Pleasure and Danger: Towards a Politics of Sexuality." In *Feminisms*, eds. Sandra Kemp and Judith Squires, 327–335. Oxford: Oxford University Press, 1997.

Varon, Jeremy. *Bringing the War Home: The Weather Underground, the Red Army Faction, and Revolutionary Violence of the Sixties and Seventies.* Berkeley: University of California, 2004.

The Venceremos Brigade. *Venceremos Brigade: Young Americans Sharing the Life and Work of Revolutionary Cuba—Diaries, Letters, Interviews, Tapes, Essays, Poetry by the Venceremos Brigade*, eds. Carol Brightman and Sandra Lawson. New York: Simon & Schuster, 1971.

The Venceremos Brigade. www.venceremos brigade.net/ (accessed 3 September 2017).

"Wages for Housework." Reprint, *Dear Sisters: Dispatches from the Women's Liberation Movement*, eds. Rosalyn Baxandall and Linda Gordon, 258. New York: Basic Books, 2000.

Walker, Rebecca. "Becoming the Third Wave." *Ms.*, January/February 1992, 39–41.

Warrior, Betsy. "Housework: Slavery or Labor of Love." In *Radical Feminism: A Documentary Reader*, ed. Barbara A. Crow, 530–533. New York: New York University Press, 2000.

Watkins, Rychetta. *Black Power, Yellow Power, and the Making of Revolutionary Identities.* Jackson: University of Mississippi, 2012.

Watson, Bruce. *Freedom Summer.* New York: Viking, 2010.

Weather. "Honky Tonk Women." National War Council Packet, December 1969. Reprint, *Weatherman*, ed. Harold Jacobs, 313–320. Ramparts, 1970.

The Weather Underground. "A Declaration of a State of War: May 21, 1970 Communiqué." 21 May 1970. Reprint, *The Weather Eye: Communiqués from the Weather Underground*, ed. Jonah Raskin, 16–18. San Francisco: Union Square Press, 1974.

The Weather Underground. DVD. Directed by Sam Greene and Bill Siegel. Free History Project, 2002.

A Weatherwoman. "Inside the Weather Machine." *The Rat*, 6 February 1970. Reprint, *Weatherman*, ed. Harold Jacobs, 321–326. Ramparts, 1970.

Whitehorn, Laura. "Introduction to the *War Before*." Archived at http://www.feminist press.org/sites/default/files/content/War_Before_Intro.pdf. 2009.

Whitehorn, Laura. Interview with author. 23 October 2014.

Wilkerson, Cathy. *Flying Close to the Sun.* New York: Seven Stories Press, 2007.

Wilkerson, Cathy. "Toward a Revolutionary Women's Militia." *New Left Notes*, 8 July 1969, 6–7.

Wilkerson, Cathy. Letter to author. 30 January 2014.

Willis, Ellen. "Lust Horizons: Is the Women's Movement Pro-Sex?" *Village Voice*, 17–23 June 1981.

Winslow, Barbara. "Primary and Secondary Contradictions in Seattle, 1967–1969." In *The Feminist Memoir Project: Voices from Women's Liberation*, eds. Rachel Blau Duplessis and Ann Snitow, 225–248. New Brunswick: Rutgers University Press, 2007.

Wolf, Susan. "Freedom Within Reason." In *Personal Autonomy*, ed. James Stacey Taylor, 258–274. New York: Cambridge University Press, 2005.

"Women in the Senate." http://www.senate. gov/artandhistory/history/common/briefing/women_senators.htm (accessed 4 July 2018).

Women of the Weather Underground. "A Collective Letter to the Women's Movement." 24 July 1973. Reprint, *The Weather Eye: Communiqués from the Weather Underground*, ed. Jonah Raskin, 68–79. San Francisco: Union Square Press, 1974.

The Women's Brigade. "Health, Education, and Welfare: An Enemy of Women, San Francisco, March 6, 1974 Communiqué." 6 March 1974. Reprint, *The Weather Eye: Communiqués from the Weather Underground*, ed. Jonah Raskin, 100–106. San Francisco: Union Square Press, 1974.

The Women's Caucus. Political Science Department, University of Chicago. "The Halls of Academe." In *Sisterhood Is Powerful: An Anthology of Writings from the Women's Liberation Movement*, ed. Robin Morgan, 101. New York: Random House, 1970.

"Women's Militia." *New Left Notes*, 12 September 1969. Reprint, *Weatherman*, ed. Harold Jacobs, 163–165. Ramparts, 1970.

Worker Student Alliance. "Revolutionaries Must Fight Nationalism." June 1969.

Works, Michael. "Young Animals Attack ROTC." *Seattle PI*, 3 October 1969.

Wright, Doris. "Angry Notes from a Black Feminist." 1970. Reprint, *Dear Sisters: Dispatches from the Women's Liberation Movement,* eds. Rosalyn Baxandall and Linda Gordon, 37–38. New York: Basic Books, 2000.

WUO. "The Bombing of the Capitol: Washington, D.C., February 28, 1971 Communiqué." 28 February 1971. Reprint, *The Weather Eye: Communiqués from the Weather Underground,* ed. Jonah Raskin, 34–39. San Francisco: Union Square Press, 1974.

WUO. *Prairie Fire: The Politics of Revolutionary Anti-Imperialism.* San Francisco and New York: Prairie Fire Distribution Committee, 1974.

WUO. "The Symbionese Liberation Army, the Hearst Kidnapping: San Francisco, February 20, 1974 Communiqué." 20 February 1974. Reprint, *The Weather Eye: Communiqués from the Weather Underground,* ed. Jonah Raskin, 34–39. San Francisco: Union Square Press, 1974.

WUO. "Weather Letter." *Rat,* 15 July 1970. Reprint, *Weatherman,* ed. Harold Jacobs, 456–461. Ramparts, 1970.

WUO. "Weather Underground Organization Bombs Kennecott Corporation: Salt Lake City, Utah, September 4, 1975 Communiqué." 4 September 1975. Reprint, *Sing a Battle Song: The Revolutionary Poetry, Statements, and Communiqués of the Weather Underground, 1970–1974,* eds. Bernardine Dohrn, Bill Ayers, Jeff Jones, 222–225. Kindle Edition. New York: Seven Stories Press, 2006.

WUO. "Who We Are." *Osawatomie,* Summer 1975, No. 2, 2.

WUO New York Region. "Clifford Glover 103rd Precinct: New York City, May 18, 1973 Communiqué." In *The Weather Eye: Communiqués from the Weather Underground,* ed. Jonah Raskin, 66–68. San Francisco: Union Square Press, 1974.

Young, Iris. *Justice and the Politics of Difference.* Princeton: Princeton University Press, 1990.

Young Lords. "Young Lords Thirteen Point Program and Platform." October 1969 and updated May 1970. Archived at Latino Education Network Service http://palante.org/YLPProg.html.

Zack, Naomi. *Inclusive Feminism: A Third Wave Theory of Women's Commonality.* Oxford: Rowman & Littlefield, 2005.

Zwerman, Gilda. "Mothering on the Lam." *Feminist Review,* No. 47 (Summer 1994): 33–56.

Index